THE SHAMAN'S COAT

Other titles by Anna Reid
BORDERLAND: A JOURNEY THROUGH THE
HISTORY OF UKRAINE

THE SHAMAN'S COAT
A NATIVE HISTORY OF SIBERIA

ANNA REID

Walker & Company
NEW YORK

First published in the United States of America in 2003 by
Walker Publishing Company, Inc.;
originally published in Great Britain in 2002 by
Weidenfeld & Nicolson

For information about permission to reproduce selections from this book, write to
Permissions, Walker & Company, 435 Hudson Street, New York, New York 10014

Library of Congress Cataloging-in-Publication Data

Reid, Anna.
The shaman's coat : a native history of Siberia / Anna Reid.
p. cm.
Originally published: London: Weidenfeld & Nicholson, 2002.
Includes bibliographical references and index.
ISBN 0-8027-1399-8 (alk. paper)
1. Ethnology—Russia (Federation)—Siberia.   2. Indigenous peoples—Russia
(Federation)—Siberia—History.   3. Siberia (Russia)—Social life and customs.   I. Title.

DK758 .R45   2002
957'.004—dc21
2002029615

Visit Walker & Company's Web site at www.walkerbooks.com

Printed in the United States of America

2   4   6   8   10   9   7   5   3   1

To Sara and Sandy

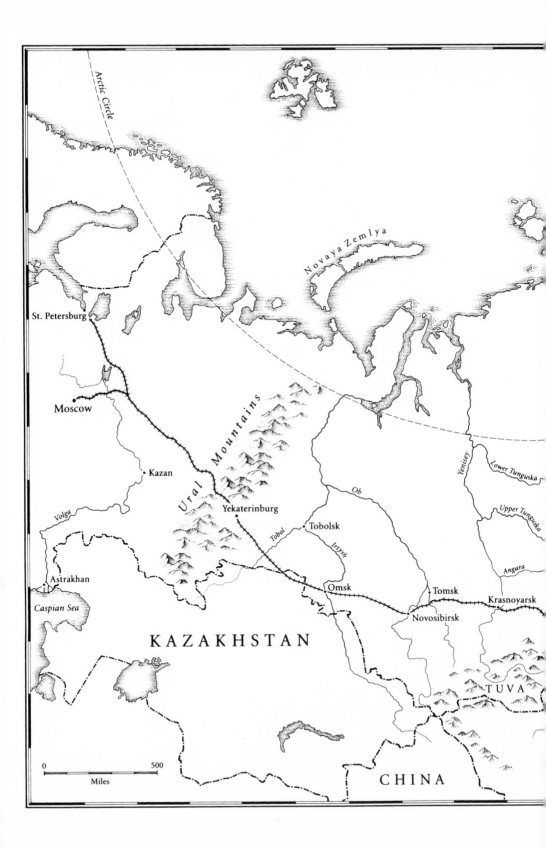

Arctic Circle

Novaya Zemlya

St. Petersburg

Moscow

Kazan

Ural Mountains

Yekaterinburg

Volga

Astrakhan

Caspian Sea

Tobol

Tobolsk

Ob

Irtysh

Omsk

Yenisey

Lower Tunguska

Upper Tunguska

Angara

Tomsk

Krasnoyarsk

Novosibirsk

KAZAKHSTAN

TUVA

CHINA

0   500
Miles

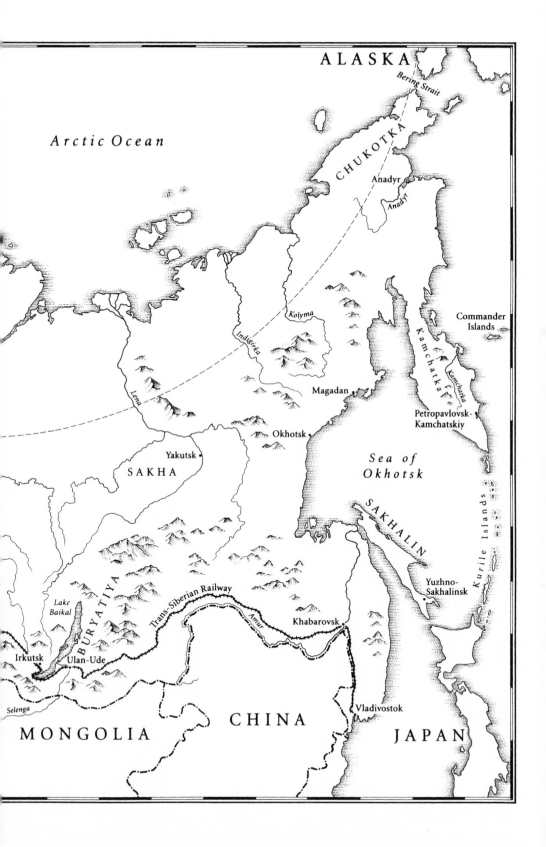

CONTENTS

ACKNOWLEDGMENTS

For their unstinting help and hospitality in Siberia, I would like to thank the following: Annabel Baddeley, Dandar Dorzhiyev, Sergey Filippov, Viktor and Svetlana Garmayev, Ludmilla Gombozhabon, Valeriya Hussar, Konstantin Khlynov, Sonya Kholmogorova, Lidiya Kimova, Dr Viktor Kuzevanov, Zoya Kyrgys, Stas Nitkuk and Margarita Buldakova, Tatyana Irgit, Dembik Oorzhak, Baibek Sat, Nadezhda Shalamova, Ivan Tanko, Zoya Yampilova and Andrey and Valentina Zarubin.

In Moscow and St Petersburg, Dr Olga Balalaeva, Dr Ludmilla Bogoslovskaya, Mariya Stanyukovich and Professor Andrew Wiget were all generous with their time and expertise. Joaquin Duran-Garach and Karl and Chiara Mayer-Rieckh gave encouragement and ideas as well as the run of their homes.

Elsewhere, Professor Bruce Grant, Robin Hanbury-Tenison, Eleanor O'Hanlon, Professor Geoffrey Hosking, Alan Leighton, Edward Lucas, John Massey Stewart, Patrick Newman, Dr Benjamin Seligman, Christine Sutherland, Andres Truuvert, Prince George Vassiltchikov and Marcus Warren all provided invaluable advice and contacts. Special thanks go to Benedict Allen and James Forsyth for permission to reproduce their artworks, to Kira Finkelstein for teaching me Russian, to George Maenchen for information on his father Otto, to Maria Kozak for her research on the Sakha national movement, to Michael Ormiston for demonstrating his collection of Siberian musical instruments, to Dr Piers Vitebsky for letting me attend his seminars at the Scott Polar Research Institute, and to Emma Wilson for reading part of the manuscript as well as guiding me round Sakhalin.

Alex and Sian Reid kindly provided me with a cottage to write in, as did Archie and Henrietta Fraser, together with translations from the Greek and Latin. The first draft of the manuscript was expertly massaged into shape by Dan Fenton, freeing it of much excess verbiage. Peter Robinson of Curtis Brown, and Richard Milner and Rebecca Wilson of Weidenfeld & Nicolson combined patience with enthusiasm throughout, and Bela Cunha copyedited with an eagle eye.

Finally, love and gratitude to my husband, Charles, who has no intention of visiting Siberia, but without whom this book would probably not have been written at all.

ILLUSTRATIONS

INTRODUCTION

At first glance the picture resembles a nativity scene. Under the low beams of a rough wooden hut a young woman stands facing us, hair bright in the sunlight that falls through a hole in the roof. A man wrapped in sheepskin peers over her shoulder, and she carries a bag marked with a scarlet cross. Bowed in front of them, back to the viewer, is a third figure. Though his face is invisible, his coat marks him out as a priest or potentate: fringed with plaited thongs and metal snakes and birds, it is exotic enough for one of the Three Kings. Once an exhibit in a museum of atheism, the painting makes its message clear. The woman is a flying doctor, come to save a savage land. The man in sheepskin is her pilot, and the figure in the coat a Siberian shaman, making obeisance before the forces of science and progress as embodied by Soviet Communism.

What everybody knows about Siberia is that it is big and that it is cold: a vast white snowfield, in the mind's eye, somewhere to the east of Moscow. Big, it certainly is. 'If it were possible to move entire countries from one part of the globe to another,' a nineteenth-century explorer correctly wrote,

> you could take the whole of the United States of America ... and set it down in the middle of Siberia, without anywhere touching the boundaries of the latter territory. You could then take Alaska and all the States of Europe, with the single exception of Russia, and fit them into the remaining margin like the pieces of a dissected map.[1]

Defined as all Russian-ruled territory between the Urals and the Pacific, Siberia occupies five million square miles of northern Asia, or a twelfth of the world's total landmass. Flying across it from end to end takes seven hours, during six of which, unless you overfly the southerly Trans-Siberian Railway, the bogs and forests below display no sign whatsoever of mankind's existence. In its deepest backwoods, survey parties still stumble across strange, shy families who have never heard of Lenin or the Second World War. And though it encompasses farmland and steppe as well as forest and tundra, for the most part it is cold indeed. Winter temperatures average minus 30–40 degrees centigrade, and can plunge into the minus 60s. In such conditions mercury turns to lead, brandy to syrup. Living trees explode with a sound like gunfire, chopped logs strike blue sparks, and exhaled breath falls to the ground in a shower of crystals, with a rustling sound called the 'whispering of the stars'.

If this big, cold Siberia of the imagination has inhabitants, they are probably Europeans: stooped files of exiled revolutionaries, prisoners of war and Gulag slaves. It is here that the mental picture of Siberia errs, for it was no more an empty land before the Russians' arrival in the late 1500s, than any other so-called New World. Pre-conquest, its population numbered about a quarter of a million, divided into over thirty different ethnic groups. Some spoke Mongol, Turkic or Finno-Ugric languages; others bore no linguistic relation to the rest of humanity at all. Unaware that the world stretched beyond their own vast horizons, they called themselves simply 'sea-people', 'forest-people' or 'men'.

Their means of existence perfectly reflected their surroundings, simultaneously tributes to and triumphs over Siberia itself. Two groups knew writing, and a few more metalwork, but all depended on hunting or herding. Along the 3,000-mile river Ob, Khant fished from leaf-shaped dug-out canoes, wore bird-skin capes and used the jawbones of pike to tattoo their bodies with waves and spirals. The forest Evenk lived in bark-covered teepees, and rode reindeer with bridle and saddle. On the Arctic coast, Chukchi hunted seals from coracles with obsidian-tipped spears, and roofed their crofts with the ribs of whales. South of Lake Baikal, Buryat galloped shaggy ponies over rolling grasslands and burned dried camel-dung inside felt yurts.

There was nothing idyllic about these lives. War and famine forced large-scale population movements long before the Russian conquest, and in the far north the old and sick routinely requested euthanasia by stabbing or strangulation. When an Edwardian anthropologist told her Nenets hosts the story of Captain Oates's heroic 'I am just going outside; I may be some time', they refused to believe her. Scott, they objected, would surely have eaten him. But for the most part, according to archaeologists and early travellers, indigenous Siberians were well-fed, healthy and even wealthy. Buryat chiefs owned tens of thousands of horses, as rich Evenk did deer, and decorated their harnesses with charms of turquoise and smoky silver alloy, bought from Bokharan traders. The practice – later to excite Marxist ideologues – of sharing hunting spoils insured against bad luck, and kinship rules guarded against genetic disorders and rescued widows and orphans. Even the stone-age tundra peoples had leisure to embroider their clothes with feathers and dyed reindeer-hair, to celebrate feasts with running races and bawdy dances, and to spend nights on end reciting rhythmic, alliterative epics thousands of verses long. For their children, they fashioned cheerful, chunky little toys: miniature sleds and cradles, fur-appliquéd footballs, rope-puzzles and ivory figures of wrestling bears and men riding wolves.

The toys are still there in the ethnographical museums, handled now only by curators wearing cotton gloves. Where it is harder to find things native Siberian is in the popular idea of Russia, in conceptions of what the country is and how she came to be. To tsarist Russians the indigenous tribes were an irrelevance, a minor stumbling-block on their march to a manifestly continent-sized destiny. To the Communists they were an embarrassment, their refusal, in most cases, to flourish under Russian rule giving the lie to the claim that the Soviet Union was a technologically advanced Brotherhood of Peoples rather than a backward empire based on old-fashioned force. From the late 1920s onwards historians denied or omitted to mention that Russians and native Siberians had ever fought at all, using terms such as 'absorption' and 'annexation' instead of 'conquest', or referring to 'voluntary unions with tribes languishing under the oppression of feudal lords'. The Russians I met while researching this book frequently assured me that their fighter-explorer Cossacks were not to be compared with the *conquistadores*, and were surprised and indignant when I riposted with the natives' numerous risings and resistance wars, used the word 'colonialism' or drew parallels between Siberia and British India.

They had a point, for though Russia really is the last European power in Asia, Siberia's relation to it is more like the American West's to the United States. Geographical contiguity blurred the distinction between motherland and colony, and quickly attracted Slav settlers, many of whom took native wives. Today, the indigenous peoples make up only 1.6 million out of a total Siberian population of 32 million, and do not form a majority in any so-called ethnic republic save for Tuva, nestled on the Mongol border. Plainly, they are too few and scattered to mount a Chechen-style war of secession, or to spark a political collapse of Russia in Asia to match that of Russia in Central Europe. But to sideline them from Russia's history, not to mention her present, remains as false and self-deluding as leaving the Maya out of Mexico, the Aborigines out of Australia, or the Sioux and Apache out of the United States.

The native Siberians believed that everything around them was animate, possessed of personality and living force. As one told a nineteenth-century anthropologist:

> All that exists lives. The lamp walks around. The walls of the house have voices of their own. Even the chamber-vessel has a separate land and house. The skins sleeping in the bags talk at night. The antlers lying on the tombs arise at night and walk in procession around the mounds.[2]

When the mountains threw rocks in the air they were fighting, and the earth shook thanks to the tunnelling action of mammoths, who expired on contact with sunlight. Mice went to sea in shells and built sleds from blades of grass. Human excrement was a ribald old man dressed in sleek brown furs, boastful but secretly afraid of being eaten by dogs. The sun was a man in glittering clothes who drove a team of copper-antlered deer, and the Milky Way a river choked with boulders. The south-west and south-east winds were an estranged couple who shouted abuse at each other as they passed; thunder the noise of heavenly infants playing on a seal-skin; the unmoving pole star the stake to which the gods tethered their horses. Even the clouds had their own homes and families, complete with vaporous tents and cooking-pots.

The native Siberians' mediators with this vital, teeming world were their shamans – in the Evenk original 'ones who know'. Gifted with vocations involuntarily through heredity or according to the whim of the spirits, they performed the usual sacred offices, presiding over thanksgiving and propitiation ceremonies, healing the sick and divining the future. Their most characteristic function was the soul-journey, undertaken while in a trance achieved by dancing, fasting or ingesting hallucinogenic plants. In the course of such a journey a shaman might turn himself into a wolf or gull, fight the spirits of famine or bad weather, retrieve a sick man's soul, summon migrating walrus, or compete with the shaman of an enemy tribe. Especially dramatic were their initiatory journeys, during which they endured dismemberment and resurrection, emerging with shamanising powers. A Sakha shaman told of how a long-tailed, iron-beaked bird carried him off to the underworld, spitted him on a pine-branch, then cut him up and fed him to the spiritis of smallpox and influenza. When the diseases had eaten their fill the bird gathered and reclothed with flesh his clean-picked bones, leaving him with the ability to heal. A Nenets shaman stumbled into a mountain cave where he found a naked man stirring a giant cauldron. The man caught him in a pair of tongs and boiled him up for three years, before reassembling him complete with eyes that could see the spirits, a throat that could sing forever, and ears that could understand the conversation of trees. trees.

Shamans acted out their soul-journeys in front of an audience, in intense and vivid pantomime. Their spirit adversaries could be heard flying about the tent, barking, growling or arguing in unintelligible languages. Angered, they shook the walls, tugged at the skins on the floor or knocked over the urine bowl. Illnesses were extracted from patients' bodies in the shape of stones, insects or thorns. 'He lays hold of the trouble,' wrote an anthropologist, 'carries it to the middle of the room, and, never stopping his imprecations, chases it away, spits it from his mouth, kicks it, drives it with his hands and breath.'[3]

Powerful shamans could spill never-ending streams of pebbles from their fists, swallow sticks, stab themselves in the stomach or walk over hot embers without apparently coming to harm.

Europeans – especially Romanticism-fuelled early nineteenth-century ones – found such performances impressive, even frightening. A Russian noblewoman who followed her husband into exile after the failed liberal revolution of December 1825 was invited to see a Buryat shaman in action:

> We all retired inside the yurt, where a white mare's skin had been spread on the floor. At first, everything was silent, then a handful of horsehair was thrown on the fire, putting it out. In the faint gleam of the red coals we could see the figure of the shaman, motionless, with drooping head, big drum on breast, and face turned towards the south . . . He gradually began to play the drum – first softly, then rising to a crescendo like an oncoming storm, with peals of thunder and squawking of wild birds. When the music swelled to its highest pitch the shaman began to leap and dance, at first on the skin and then, becoming more rapid, gliding all over the floor of the yurt, beating the drum furiously, jumping about . . . His eyes were closed, his hair tumbled, his mouth strangely twisted, saliva streaming down his chin . . . His fury rose and ebbed like a wave, now smooth, now frantic and frenzied . . . After what seemed to us quite a long time, he finally slowed down. We were told that the ceremony was now over. With a final leap, the shaman collapsed onto the white mare's skin and was carried out of the tent by two assistants.[4]

Vital to the whole drama, according to most Siberians' beliefs, was the shaman's charm-laden coat. Bird-shaped pendants allowed him to fly, the metal antlers jutting from its shoulders gave him the swiftness of a deer, and its trailing thongs represented snakes, enabling him to squeeze into small spaces. The iron bars hanging from the coat's sleeves were arm-bones and the chains hanging down its back vertebrae, recalling his initiatory dismemberment. The whole assemblage jangled fearfully and weighed up to fifty pounds. One of the marks of a true shaman was that he found it easy to pick up.

The state of Siberian shamanism, I thought when embarking on this book, would be an indicator of the extent to which the indigenous peoples had preserved their identities under Russian rule. The tsars tried to replace shamans with priests. The Communists ostracised and imprisoned them, and under Stalin shot them or threw them out of helicopters, saying that if they could fly, now was their chance. If shamanism had survived all this, other aspects of native Siberian culture probably had too.

My first stop was St Petersburg's Institute of Anthropology and Ethnography, across the Neva from the Winter Palace. The anthropologists to whom I had introductions shared an office filled with dusty card indexes and reflected light from the river. The expert on the Ket blinked owlishly, beads and spectacles tangling across her downy bust. The Altai specialist was tiny as a child, wore her shirt buttoned up to the neck and her hair in a Bolshevik crop; I would not have been surprised to see razor-blades snap from the points of her shoes. Perched behind tall typewriters, they eyed me without enthusiasm. If I was one of those New Age Western shaman-seekers, their looks said, I had come to the wrong place.

Back in the 1970s, when they did their fieldwork, shamans still existed, just. 'Despite all the Russians did,' said the Altai lady, 'shamanism survived – in secret, underground. It never became extinct because there was always a succession, a teacher who might take you on as an assistant. But, of course, genuine shamans were very few.' Native Siberians could be persuaded to discuss shamanism, the Ket lady chipped in, only after long preliminaries. Once, she had managed to lead a conversation all the way from ski-design to the 'seven drum system', whereby shamans graduated to stronger instruments as they perfected their soul-journey technique, and back to weaker ones as they grew old and frail themselves. She smiled at the memory: 'When I understood I wanted to rush out and stand on my head! It was a marvellous moment!' Though it was not possible openly to discuss such findings, 'you could put things so that other people in the field understood. One of the tricks was to write in the past indefinite, even though you had gathered the material that very year. It was a way of protecting your informants, in case some Party fool read it and made trouble.' As for finding shamans today, neither woman held out much hope. Real shamans did not talk to strangers, and the new breed were a waste of time. They had been to see a Sakha so-called shaman perform at the Palace of Sport: 'He had the coat, the cap, the drum. But it was just a performance. There was nothing genuine about it.'

Attending a conference on shamanism in Moscow, I began to worry that the Petersburg ladies might be right. Though organised by the Academy of Sciences, it was funded by Californian shamanists of just the sort they despised. Before lunch, earnest Russian Academicians delivered weighty papers on Sami Chants and Sakha epics. After lunch, even more earnest Americans took to the rostrum with 'bio-extrasensories', 'super-abilities' and 'psy-surgery'. At the back, ostentatiously bored, sat a row of real live shamans – plump, middle-aged Asian women, tricked out in nylon robes, neo-Celtic jewellery and gypsy scarves. Everyone woke up slightly for Dr Michael Harner, the renegade academic anthropologist who, having tried out his Ecuadorean subjects' hallucinogens back in the 1960s, is currently Western shamanism's leading guru. Shamanism, he told us, contributed to 'deep ecological understanding' and to 'the potential of humankind to transcend materialistic boundaries'. But it could not be understood via 'Western paradigms'; to grasp it one had to participate. His San Francisco-based Foundation for Shamanic Studies offered a range of Harner Method courses, from a basic weekend Way of the Shaman workshop at $225 ('Wear comfortable clothing, warm socks, and bring a cushion and/or blanket') to a three-year Advanced Shamanism and Shamanic Healing Program including Divination, JourneyWork and Soul Retrieval. Trainees could invest in a high-quality, reasonably priced beginner's kit of book, CD and 16" RemoUSA FiberSkin Buffalo Drum. ('Excellent for drumming in those April showers, and on adventure treks where fires to dry skin drums may not be appropriate, or electrical outlets for hair-dryers may not exist.') The day was due to end, I noticed as I sidled out, with healing and hypnosis demonstrations, before the Academy hit back with Folk Music and a *Banket*.

It was not an encouraging start. But then perhaps, as the good doctor suggested, I was approaching shamanism from the wrong angle. It had never been an organised religion, had never possessed formal entry requirements or sacred texts. And shamans had always taken payment for rituals – indeed, their rituals were reckoned to be useless if payments were not made. In short, anyone was a 'genuine' shaman who sincerely believed himself to be one, and was accepted by his community as such. Like the keen young Komsomol leaders who denounced shamans as capitalist exploiters, the Freud-inspired anthropologists who wrote them off as schizophrenics, or the Enlightenment scientists who scolded them for using ventriloquy and sleight-of-hand, I had failed, perhaps, to get the point. After all, the Church of England passed round the plate on Sundays, and I did not expect thunderbolts when taking communion.

Shamanism, moreover, was far from the only sign of native Siberian renaissance. In the hopeful early 1900s, when it looked as if Russia might turn into a Western-style constitutional monarchy, national movements flourished among the larger Siberian peoples as among Czechs and Ukrainians, Indians and Javanese. During the civil war that followed 1917's Revolution they formed partisan armies and fought for political autonomy, sometimes for outright independence. Since Communism's collapse history had in a muted way been repeating itself. In the late 1980s and early 1990s there had been race riots in several Siberian cities, and the parliaments of three ethnic republics had adopted constitutions giving themselves the right to secede. Sakha wanted ownership of their diamond mines, Buryat were rebuilding their Buddhist monasteries, and Khant were protesting against oil companies' destruction of the tundra. Out beyond the Urals, would I find only Russians with Asian faces? Or had the shaman donned his coat again? Might he be showing the flying-doctor the door?

CHAPTER I

SIBERIANS AND *SIBIRYAKI*

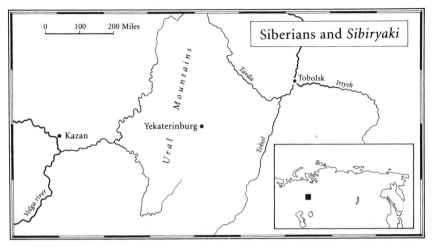

In Europe we were hangers-on and slaves, but in Asia we are masters.
In Europe we were Tatars, but in Asia we too are Europeans.
                                            – Fyodor Dostoyevsky, 1881

On an island in the middle of a river in the middle of a forest, soldiers lie sleeping around a smoky fire. They have stacked their pikes in pyramids, like corn-stooks, and made racks from forked branches for their muskets, to keep them off the wet ground. Their boats, high-masted and with prows carved in the shape of animals' heads, ride at anchor close to shore. Over the page, the scene springs into action. Mounted warriors armed with curved scimitars have forded the river and taken the camp by surprise. Half-asleep, the soldiers stand no chance. One is being beheaded, others stabbed or shot through with arrows. The soldiers' leader, bearded and twice the size of the other figures, stands at the water's edge, pulling an escape vessel to shore. A handwritten caption in Old Slavonic tells us that he fails:

> Yermak, seeing the killing of his men and no help from anywhere to save his life, ran to his boat. But he could not climb into it for he

was clad in the two royal coats of mail, and the boat had floated away from the bank so that, unable to reach it, he was drowned.[1]

The manuscript tells the story of the first Russian invasion of Siberia. A storyboard-style sequence of hand-drawn sketches, one would expect it, if it were French of English, to date from the Middle Ages. But it is Russian, and in autocratic Muscovy printing-presses were kept out of private hands and monks remained the chief recorders of history well into the 1700s. So although the invasion happened only just over 400 years ago, our sources on it are few, packed with church propaganda, and mostly of dubious authorship and date. Of the four extant chronicles on the subject, the earliest was written at least fifty years after the event, and they disagree so often that reading them, as a Russian writer puts it, is like listening to 'the uproar of drunken Cossacks bursting into reminiscence, interrupting each other and cutting each other off'.[2]

As far as we can tell, the ambush described above took place in August 1585, seventeen months after the death of mercurial, sadistic Tsar Ivan IV – 'the Formidable' to Russians, 'the Terrible' to English-speakers. Thanks to Ivan's wars, Muscovy already stretched from the White Sea to the Caspian. But it was poor, backward and so lacking in settled laws and institutions that it qualified more as a power than a state. Until a century previously it had paid tribute to Genghiz Khan's Mongol Horde, and as recently as 1571 the Ottoman-backed khan of one of the Horde's Muslim successor states, Devlet Giray of Crimea, had raided Moscow, carrying away thousands of Slav slaves. So although Russians already called their capital the Third Rome, and their princes Caesars, to the rest of the world these imperial claims seemed empty boasts. As for what lay beyond the Urals, they were as much in the dark as everyone else. The odd wanderer who did venture east brought back tales of tribesmen who froze to the ground in winter, spent the summers at sea lest their skins split, and had mouths on top of their heads, eating by placing food under their hats and shrugging their shoulders.

The man who changed all this was Yermak Timofeyevich, the bearded giant who drowned under the weight of his chain-mail while fleeing a midnight attack. The chroniclers' sole comment on his personality is predictably flattering: he is 'most courageous, shrewd and humane; well-favoured and endowed with every kind of wisdom; with a flat face, black beard and curly hair; of medium stature, thickset and broad-shouldered'.[3] Courageous he must have been; humane he was not. According to the only account of his origins, he came from a family of highwaymen and spent his youth at the head of a robber band that preyed on Volga shipping. When he turned up in the Urals in the late 1570s he was probably on the run from troops sent to put down river piracy. One chronicler certainly thought so, sketching Yermak's men being executed by Ivan's soldiers.

Russian settlement of the Urals dated back to 1517, when wealthy boyars, the Stroganovs, were granted a royal charter to mine them for iron and salt. By the 1580s they had semi-independent jurisdiction over a string of forts stretching east to the river Tobol. Whether the Siberian expedition was their idea or Yermak's is unclear. A charter of 1574 specifically instructed them to build and garrison new forts, which suggests that they may have invited Yermak to help them. On the other hand, one chronicle has Yermak squeezing them for supplies with menaces: 'O man, you do not know that even now you are dead; we shall take you and shoot you to bits. Give us ... for 5,000 men in all, three pounds of gunpowder and lead, and a gun for each man ...'[4] Another chronicle does not mention the Stroganovs at all. Nor do we know what Yermak's own aims were. According to the monks he set off to conquer pagan lands for the greater glory of God and Muscovy. Likelier, he was simply out for plunder.

Waiting for Yermak on the other side of the Urals was a far more respectable figure: Khan Kuchum of Sibir. A descendant of Genghiz, Kuchum ruled another of the Muslim princedoms left behind by the retreating Horde. Two of them – Kazan on the Volga and Astrakhan on the Caspian – had fallen to Ivan in the 1550s. But the Girays' Crimea and Kuchum's Sibir stood firm, the first blocking Russian settlement of the grasslands north of the Black Sea, the second the river passages east into what would later be called Siberia. Though hardly the hub of the Muslim world – an Ottoman historian described Kuchum as an insignificant backwoodsman, and his subjects as 'strange, of astonishing appearance, speaking an incomprehensible language, without religion or rite, almost like animals' – [5] Sibir was wealthy and not without sophistication. Its 20,000 or so inhabitants, a Mongol-Turkic mix loosely known, like those of Crimea, Kazan and Astrakhan, as Tatars, wrote in Koranic Arabic, traded with Bokhara and Samarkand, and took tributes of fish and furs from local Khant and Ket. According to the chroniclers, Kuchum owned treasure, cattle, mullahs and warriors 'as numerous . . . as the mountains and forests, as countless as the sands'. His hundred wives, 'and youths as well as maidens'[6] lived in camps conveniently disposed around his fortified capital of Isker, on sandy bluffs above the river Irtysh. Having come out top of a dynastic feud to take the throne, he soon felt strong enough to provoke Muscovy. In 1571, taking advantage of Devlet Giray's raid on Moscow, he discontinued nominal tribute payments, and two years later allowed his nephew Mamektul to attack Russian settlements in the Ural foothills and assassinate an envoy. It may have been in response to this that the Stroganovs mounted Yermak's campaign.

Kuchum first heard of Yermak's arrival in Sibir in the winter of 1581 or 1582, from a Tatar whom he had captured in the Urals and released again with gifts and friendly messages. Yermak headed somewhere between 540 and an improbable 8,000 men, including priests, scribes, trumpeters and a purser-monk who 'did not wear black robes but kept to the rules, and cooked porridge, and knew about the stores'.[7] They travelled in flat-bottomed boats that could be sailed, rowed, towed or carried overland, and were subject to harsh discipline. Defaulters were whipped, lechers chained, and deserters tied up in sandbags and drowned. They were also, as they took care to demonstrate, supernaturally armed. 'When they shoot from their bows,' the amazed Tatar told Kuchum, 'there is a flash of fire and great smoke issues, and a loud report like thunder in the sky. One does not see arrows coming out of them . . . Our scale-armour, armour of plates and rings, cuirasses and chain-mail do not hold them; they pierce all of them right through.'[8]

On hearing the news, Kuchum and his courtiers became 'distressed and very sad', for they realised that Yermak's friendly greetings were a smokescreen, and that he would 'soon come and plunder them'.[9] They were right. The following spring, the Russians sailed downriver out of the mountains and into Sibir. In May they forced a passage along the river Tavda; in August they captured a Tatar stronghold at the Tavda's confluence with the Tobol, and in October they reached Isker. The battle for the town lasted three days and cost them 107 lives. Their first attack failed, but during the second Mamektul was wounded and his Khant vassals deserted. Watching the carnage from the top of a hill, Kuchum called down fire and famine on Yermak's head, lamented that a plebeian should have put him to shame, and 'ordered his mullahs to shout their prayers . . . because their gods were asleep'.[10] At nightfall he fled with his court, so that when the Russians entered Isker the following morning they found it eerily silent.

Among the loot Kuchum left behind was a fortune in furs, 5,200 of which Yermak despatched to Moscow. Coinciding with Muscovy's defeat in the long wars for the Baltics against Poland and Sweden, their unexpected arrival delighted Ivan, who had earlier chided the Stroganovs for making 'mischief between the Siberian sultan and us', and for hiring 'robbers to serve in your forts without our permission'.[11] He ordered thanksgiving services, distributions of alms and the despatch of reinforcements to Isker, bearing rewards of cloth and money for Yermak's followers. Yermak received a pardon for his earlier piracy, a fur coat 'from the Tsar's own shoulder', a goblet and two chain-mail tunics, embossed in bronze with double-headed eagles.

While Ivan celebrated, Yermak and his men were running into trouble. Constant skirmishing so reduced their numbers that they could no longer safely venture outside Isker, and two winters running, food ran so short that they 'were forced to eat human flesh, and many died of hunger'.[12] The arrival of Ivan's reinforcements in November 1584 made the situation worse, since there was no food for them either. Yermak's drowning, weighed down by Ivan's chain-mail, was the last straw. Of the ambushed party, a single man made it back to Isker with news of the disaster, causing the town's 150 or so remaining Russians to abandon it and head for home.

But the tsars now knew that Sibir was both rich and weak. New expeditions followed, the Tatars fell out among themselves, and within a few years the khanate had again fallen into Russian hands. Kuchum's successor Seydak was defeated by means of a squalid trick. Out hawking near Isker, he accepted an invitation to enter the fort and parley, whereupon his followers were served drugged wine and massacred. 'Henceforth,' wrote a chronicler, 'there was great fear among all the infidels of the Siberian land, and all the Tatars, both near and far, did not dare to go to war against the sovereign's cities.'[13] Though not quite as tidy as that, the fall of Sibir was indeed one of history's great turning-points, for with the khanate gone no polity existed capable of permanently halting men with muskets anywhere between the Mongol steppe and the Arctic Ocean, or the Urals and the North Pacific.

Having abandoned Isker, Kuchum retreated south with a dwindling band of followers. In 1597, after the Russians had sent two expeditions against him, he proposed a truce. 'Since the coming of Yermak, I have tried to resist you. I did not give Sibir to you; you have seized it for yourselves. Now let us try for peace; perhaps it would be better.' He begged also for the release of Tatar merchants who had been bringing medicine for his failing eyes. The contemptuous reply came from his own turncoat son Abdul-Khair, who advised him, since he was 'in great need and poverty, wandering the steppe like a Cossack with just a few men', to surrender in exchange for Russian favours. The following year a third punitive expedition found Kuchum camped on the river Ob. In a battle lasting from dawn to noon 150 of the khan's men were killed, and most of his family, including eighteen wives and daughters and another five sons, captured. Kuchum escaped, still pathetically defiant: 'I did not go to the Sovereign when I was well and had a sword, so why should I go now when I am deaf and blind, and without any subsistence? They took away my son Asmanak; if I lost all my children but still had Asmanak I could live, but without him I shall go to the Nogais.'[14] No more was heard from the khan of Sibir, for shortly afterwards the Nogais, a Tatar people to the south, murdered him for fear of Russian reprisals.

Kuchum's stand was unusual. On conquering Kazan and Astrakhan, Ivan had successfully bought the allegiance of the bulk of their defeated nobility. Ivan's successor Fyodor did the same in Sibir.

Kuchum's relatives were given lands and titles, and their retinues gifts of money, food and cloth. Some 300 lesser princes moved to the Russians' new fort of Tobolsk, took baptism and entered salaried government service. Over time such families were assimilated into the mainstream Russian nobility, as proven by the long list of famous Russian surnames with Turkic or Mongol roots. By the 1820s, a traveller to Tobolsk was able to write that Russian exiles' children were 'as little to be distinguished from their neighbours, as the posterity of Tatar princes'.[15] The *bon mot* with which Savoy's ambassador to Petersburg, Joseph de Maistre, is said to have regaled Napoleon – '*Grattez le Russe et vous trouverez le Tartare*' – was genetically as well as metaphorically true.

Ordinary Tatars were not so forgetful. According to one of the later chronicles, written about 1700, they dreamed of recapturing Sibir, taking comfort from the legend that a hairy white wolf as big as an ox would one day emerge, roaring, from the Irtysh, frightening the Russians away. An eighteenth-century German traveller wrote that 'even the meanest people' prided themselves on their genealogies, and would 'warm their imaginations with raptures on the ancient splendour of the Tatarian empire, and often break out in wishes and ardent longings for the re-establishment of their former power'.[16] In the mid-1800s, Siberian Tatars still preferred to call the town of Tyumen 'Chingistora', after Genghiz, and ethnographers collected ballads that inverted history by making Yermak Kuchum's sly servant-boy.

While in death Kuchum dwindled to a footnote, Yermak turned into a national hero, accumulating as many mythical accretions as a St George or Robin Hood. In old Cossack songs he turns up in a variety of unlikely guises: as a courtier, as a prisoner of the Turks, as a comic trickster who deceives the Tatars by making dummy soldiers out of straw, and as one of the *bogatyri*, the mythical warriors of medieval Rus. Siberia's first prelate, Archbishop Kipriyan of Tobolsk, made him a saint, gathering relics and enrolling his soldiers into the company of Orthodox martyrs. Kipriyan also commissioned the first miracle-packed chronicles, according to which Yermak's campaign was aided by frequent visions of Christ, at the sight of which the Tatars' best archers dropped dead, their bows shattered. Even Yermak's corpse, the monks claimed, smelt sweet for six weeks, spouting fresh blood and shunned by birds of prey. The awestruck Tatars were said to have buried him beneath a spreading pine and to treasure earth from his grave for its power to heal the sick and bring success in battle.

The mythologising stuck. Eighteenth-century historians (mostly imported Germans) portrayed Yermak neutrally or negatively, stressing his robber origins and ignominious end. But the first home-grown Russian histories, appearing from the 1830s onwards, turned him back into a hero. Pushkin, just before his death, was planning an epic poem about him, and a popular play of the 1840s had the old river pirate soliloquising with his latest breath on how 'clear and bright/Is your future destiny, Mother Russia!' before falling 'silent in ecstasy' as the curtain descended.[17] For the Soviets, he made a splendid example of the proletariat's vanguard role in history, and they gave him a Yermak power station, several Yermak ice-breakers and the towns Yermaka, Yermaki, Yermakova and Yermakovskoye.

The inflight movie on the plane from Moscow to Sibir was *Some Like It Hot*, accompanied by rye bread, cucumber and soapy mineral water, served on battered aluminium trays. The Tupolev's engines kept up a homely rumble, and the sun sparkled on the scratches on the window-panes. As we came in to land, no bossy loudspeaker said to belt up or stow bags in overhead lockers, the unoccupied seats flopped forward in unison and a canteen of cutlery jingled down the centre aisle. On the runway our baggage tumbled on to potholed tarmac awash with meltwater and the cawing of rooks.

From a predatory circle of taxi-drivers I picked out a middle-aged man with a big old Volga. We negotiated a fare – far too much, but then I was a foreigner – and set off for Tobolsk. From the air, Kuchum's old khanate had resembled a bearskin, each pine a magnified bristle, each road or pipeline the graze of a hunter's bullet. On the ground, it resolved into flooded fields, dirty snowdrifts, lapwings wheeling round telegraph poles, an ice-breaker nosing under a bridge. Cafés knocked up from the long-distance lorry containers Russians call *vagonchiki* advertised borscht and blinis, and skinny, grubby children yelled as they pushed their bicycles down quagmire lanes. Between villages, bridal birches swayed slim and satiny, their branches etched in drypoint against the white sky.

Jolting along, I flipped through a book by one of the best commentators on Siberia, the nineteenth-century liberal Nikolay Yadrintsev. The Russians who settled in Siberia, the *Sibiryaki*, were, he thought, different from European Russians: cannier, more self-reliant and less obedient to authority. I asked the driver if he agreed. Pleased with the question, he jammed a Peter the First cigarette between his teeth, twisted in his seat and raised a fist. 'A *Sibiryak*? He's strong. He's got a beard, and big shoulders, like this! He can kill a bear just with a knife. Women love him! And he loves women!' *Sibiryaki* were cheerful, open, they liked a song and a drink. European Russians were 'pragmatic, closed. A Muscovite will smile, and all the while he hates you. We just say what we think.'

Tobolsk was this man's Siberia's, Russian Siberia's, foundation-stone. It began as the first Russian fort east of the Urals, built by the soldiers who avenged Yermak from the timbers of their dismantled boats. The chroniclers portrayed it as a heavenly city, endlessly appearing in visionary splendour to discouraged Russians and uppity Tatars. It was the home of Siberia's first monastery, and of its first, inanimate, exile, the Uglich Bell, whose clapper Ivan tore out for proclaiming the assassination of his son Dmitriy. There to observe the transit of Venus (vital to the calculation of longitude) in the spring of 1761, the French astronomer and abbé Jean Chappe d'Auteroche thought it a pretty place, at least from a distance. Perched on landslide-prone cliffs above the Irtysh, the upper town boasted battlements, brick-built houses for the governor and archbishop, and a cluster of golden-domed churches. The lower town was a muddle of rough-hewn fishermen's huts, so muddy that he had to go everywhere by carriage. Though there was no shortage of handsome girls; there was of good conversation. The governor took an intelligent interest in astronomy, but the archbishop 'was always in a passion at the idea of the motion of the earth',[18] and tried to convert d'Auteroche's Lutheran servant by throwing a plate at his head. As for the townspeople, they decided that d'Auteroche had conjured up the spring floods with his magical instruments, and threatened to demolish his observatory.

By the time the Prussian geographer Adolf Erman passed through in 1828, Tobolsk was larger, tidier and a touch worldlier. He admired its smart new customs house, bazaar full of Chinese and European manufactures, schools operating on the modern Lancastrian system, and frequent military balls, at which Tobolskians had just learned to waltz – though they still sang along to the band, he noted, as though at a country dance. Politically, meanwhile, the town was turning into a backwater. Governor-generalship of the new province of Eastern Siberia had gone to Irkutsk, just west of Baikal, and in 1839 Western Siberia's administration was transferred to the fast-growing city of Omsk. By the 1890s Tobolsk was sufficiently obscure to be bypassed by the Trans-Siberian Railway. In August 1917 the head of the moderate, doomed Provisional Government, Aleksandr Kerensky, hit upon it as a safe place to stow the imperial family. 'I chose Tobolsk,' he wrote later, 'because it was an out-and-out backwater ... had a very small garrison, no industrial proletariat, and a population which was prosperous and contented, not to say old-fashioned.'[19] Until their transfer to Yekaterinburg in April 1918, the Romanovs lived under house arrest in the former governor's mansion. As power slipped away from the Provisional Government to the Bolsheviks, the soldiers guarding them turned increasingly hostile, scratching obscenities into the fence surrounding the yard where Alexandra took exercise and stripping Nicholas of his epaulettes. But the Tobolskians remaining touchingly loyal, gathering to cheer when the Grand Duchesses appeared at a window and bringing gifts of cakes and eggs. When the family ran out of cash a local merchant offered a 20,000-rouble loan, and at Christmas the priest of the church where they were allowed to take communion risked arrest by saying prayers for their health.

Eighty years later, Tobolsk felt half-dead. From the ramparts of its small cliff-top kremlin, the streets radiated crisp as a Canaletto, each haywire fence and snow-muffled roof precisely drawn in the scalpel-sharp light. Beyond, locked in freeze-frame immobility, shimmered the frozen Irtysh, and beyond that grey-brown forest stretched flat and seamless to the horizon. There were no cars, few people and disconcertingly little noise.

Down in what used to be the commercial district, every visible object – buildings, signposts, bus shelters, street-lights – was in a state of decay verging on dereliction. Of a row of brick warehouses, all that remained were smoke-blackened shells. Wooden cottages lurched between puddles the size of ponds. One church had lost its windows, a second its roof. In a third, builders were at work. It was, the foreman explained, a Catholic church, built at the turn of the century to serve exiled Poles. The Communists sliced off its spire and used it as a cinema, but now it was being refurbished with funds from Catholics abroad.

Was the city council contributing?

The builder – a Pole – snorted and flapped his enormous hands: 'What do you think? They've got no faith; they're nothing but alcoholics.'

This was unfair, since in the better-kept upper town, on the steps of Archbishop Kipriyan's St Sofia cathedral, a service was under way. Beneath a chorus of lapis domes the faithful clustered in a drab, padded huddle, their sung responses dissipating in the bright, still air. Inside, the walls were crisp with new plaster and the iconostasis gaudy with acrylic paint. In Soviet times, a monk told me, the cathedral was used as 'a stable, it was full of dung'. Another said that was nonsense, that it had been a vegetable store. They agreed that it once housed a miraculous icon: 'It was covered in gold. The Communists took it away somewhere, no one knows where. People say that maybe it's in Australia.' In the porch an old man with narrow, china-blue eyes and a photographer's dream of a face practised his patter to the clangour of bells: 'Give me a kopeck and God will give you health and happiness and good luck. Show me a dollar, a green dollar. Go on, I've never seen one, give it to me as a present . . .' A small girl bounced in front of him. I should not give money to beggars, she admonished, shaking her earrings, for they weren't good, they were all drunks. The first place I should see was the museum, and she, Katya, would take me there.

Housed in the old archbishop's palace, the museum was worth seeing. Its mahogany cabinets were filled with butterflies and pottery shards redolent of pre-revolutionary civic pride. A local merchant's family who gave over their house to Nicholas's retinue in 1917 were commemorated by the contents of their drawing-room: an upright piano, a faux-bamboo chaise-longue, sepia photographs of steam-barges and a group portrait of the family itself – plump, slightly crumpled and unmistakably Tatar-eyed. Best of all, in Katya's opinion, was a travelling exhibition of anatomical curiosities: a two-headed human foetus, puckered anus winking obscenely through the pickling fluid; mutant calves, contorted like figures from the Kama Sutra; eyeless, noseless babies, their blanched, misshapen heads garnished with lacy mob-caps. A woman with peroxide hair was giving a party of schoolchildren a tour. 'If you have sex too young, or go out in winter without tights on,' she said, pointing at a fungoid lump with her baton, 'this is what happens to your womb.' Cancerous breasts, floating in pulpy cross-section, were caused by 'stress, and quarrels in the family'.

Afterwards, Katya took me to a café. The owners, she said grandly, were 'Armenians, but good people'. Sliding twinkly clips in and out of her hair, she announced that she was aged eleven and 'genuine Russian', though with her street-child skinniness and sparkle I would have put her at seven or eight and part-Tatar or gypsy. Her mother, she said, sold vegetables in exchange for flour and bread, and her father drank. 'His roof moved' – tapping her head – 'and he ran into the courtyard with an axe. Now he's normal again.' Of her four siblings two lived in a children's home, but she went to proper school, where she liked drawing and maths best. How old was I when I had my ears pierced? She did hers herself with a pin, and it hadn't hurt at all. Had I met Madonna? Leonardo di Caprio? That girl across the street pulling a sled was Natasha. Yesterday she beat up Dasha and took his *shapka* and threw it in a puddle. Outside, I gave Katya a bag of oranges and a 100-rouble note. She grinned, stood on tiptoe to kiss my cheek and whipped round the corner like quicksilver, her story flicking after her like a thousand and one half-told Siberian tales.

Tobolsk's museum had few reminders of the Tatar past: necklaces of coins, a high-pommelled saddle inlaid with ivory, a gravestone carved with the words 'gone from the land of the flesh to the land of eternity' in Arabic. But the city was never without Tatars, as foreign visitors all remarked, usually to compare them favourably with the Russians. 'The Russe,' wrote Giles Fletcher, Elizabeth I's ambassador to Muscovy, 'neither beleeveth anything that another man speaketh, nor speaketh anything himselfe worthy to bee beleeved. These qualities make them very odious to all ther Neighbours, specially to the Tartars, that account themselves to be honest and just.'[20] Johann Gmelin, a German naturalist and member of the Danish explorer Vitus Bering's expedition in search of the North-East Passage in the 1730s, praised his 'efficient, calm and willing'[21] Tatar boatmen, who toiled uncomplainingly day and night and never broke bread or hoisted sail without a prayer. D'Auteroche was impressed with the Tatars' cleanliness and dignity. 'Their houses are as neat,' he reported, 'as those of the [Russian] Siberians are dirty . . . They are tall, strong, and well made, and their dress is perfectly becoming. Notwithstanding the mildness of their countenances, they have still the appearance of a warlike and independent people.'[22] The accompanying illustration in his beautifully produced travel book shows a Tatar dandy sporting a cane, curled moustache and fashionably blasé expression. John Ledyard, a young American who had sailed with Captain Cook and wanted to get into the Russo-American fur trade, agreed. 'The Tatars', he wrote to his patron Thomas Jefferson, 'are universally neater than the Russians, particularly in their houses', though their increasing Russification was to be regretted since 'the coat of civilisation sits as ill upon them, as upon our American Tartars'.[23]

Today there are altogether over five million Tatars in Russia, 1.8 million of them in the 'ethnic republic' of Tatarstan – once the khanate of Kazan – on the upper Volga, where they make up half the population and have limited freedom to pass their own laws and set their own taxes. In Sibir, they have long fallen into a minority. To find them I enlisted Alik, a young half-Russian, half-Tatar postman whose cornflower-blue eyes contrasted handsomely with a happy-go-lucky Asian face. He did not think much of Islam – 'All these mullahs are old Communists. In my village the head accountant suddenly said he was a mullah. What kind of mullah is that!' – and if he had a patron saint it was Princess Diana, simpering from a sticker on the dashboard of his van. But he did know the way to the poor quarter of the lower town that locals called the 'Tatar Republic' and to the shabby side-street that hosted Tobolsk's mosque.

Plain and foursquare in utilitarian brick, it looked more like a village hall than a religious building. Inside, cast-iron radiators belched softly and dainty old ladies wearing snow-white headscarves told beads to the patter of rain on the roof. One was doing stretching exercises: 'People complain to God about their health! And I say to them, "Touch your toes!" ' Another wiggled her feet so that we could admire her tinsel socks. Presently the mullah appeared, in a crimson hat the size and shape of an upturned wastepaper basket. Before the revolution, he said, there were two mosques in Tobolsk. Through the 1920s the Communists let them stay open, but come Stalin one was pulled down and the other was turned into a prison, then a cinema, then a House of Pioneers. Their mullahs were accused of spying or sabotage and shot. After Stalin's death, Islam was made legal again, but training was rationed and the clergy kept under the Party's thumb. The city government gave permission to reopen this building only in 1989, at the tail-end of Gorbachev's perestroika. Saudi missionaries promised money for repairs, but it never arrived, so local volunteers did all the work themselves.

What, I wanted to know, were relations like between Tatars and Russians? It was a delicate question, and the ladies twittered and jostled. 'Nobody bothers about nationality,' said one. 'It doesn't make any difference. All we care about is whether someone's a good person or not.' Another thought that Russians had no sense of humour; a third was against mixed marriages. Couples got on fine to begin with, 'but when they get older they start to argue about which nation is best. The worst is if a child dies, because then they can't decide which cemetery to put him in. They have to think, Are our children Tatar or Russian?' And what about Khan Kuchum, and his battle with Yermak? The first lady was firm: 'Ordinary Russians and Tatars always got on very well. Any fighting, it was all their leaders' fault.'

Kuchum's old capital of Isker lay ten miles upriver from Tobolsk. Slaloming round potholes, Alik pointed out the sights. This *was* a collective farm, he said, *was* a tractor station, *was* a timberyard. Isker, it turned out, was in the past tense too. By the 1730s all that remained of it were three mud walls. Now, the site's only noteworthy building was an Orthodox monastery, crumbling white and verdigris amid more silence, more trees, more wet snow. Here, too, builders were at work: red-bearded giants who rapped freckled knuckles on the chipboard coffins draped with old curtains in which they were reburying the skeletons – of monks shot by the Bolsheviks, they thought – they had found in a mass grave out in the yard.

The Tatar village next door did not have a mosque, but it did have a mullah. A man herding a cow and a calf showed us the way, grumbling between thwacks of his stick on the animals' bony rumps. 'Mullah? You mean Anatoliy. All these new religions, you can't tell them apart. And the young people don't know anything. You know what they think happened to the monastery? They think it was bombed by the Fascists!' We hopscotched through a mud-bath to Anatoliy's front door, and pulled off our boots in a lean-to stacked with firewood, shovels, churns, back-issues of *Sovyetskaya Sibir* and a gas-stove that looked like salvage from a deep-sea wreck. In the living-room, busy lizzies spilled from condensed-milk cans, and a glass-fronted cabinet displayed the same china tea set – orange with white polka dots – to be found in every living-room from Lviv to Vladivostok. The only Tatar touch was the mullah's wife, a tiny old woman with cheekbones wide as a Persian cat's, who sat ballerina-straight on the edge of their bed in front of the television, watching blondes thrash about the screen to thumping Russian rock.

The mullah's real name was Kadriguli – in Tatar, 'Flower of God'. When he was called up for the war, he explained, 'they just put Anatoliy in my passport and it stuck'. In 1945 he returned home and started work – officially as a tractor-driver, unofficially as village mullah in place of his father. He had never had any religious training nor learned Arabic, but knew enough to scrape by. 'I remembered all the customs, so when someone died, or wanted their child circumcised, I told them what to do.'

Didn't this get him into trouble?

'They prohibited the faith, but really it all depended on the local administration. Bad Communists didn't allow any religion; good ones did.'

His wife exploded like a firecracker: 'Of course the Communists were good! With them, there was order, discipline! We got up early and went home late, but we got paid! Now we don't have any money, and everyone's home at midday! Perfect Communism! Nobody works!'

Having swept aside Kuchum's khanate, the Russians pushed on east with extraordinary speed. First they established themselves along the Ob and its tributaries, then along the Yenisey, and in the 1640s and 1650s along the Lena, Indigirka and Kolyma. In 1639 Ivan Moskvitin became the first Russian to see the Pacific, 166 years before Lewis and Clark debouched on to the mouth of the Columbia river, and a mere fifty-eight after Yermak first breached the Urals.

What drew them on, swiftly and surely as gold drew the *conquistadores* to Peru, was fur, especially that of the ferret-like sable. Blacker than night, softer than a snowfall, sable pelts had been the ultimate status symbol since history began. The heroes of the Icelandic sagas used them to bind their wounds; Kubla Khan, so Marco Polo tells us, to line his audience tent. They may have been the ancients' Golden Fleece. In medieval England sumptuary laws reserved them for the high nobility.

In the 1500s European demand for fur expanded, thanks to the influx of New World bullion and rise of a showy new merchant class. Chief supplier to the growing market was Russia, whose European forests were soon hunted out. But in Siberia, travellers whispered, fortunes in fur were still there for the taking. Its sable were so fat that their fur dragged on the ground, so tame that they could be bludgeoned to death with sticks, and so numerous that the natives used their skins to cover their snowshoes, happily exchanging a kettle-full for the kettle itself. Exaggeration aside, a single lucky hunt could indeed set a man up for life. In 1623 a Siberian official reported the theft of two black fox pelts, one worth thirty roubles, the other eighty. With this money, he calculated, the thief could buy himself fifty acres of land, a cabin, five good horses, ten cows and twenty sheep, and still have half his takings left over.

There duly appeared in Siberia a heterogeneous breed of trapper-

fighter-explorers, not unlike the French woodrunners who first pene-
trated Canada. In theory, they divided into two categories: commercial operators, self-financed or under hire to merchants, and
'servitors' – mostly the unruly soldiers known as Cossacks – in salaried
government service. In practice, they behaved so similarly and worked
together so often as to be virtually indistinguishable, giving rise to a
continuing debate over whether Siberia's conquest was primarily
the result of conscious government policy or of haphazard private
enterprise. Both groups went armed, and both, as noted by an English
merchant trying to break into the fur trade himself, were superlatively
tough:

> I believe such men for hard living are not under the Sunne: for no
> cold will hurt them. Yea, and though they lye in the field two
> moneths, at such times as it shall freeze more than a yard thicke, the
> common Souldier hath neither Tent nor anything else over his head
> ... every man musts carrie and make provision for himselfe, and his
> Horse for a moneth or two, which is very wonderfull. For hee
> himselfe shall live upon water and Oate-meale mingled together
> cold...[24]

Like their Canadian equivalents, they travelled as far as possible by
river, dragging their boats from headwater to headwater and building
wooden forts, fortified with stockades of sharpened logs, at strategic
confluences and narrows. From these they set off on fur-gathering
expeditions, in the course of which they both trapped themselves
and extracted pelts, by violence or by barter, from nearby native
settlements. Seduced or subjugated, each tribe's duty regularly to
produce furs in the future was made official by the imposition of an
oath upon its leader. If he made war or failed to pay tribute in full,
the Buryat chief Bului swore in 1642, 'the sun will not shine on me,
I will not walk the earth, I will not eat bread, the Russian sword will
cut me down, the gun will kill me, fire will destroy all our villages
...'[25] Taking their oaths, Sakha walked between the two halves of a
dismembered dog; Altaians drank from vessels containing gold coins.
For added security the Russians held one or two of each chief's
relatives permanently hostage, releasing them only in exchange for
substitutes. Backsliding got short shrift. A furious letter of 1645 from

the commander of Yakutsk fort to the above-mentioned Bului detailed what rebels could expect. Bului, he wrote, had murdered Russian tribute-collectors, burned hayfields and stolen horses and cattle. Unless he gave himself up immediately, soldiers would be sent against him: 'These men will be instructed that not only you and your wives and children and tribespeople are to be killed because of your treason, but your livestock are to be destroyed and your yurts burned relentlessly . . . And you will have brought this destruction upon yourselves.'[26]

What makes the motives for Siberia's conquest plainest are the volumes of correspondence between Moscow, fort commanders and Cossack expedition leaders. The orders given Vasiliy Poyarkov by Yakutsk's commander in 1643 were typical. Proceeding south, he was to 'collect the Sovereign's tribute and search for new non tribute-paying people, and also to search for silver, copper and lead ores, and for grain'.[27] Over the next four years, Poyarkov sailed 4,000 miles to the mouth of the river Amur and back, losing most of his men to shipwreck, starvation and native attacks on the way. But in the report he wrote on his return he hardly mentioned that the Amur was now known to empty into the Pacific, concentrating instead on the crops grown by its local peoples and its sad lack of precious metals. Five years later, the Cossack Semyon Dezhnev made an astounding 2,000-mile voyage, at the cost of the lives of seventy-eight out of his ninety men, round the Chukotka peninsula, becoming the first European to find the North-East Passage between Asia and America. Instead of trumpeting this epoch-making feat, his report dwelt on the iniquities of a rival, the back pay owed him by the government and the debts outstanding between his surviving Cossacks: Grigoriy had paid one sable for berries and a flint, Vasiliy four sable for caviar and meat, Fyodor eight roubles for twenty fish, a pound of lead, an amulet, a hat with a red top, a bowstring and a pipe.[28] A Croat Jesuit exiled to Tobolsk in the 1650s heard rumours that Cossacks from Yakutsk had discovered that Siberia was 'washed on the east by one continuous ocean'.[29] Otherwise, all memory of Dezhnev's historic journey was lost until the 1730s, when one of Bering's scientists stumbled across his papers in the Yakutsk archives.

Haphazard as it was, the conquest of Siberia transformed Muscovy, helping turn it from an obscure princedom on civilisation's fringes into a great European power. Until the end of the seventeenth century, one historian estimates, the fur trade contributed more to the country's economy than any other single activity save agriculture. At the trade's peak in the 1650s, the government drew from it somewhere between a tenth and a third of total state revenues. In large transactions furs substituted for precious metals, as they also did in foreign diplomacy. In 1595 Boris Godunov was embarrassed by a request from the Holy Roman Emperor, Rudolf II, for military assistance against the Turks. Not wishing to jeopardise trade with Constantinople, he compromised by sending Rudolf the pelts of 337,235 squirrel, 40,360 sable, 20,760 marten, 3,000 beaver and 1,000 wolves. Their display – not counting the squirrel skins, which had to be left in wagons outside – took up twenty rooms of Rudolf's palace in Prague. Forty years later, when renegade Ukrainian Cossacks seized the Ottoman port of Azov, Tsar Mikhail smoothed things over with the Porte by showering it with 8,000-roubles' worth of sable for the Sultan and another 2,000-roubles' worth for his viziers.

Within a few decades, the more accessible parts of Siberia were hunted out in their turn, and the fur take fell. By 1649, trappers were complaining that on rivers where they used to catch a hundred or more sable each season, they now took only fifteen or twenty. Native tribute had to be cut from twelve sable pelts per man per year to three. At the same time, the Hudson's Bay Company started to compete for the European market, and tax reforms began to bring funds from other sources into the budget. By 1701, furs made up less than 3 per cent of government revenues.

In the meantime, though, Siberian furs had not only lured Russia into Asia, but helped politically to consolidate the Russian state. Had they not brought income into the imperial treasury when they did, historians argue, Muscovy might never have emerged from its 1598–1613 Time of Troubles, during which it saw five different pretenders take the throne, was invaded by Sweden and Poland and lost a third of its population to warfare, famine and disease. By easing Mikhail Romanov, the boyar who emerged from the mess, into his thirty-two-year reign, they helped establish the dynasty that held the country together for the next three centuries. When Yermak crossed the Urals in the 1580s Muscovy's Third Rome pretensions had seemed absurd. A century on it had seized eastern Ukraine from Poland and was poised to take Finland and the Baltics from Sweden. The title Caesar or 'Tsar' was no longer a joke.

In Siberia the Russians had won themselves a continent, a land on which the sun never set, one of the biggest empires the world had ever known. Their stupendous achievement took some time to sink in. Until the late 1600s, they treated it as a rich landowner might a distant estate: as a useful source of income, but not worth bothering about so long as the peasants stayed quiet and the rents kept coming in. So unattractive was Siberia, went a joke, that it must have been God's botched first attempt at creation, or something he scrambled together with the leftovers when he had finished everything else. As Western ideas started percolating into Russia, curiosity increased. Peter the Great sent scientific expeditions to Siberia; Empresses Anne and Catherine did the same, and encouraged peasant settlement.

But even during Russia's most self-consciously imperial phase, Siberia's place in the national imagination was oddly insecure. 'Siberia is simply Siberia,' grumbled a nineteenth-century governor, 'and has nothing in common with India.'[30] Though salon painters turned out endless oils of languid Samarkand tea-houses and beetling Caucasian crags, none was moved to romanticise Buryat yurts or the cliffs of the river Lena. Similarly, Tolstoy wrote no Prisoner of the Altai, and no Lermontovian duels took place in Tomsk or Irkutsk.

The reason, of course, was that people like Tolstoy and Lermontov never went to Siberia – at least, not voluntarily. Almost as soon as it was discovered, its image as a land of opportunity, of abounding natural resources, was overlaid with a darker vision: Siberia as Dostoyevsky's *House of the Dead*, Gorky's 'land of death and chains', Solzhenitsyn's *Gulag Archipelago*. For runaway serfs and schismatics, as for fortune-hunting Cossacks, it was a place of escape, of new beginnings. But for the convicts, prisoners of war and political exiles who made up one in ten of its population by the late 1600s, it was the death of hope, the unhappiest of endings. 'I ceased,' the Decembrist Nikolay Basargin wrote on hearing his sentence of exile, 'to consider myself an inhabitant of this world.'[31] Siberia was Russia's New World, her bright fur-, gold- or oil-fed future. But it was also her dark past, her cupboard full of skeletons, a sinister hinterland where grotesque officials riffled their takings to the howl of wolves and rattle of convict fetters.

The image of its Russian colonists, the *Sibiryaki*, was similarly confused. For nineteenth-century Slavophiles the isolated, old-fashioned *Sibiryak* embodied unpolluted traditional values. To reach Tomsk and Irkutsk, wrote one, Western ideas had to travel thousands of versts on horseback, in the course of which they crusted over with hoarfrost and acquired a strong Siberian accent. Just as it was simple, faithful Holy Russia's mission, Slavophiles thought, to redeem decadent Europe, Siberia's virginal innocence would be the saving of decadent Moscow and Petersburg. The theme was taken up again in the 1960s by Siberia's ethnic-Russian 'village writers', who extolled country at the expense of city in stories featuring awkward meetings between urbanised children and rural parents, and village eccentrics' doomed stands against authority. 'Humanity,' wrote the best-known of them, Valentin Rasputin, 'could turn over a new leaf by leaning on Siberia.' He found the *Sibiryak*'s geographical analogue in the transparent waters of Lake Baikal, using mystical language to turn it into the centrepiece of the nascent Russian conservation movement:

> It's impossible to give a name to the regeneration that occurs in people when they're near Baikal ... Here he stands and looks around, is filled with something and carried off somewhere, and can't understand what's happening to him ... Something in him cries, something exults, something plunges into peacefulness, something becomes orphaned.[32]

But in other ways, the *Sibiryaki* were not very Russian at all. Tough, enterprising and free from serfdom, they struck many as more like pioneer Americans. 'The further we moved into Siberia,' wrote Basargin:

> the more it improved in my eyes. The common people seemed freer, more skilful, even better educated than our Russian peasants,

especially more so than our estate serfs. They better understood the dignity of man, and valued their rights more highly. Later, I several times heard from persons who had visited the United States and lived there that Siberians have many similarities with the Americans – in their manners, in their customs, and even in their way of life.[33]

From exile in London, the socialist Alexander Herzen pronounced the Siberian peasant to be 'well-formed, healthy, clever and prudent', and 'much more martial, dextrous and able to offer resistance than his Great Russian brother'. If it were not for autocracy, which produced nothing save by the stick, they would develop Siberia 'with American rapidity'.[34]

The Siberia-as-America story reached its apogee in the 1850s, during which the Crimean War alienated Russian liberals from France and Britain, and Russia and America consolidated their respective Pacific seaboards. 'Both countries,' gushed Herzen, 'abound in strengths, flexibility, a spirit of organization, and a persistence which knows no obstacles. Both are poor in history; both begin with a complete break with tradition . . .'[35] Bringing trade, investment and a 'breeze of civic freedom',[36] the Amur would turn into Russia's Mississippi, Mongol steppe into Kentucky bluegrass, Nikolayevsk into San Francisco. The connection would take physical shape – as President Lincoln outlined in several State of the Union Addresses – in the form of a telegraph-line joining Europe with America via the Bering Strait. A team of Western Union employees spent two years, from 1865 to 1867, surveying and felling trees for telegraph poles in the far north-east before news got through to them, more than six months late, that a cable had been laid under the Atlantic, and that their work had all been in vain.

Politically, Siberia-as-America was a wish-fulfilment fantasy, a pro-jection on to Siberia of the sort of Russia that would never come to pass in reality. But physically, there was enough truth in the idea for American travellers constantly to compare Siberia's roughhouse mushroom cities, filled with claim-stakers, gold-panners and brothel-keepers, with similar ones back home. Even today, its forest-girt log cabins instantly recall Laura Ingalls Wilder's *Little House in the Big Woods*, and its southern grasslands, featureless save for the occasional fly-bitten horse hitched to a rail outside a corrugated-iron shack, the backdrop to a hundred Westerns. With a bit of imagination, the fretworked merchants' mansions of Tomsk and Irkutsk can even be transformed into New England sea-captains' clapboard – though whereas America's versions can hardly breathe for blue plaques, Siberia's have degenerated into squalid tenements.

In the 1860s the two contradictory threads – Siberia as Russia's saviour because of its Russian-ness, and Siberia as Russia's saviour because of its American-ness – converged in a regionalist movement. Drawn from the Siberian-born, Petersburg-educated provincial intelligentsia, the regionalists argued that Siberia was distinct enough from European Russia to be allowed a degree of self-government. Failing that, customs barriers should be lifted, more funds provided for roads and schools, and the exile system that filled it with roving criminals scrapped. It was not a new idea. In 1849, during the Europe-wide popular revolts known as the Springtime of Nations, the governor-general of Western Siberia had warned Nicholas I that the *Sibiryaki* took a dangerously proprietorial view of their natural resources, and should be allowed no contact with foreigners lest it awaken in them 'the desire for the establishment of an independent country'.[37] This time as then, the monarchy's response was a crackdown. In 1865, when a pamphlet came to light calling for an independent republic, the regionalists were rounded up and sentenced to lengthy terms of imprisonment – not, for once, in Siberia.

Where did the real Siberians, the native peoples, fit into all this? The answer, usually, was nowhere very much. Russians' perceptions of them progressed through familiar stages. For the Cossacks, they were an economic resource; for Enlightenment scientists, natural curiosities; for Romantics, noble savages; for empire-builders, an excuse – so as to rescue them from cruel Chinese or Japanese rule – to conquer new territory, and a canvas on which to display civilising prowess. Pre-revolutionary travel writers usually only featured them as a side-show: the flutter of rags on a wayside bush or glimpse of yurts from a train window. When they padded out such fleeting observations, it was with a mish-mash of old saws and sloppy generalisations. The natives, they said in one breath, were ferocious and hospitable, lazy and energetic, childish and possessed of ancient wisdom. Even the immaculate Anton Chekhov fell into confusion on the island of Sakhalin, describing the Nivkh as simultaneously cheerful and mournful, honest and liars, scared of and brash towards authority.

In Petersburg's State Russian Museum, a treasure-house of Russian arts and crafts, the sole evidence of the native Siberians' existence is an eighteenth-century ivory. Carved, judging by its directness and vigour, by an indigenous artist for the Russian market, it depicts hunters going about their traditional business − shooting a wolf, baiting a bear-cub, butchering a deer − around a tent. The only inactive figure is a European, in tricorne hat and breeches. The Hermitage's only nod to the indigenous peoples is a china figurine of an Itelmen girl, one of a series of 'national types' produced by the Imperial Porcelain Factory in the 1780s. Winsome and rosy, with a cornucopia of fish spilling at her feet, she is as charming and as bogus as the prancing deer and graceful shamanesses of the early Siberian travel books, whose illustrators never left Paris or London. Even the regionalist Yadrintsev, passionately defending native rights in a book titled *Siberia as a Colony*, termed the native peoples *inorodtsy*, or 'aliens'. 'Indigenes', in his vocabulary as in Rasputin's, meant old-established Russian colonists. In the Gulag the word 'aborigine' was used by the tough ex-soldiers exiled after the Second World War to denote the frail intellectuals swept up by the purges of the 1930s. In the brilliant, harrowing stories Varlam Shalamov wrote about his seventeen years in the Kolyma camps, the Sakha, whose homeland Kolyma is, are a wholly offstage presence, their existence implied only by the appearance of a Sakha dog, which the starving prisoners kill and eat.

There were exceptions. Condemned to remote settlements for years on end, nineteenth-century exiles often staved off despair by turning themselves into ethnographers. Outcasts themselves, they empathised with their subjects. 'Constantly longing to return to my native land,' wrote the Polish nationalist (and brother of Józef) Bronisław Piłsudski, 'I naturally felt attracted towards the natives of Saghalien, who alone had a true affection for that country' and who, like the Poles, had been invaded by 'an utterly different form of civilisation'. Their predicament reminded him of his schooldays in

Russian-ruled Vilnius, where 'cruel attempts were made to force . . . contempt for our past and our national culture, and coerce us into speaking the foreign intruder's language'.[38] The lively, humane and mind-bogglingly comprehensive studies such men produced are classics of the discipline.

Nor were native Siberians entirely ignored by novelists, the nearest Russia has to a Kipling or Fenimore Cooper being Vladimir Arsenyev. Posted to Vladivostok as a young army officer in 1900, Arsenyev made three long expeditions into the Ussuri forest looking for possible Japanese invasion routes. Sidetracked into ethnography, he became director of the Khabarovsk city museum, and during the revolution kept his head down writing a children's book based on his Ussuri adventures. Published under the title *Dersu Uzala*, the book was an international bestseller, winning plaudits from the Norwegian explorer Fridtjof Nansen and invitations to lecture in Japan. With Stalin's rise to power, Arsenyev's foreign contacts turned into liabilities. In 1930, having been interrogated several times by the security service or GPU, he escaped arrest by dying of heart disease. His widow was shot as a Japanese spy, and his seventeen-year-old daughter given ten years in a labour camp for 'anti-Soviet propaganda'.

Dersu, though, lived on, becoming the archetypal Siberian native to generations of Russian schoolchildren. His exact nationality is somewhat vague: Arsenyev described him as a Nanai, but based him on a variety of characters, including his Chinese guide. The actor who plays Dersu in Akira Kurosawa's 1975 film version is Tuvan – suitably Asiatic-looking in other words, but from a region of Siberia as far away from the Ussuri as Moscow is from Madrid. In the book, Arsenyev's Cossacks initially mistake him for a bear: ' "No shoot, me man!" came a voice out of the darkness, and a moment later a man stepped into the light of the fire.'[39] Invited to join their expedition as a tracker, he quickly proves invaluable, using his ancient forest and medicinal skills to save them from flood, storm, quicksand and fever. Reserved and melancholy, he shows anger only when they shoot game for sport, and scolds blunt knives and spitting logs as if they were human beings.

In reality, even by Arsenyev's time, wise, loyal Dersus were rare. In Khabarovsk in 1913, Nansen was struck by the elegance of the Evenk canoes in Arsenyev's museum, and by the similarity of their sleds to the ones he had designed for his own expeditions. But the only actual native people he met were a pair of dockside drunks. 'In their dress,' he lamented, 'they were entirely Russian: and as in addition one of them had absorbed so much Russian vodka that he fell prostrate before us and kissed the ground under our feet, there was not much enjoyment to be got out of them.'[40] Arsenyev himself was convinced that the indigenous peoples had been so degraded by European contact that they would soon become extinct. At the end of his book Dersu starts to go blind, so Arsenyev moves him into his flat in Khabarovsk. Predictably, the scheme is a disaster. Dersu hates sleeping indoors, cannot understand having to buy water, and gets arrested for felling a tree in the park. Fleeing back to his beloved forest, he is murdered in his sleep by thieves. Arsenyev buries him beneath twin cedars, but when he revisits the spot two years later the grave has disappeared: 'Several efforts I made to locate the grave, but in vain. My cedar landmarks had vanished. New roads had been made. There were quarry faces, dumps, embankments . . . all around bore the signs of another life.'[41]

Eight decades on native Siberians puzzle Russians as much as ever. Natasha, a 21-year-old with a face like a china doll's and a river of black hair, is a graduate student at Moscow's Academy of Sciences. She is also an Even, one of a 17,000-strong nationality from the far north-eastern tundra. Blowing the froth off a cappuccino, she explains what that entails. Muscovites, she says, are either amazed by her ethnicity, or patronising: 'Either they don't know anything about the indigenous peoples at all, or they treat you as an exotic. They don't see you as a person, an individual.' The Chechen-obsessed Moscow police stop her several times a week. 'When the *militsiya* look at my passport and see the word "Even" they can't believe it. They say I must be from Uzbekistan or somewhere. They think that if you're from the north you've got slitty eyes, that you live in a tent making friends with bears.'

Back home in Magadan, the dying mining-town that was once the capital of the Kolyma Gulag, her schoolteachers were little better. 'Even got put down as Evenk, and Evenk as Even. They'd say, "What difference does an extra letter make?" Or they'd just put you down as a Yakut.' Defining herself got even harder with the collapse of the Soviet Union. 'It made sense to say "I'm a Soviet." But it's impossible for me to call myself a *Rossiyanka*, a Russian. It's not a category I fit into. But then if I'm not Russian, how can I belong to a Russian state?' It is a familiar theme, expressed in vocabulary that Natasha has picked up from the Greenpeace office where she works part time. But that does not detract from its truth. On a continent that was theirs before Russia existed, native Siberians are not extinct, but excluded.

THE KHANT

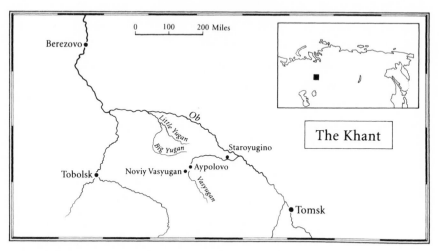

A berry and a bunch of grass lived together.
Once they went to bed.
In the morning they got up, and the berry said to the grass 'You,
    grass, make a fire!'
And the bunch of grass started building a fire.
The flames flared up, and the grass flared up too.
The berry lay on the floor rocking with laughter.
It laughed and laughed until it split its sides.
Their house burned down.

– Khant folktale, 1950s

The river Ob, wide, brown, meandering mightily among leafy islets, has cast a spell on our hydrofoil. On deck men in paint-spattered trousers and cork life jackets smoke in silence, shifting only to point out the rise of a fish or the current's churn past a tethered buoy. In the cabin children flop across their mothers' laps, and a teenager parades a Siamese cat on a leash up and down the centre aisle. It is apparent that he is proud of his cat, showing it off, and it is indeed a lovely creature, with *café au lait* fur and aquamarine eyes. When the engine cuts, sky and water tilt gently upwards, silence washing over us like the floodwater drowning the willows on either bank. The trees part and a village drifts alongside, strung along a low scarp of soft brown earth. Then the cabins and fences spin away, and we are skimming again between mazy walls of green. It would be no surprise if parrots flashed out of them, or a hail of arrows.

On the map the Ob resembles a centipede, its sinuous 3,000-mile length the insect's body, dozens of tributaries its legs. Flowing northwards through Western Siberia, the river's middle reaches are the homeland of the Khant, originally known to Russians, in what has become a derogatory term, as Ostyaks.

Related to the Finns and Estonians, they lived, before the Russian conquest, from fishing and hunting. In winter, they sheltered in log-built, turf-roofed crofts; in summer, in bark-covered bivouacs at riverside fishing-camps. Their most sophisticated artefacts were their bows. Six feet tall, they were made from sandwiched strips of cedar and birch, and equipped with an armoury of arrows: forked for birds, blunt-headed for fur-bearing animals, or specially feathered so as to imitate a swooping hawk or frightened duckling. Cruder were their gingerbread-man-shaped wooden fetishes, which they housed in raised shrines and placated with sacrifices of deer and captured enemies. Their most elaborate ritual – as for most native Siberians – was the feast that followed a successful bear hunt. Carried in procession back to the village, the dead animal was offered food and drink, and entertained with songs and dances. After several days' celebration its body was reverently butchered and eaten, and its cleaned skull set on a pole as a guardian totem.

But bears' skulls were no match for muskets, as the Khant were among the first native Siberians to discover. A chronicle records an encounter with Yermak's Cossacks:

> In the morning the Ostyaks came up to the [Russian] stronghold and brought with them an idol. They had this instead of a god, and this idol was famed in their land. They set up this idol beneath a tree and began to sacrifice before it. They expected that by its aid they would capture the Christians and put them to death. While they were sacrificing, the Russians fired a cannon from their stronghold,

and smashed into many pieces that tree, beneath which was the idol, and this idol itself. The pagans were terrified, not knowing what this was, and they thought someone had let fly from a bow, and they said to each other: 'These are indeed powerful archers, as they have smashed such a tree.'[1]

'From this hour', the chronicle goes on, the Khant 'returned to their homes', living 'like animals in wild forests, keeping out of sight of the Russian people ... And to this day it is their custom to flee and disappear when our peoples come.'[2]

It was a sensible reaction, for until at least the mid-1800s Russian rule of Siberia was brutal, rapacious and corrupt. Unfashionable and uncomfortable, Siberian postings tended to attract the mad, bad, drunk or disgraced. A man who left Moscow as a common soldier, it was said, became a sergeant in Tobolsk, a captain in Yakutsk and a colonel on Kamchatka. Paid a derisory salary, he was expected to support himself by *kormleniye* – literally translated as 'feeding' – off the local population, a system of state-sanctioned graft abolished by Ivan the Terrible in European Russia, but given a new lease of life east of the Urals. Distance made controlling Siberian officials almost impossible, as illustrated by a decree of Peter the Great. 'Written laws,' the tsar thundered, 'should not be treated like playing cards. This *ukaz* seals all orders and regulations like a stamp, so that nobody can act according to their own whims or in breach of instructions. If something in the regulations is unclear then one should not define or decide anything independently, but report to the Senate.' But as long as the round trip to Tobolsk took ten weeks, to Tomsk seven months, and to Yakutsk two years or more, such declarations were as flimsy as the silk they were printed on, and officials behaved as they pleased. A prime example was Peter's own appointee as governor of Tobolsk, Matvey Gagarin. During his nine-year reign he burned arsonists alive, minted his own coins and made such a fortune from smuggling that he was able to shoe his horses with silver and hang an icon of the Virgin encrusted with 130,000-roubles' worth of diamonds over his bed. Furious, Peter summoned him back to Petersburg, ordering that he be publicly hanged and left to dangle until the rope rotted, at which point it was to be replaced with a chain.

Eighteenth-century travellers to Siberia came home full of tales of official ignorance, dishonesty, laziness and vice. According to the German naturalist Gmelin, the commander of Krasnoyarsk fort enlivened his suppers with drinking competitions, at the close of which the guest who found himself 'most like a beast'[3] received a prize. Visiting a nearby village with the same man, Gmelin noticed that the peasants who came to pay their respects rarely failed to hand over a few coins, discreetly wrapped in paper. Nerchinsk's commander was just as bad, being 'wholly occupied in his own interest',[4] and thinking of nothing except how best to force gifts out of the local inhabitants. The previous year, Gmelin was told, he had returned from a tour with 1,000 sheep, 100 horses and 80 camels. As for the soldiery, they were often no better than the bandits they were supposed to suppress. On the road back to Petersburg in 1742, Gmelin found two villages he had passed through earlier deserted, because 'a detachment of the Cossack horde had pillaged and burned them, and carried off all the inhabitants that they had not massacred'.[5] Though fresh troops had been sent after the renegades, the authorities dared not pursue them into the mountains for fear of more rebel bands.

In Petersburg such criticisms were not appreciated. Hence the contrast between Gmelin's account of Siberia, published after his return home to Germany, and that of his travelling companion Gerhard Müller, who stayed on at the Imperial Academy of Arts and Sciences, under strict censorship and in government pay. Where Gmelin makes cracks ('when a Tomskian has money, he spends half of it on public women, and gets drunk with three-quarters of the rest') Müller is prudently factual, sticking to dusty archives and to the minutiae of native ritual and dress.

Most damning of the eighteenth-century travellers was the French astronomer Chappe d'Auteroche, whose *Voyage en Sibérie* interspersed routine complaints about capsized sleds, thieving servants and smelly post-stations with diatribes against the whole of Russian government and society. Russia could not become a great country, he argued, until she forswore despotism, which 'debases the mind, damps the genius, and stifles every kind of sentiment'.[6] Standing in the same relation to the monarch as serfs to their master, her citizens were so paralysed with fear and mutual distrust that they answered the most innocuous questions with 'God knows, and the Empress', and kept 'total silence ... upon everything which may have the least relation either to the government, or to the sovereign'.[7] In her courts, justice was publicly sold, her clergy were so drunken and libidinous that they were 'often found in the streets unable to walk home',[8] and her naval officers so ignorant of navigation that their ships rotted in port. 'In Russia,' d'Auteroche summed up, 'no person dares venture to think.'[9]

To get revenge, Catherine the Great turned to the compliant Müller, who provided materials for an *Antidote* to d'Auteroche's book, published anonymously in 1772. Written, most think, by the Empress herself, the *Antidote* opens with a dedication to its own author, the 'pride and delight of her subjects, and the admiration of Europe'. In sprightly fashion it goes on to tear d'Auteroche's book apart. The Frenchman's criticisms are 'mere prattle, or strains of rancour and animosity'.[10] He is guilty of generalisation, exaggeration and inconsistency; of disapproval of 'every thing that is not done as in France'; of ingratitude 'against a nation that loaded you with civility';[11] of underpaying his servants; and of moaning on, in a feeble Parisian way, about the weather: 'His lamentations about the cold are without end ... As other men kept alive about him, our Abbé need not have despaired of living also.'[12] Some of Catherine's shafts smack of desperation. On peasant drunkenness, for example, d'Auteroche is said to be out of date, since the price of brandy is rising, and public morals therefore 'daily more and more improve'.[13] Russian priests are less debauched than French ones because they are poorer and married. Elsewhere, she scores palpable hits, rounding off with the observation that like many another so-called Russia specialist, d'Auteroche spent only a few months in the country and could not speak the language.

The British Library's copy of this splendid book belonged to the wealthy naturalist Joseph Banks, who made his own observation of the transit of Venus, eight years after d'Auteroche, with Captain Cook on Tahiti. One imagines him reading about lice and blizzards in his luxurious study in Soho Square, and thanking fate that it was d'Auteroche who got Siberia, and he the South Pacific.

In the 1800s Siberia's administration began slowly and haltingly to improve. Chiefly to thank were the reforming efforts of Mikhail Speransky, Siberia's governor-general from 1819 to 1821. Alexander I's unofficial chief minister from 1808, Speransky came to Siberia the traditional way – as an exile. In 1812 rivals resentful of his low birth and egalitarian reforms to the patronage system engineered his dismissal and banishment to Perm in the Urals. Four years later Alexander called him back into service and sent him first to the provincial town of Penza, then as Siberian governor-general to Tobolsk, with a brief to 'correct everything that could be corrected' and draw up guidelines for the territory's future.

The result was a raft of new laws overhauling almost every aspect of Siberian life. Administratively, Siberia was split in two, with charge of the new province of Eastern Siberia going to a second governor-general based in Irkutsk. To curb their powers, the governors were forced to consult advisory councils, half of whose members were appointed by Petersburg. Supplementary legislation modernised the tax system, encouraged peasant settlement, cut the red-tape hampering trade, made it harder for officials to act as loan sharks, regularised the treatment of exiles and clarified the status of the Cossacks.

There was a gap, however, between what was laid down on paper and what happened on the ground. On arrival in Tobolsk, Speransky had discovered that petitioners were so terrified of local officialdom that they dared approach him only in secret, on secluded forest roads. Though he had investigated complaints against 681 officials, he had managed to punish seriously only forty-three of them, thanks mainly to the shortage of suitable replacements. ('He discharged the old rogues by hundreds and engaged new ones by hundreds,' wrote a caustic observer.)[14]

Implementing his reforms was equally difficult. His advisory councils proved toothless, as did his measures to encourage peasant immigration, which did not significantly increase until the abolition of serfdom in the 1860s. Plans to foster a responsible local aristocracy by giving Siberian estates to retiring colonial officials foundered also, since they continued to go back home to European Russia at the end of their postings. Communications remained agonisingly slow: mid-century, the quickest way to get from Petersburg to Kamchatka was by taking a ship across the Atlantic to New York, a train across

America and a second ship across the Pacific. Though Speransky was eventually rehabilitated and allowed back to Petersburg, hindsight nails him as one of Russia's long list of failed would-be modernisers by administrative fiat. Tolstoy gave him a cameo role in *War and Peace*, making his plump white hands and artificial laugh the catalyst for Prince Andrey's disillusion with the world in general and government-sponsored reform in particular. There is something of him, too, in Anna Karenina's desiccated paper-pusher of a husband, whose Native Tribes Organisation Committee – convened to investigate the indigenes from the '1) political, 2) administrative, 3) economic, 4) ethnographical, 5) material, and 6) religious points of view' – is a metaphor for impotence and sterility.

Outsiders' comments on nineteenth-century Siberian government were mixed at best. Exiled to Vyatka, just west of the Urals, for singing comic songs at a student dinner, the 23-year-old Herzen was put to work among 'grotesque and greasy, petty and loathsome'[15] government clerks. 'They were to be bribed,' he wrote disgustedly, 'with twenty to twenty-five kopecks, sold documents for a glass of wine ... and degraded themselves in every possible way.' Petersburg's spatter-gun directives had no more effect than 'grape shot ... All the measures of government are enfeebled, all its intentions are distorted; it is deceived, fooled, betrayed, sold, and all under cover of loyal servility and with the observance of all the official forms.'[16]

Thirty years later another young liberal, Prince Pyotr Kropotkin, found that little had changed. An idealistic graduate of the court's Corps of Pages, he arrived in Irkutsk expecting to join in a great work of reform, as initiated by Eastern Siberia's newly recalled governor-general, the visionary imperialist Nikolay Muravyov-Amursky. Detailed off to investigate a corrupt and violent police chief, Kropotkin managed to collect enough evidence from frightened witnesses to have the man sacked. 'What was our astonishment,' he wrote in his memoirs, 'when a few months later, we learned that this same man had been nominated to a higher post in Kamchatka! There he could plunder the natives free of any control, and so he did. A few years later he returned to St Petersburg a rich man.'[17] One of his later jobs was to draw up an aid programme for famine-stricken Cossacks:

All the measures I recommended were accepted, and special grants of money were given for aiding the emigration of some and supplying cattle to others ... But practical realization of the measures would go into the hands of some old drunkard, who squandered the money and pitilessly flogged the unfortunate Cossacks so as to convert them into good agriculturalists.[18]

Puncturing Kropotkin's faith in the state's ability to reform itself, his experiences helped turn him into one of Europe's leading anarchists. Having served gaol terms in Russia and France, he spent the last thirty years of his life in Britain, where he got into trouble once, for not having a dog licence.

According to the law, it was Siberian officials' duty to see to it that the native peoples were humanely treated as long as they remained peaceful and paid their tribute on time. From the 1600s onwards, tsars issued order after order instructing that they be not cheated, turned into debt- or sex-slaves, sold alcohol or deprived of their hunting-grounds. But as their very repetitiveness suggests, such rules were seldom obeyed, and even when they were, authorised exactions alone constituted a destructive burden. Diverted from food-gathering by the need to trap fur-bearing animals for tribute, native Siberians became dependent on Russian vodka, tobacco, bread and sugar, increasingly so as sable ran out. 'We have to travel to far-off places now, in every direction,' a Sakha clan complained, 'because all the animals have been killed or driven away, and it is only with great hardship that we can trap.'[19] Nor did tribute calculations keep up to date with human population falls, leaving tribes hit by famine or disease with even heavier obligations.

Native Siberians, like Russian serfs, were also required to pay labour dues, mostly in the form of transport services. They were especially hard on the Sakha, who had to provide a porterage service over 500 miles of bog and mountain from Yakutsk to the Sea of Okhotsk, and on the Buryat, whose lands encompassed the trade route to China. An embassy to Peking of 1804 required 500 Buryat horses at each relay stop, and a Decembrist discovered that the Buryat with whom he stayed the night during a march to a new prison had been obliged to move their yurts hundreds of miles for the occasion. Foreign travellers were embarrassed by the beatings their Cossack escorts meted out to drivers – Russian and native alike – along the post-roads. 'It was his constant practice', the eccentric Scottish explorer John Cochrane wrote of his 'good and active Cossack' in the 1820s, to 'beat and otherwise ill-treat those whose business it was to provide horses, pulling them by the hair, ears and nose, and this without the least apparent necessity or provocation'.[20]

Another burden was the Orthodox clergy. Initially the tsars discouraged missionary activity, because baptised natives ceased to be liable for tribute. Peter the Great reversed this policy, encouraging large-scale conversions while keeping tribute obligations in place. A trial expedition up the river Ob was driven back by angry Khant. In 1710 Peter ordered Metropolitan Filofey of Tobolsk to try again:

> Find their seductive false god-idols, and burn them with fire, and axe them, and destroy their heathen temples, and build chapels instead of those temples, and put up the holy icons, and baptise these Ostyaks ... and if some Ostyaks show themselves contrary to our great sovereign's decree, they will be punished by death.[21]

A Ukrainian priest, Grigoriy Novitsky, wrote an account of the resulting three-year campaign. The Khant, he recorded, fought, fled, tearfully pleaded that their wives and children be spared baptism, or 'covered their ears with their hands, like vipers'.[22] They were especially distressed at the destruction of their fetishes, which they hid or tried to bribe the Russians to leave alone. By the end of the expedition, Novitsky claimed, he and his colleagues had made 40,000 converts. 'All idols, all soulless wooden gods and disgusting places of worship were ruined and burned. And all these idols fell as if struck by a fatal sickness. They vanished like burned trees.'[23]

The Khant recorded their version of events in a ballad. The narrator – possibly a chief Satyga, mentioned by Novitsky – is awoken from sleep by a roll of thunder. Leaping up he sees a 'beautiful boat with a prow like a chicken's beak', which he shoots at and temporarily forces to retreat. When it looses a second thunder-clap he faints and is seized, 'helpless as a summer duckling', by a pair of Cossacks:

> On me, whose father never wore iron,
> They have put fetters.
> Me, man that I am, they have thrown,
> Into a horrible hole fit only for dogs.

Imprisoned in Tobolsk, he capitulates, buttoning himself into a European jacket and accepting baptism:

> Around my neck,
> They have hung a four-cornered golden cross,
> The dish overflowing with horse-fat that my father used to offer
>   the gods,
> Will no more be offered, not even in a thousand days.[24]

Large-scale crusades such as this were few. They were expensive, they hindered tribute-collection, and it was hard to find priests willing to participate (Novitsky was killed in a Khant ambush). But lower-key harassment remained common. The Archbishop of Tobolsk, according to d'Auteroche, 'constantly persecuted the Mahometans and Pagans in the confines of Tobolsky, in order to convert them to the Greek religion'.[25] Tatars on the Ob told Gmelin that clerics accompanied by armed guards periodically landed in boats, dragged them out of their huts and threw them into the river. 'When they got back to the bank,' Gmelin noted drily, 'crosses were hung around their necks, and they were Christians.'[26] A priest speaks for himself:

> In the last year of 1747, in the months of April and May, I beat the new Christian, Ostyak Fedor Senkin, with a whip, because he married off his daughter . . . during the first week of Lent. I also beat his son-in-law with a whip, because he buried his deceased son himself, outside the church and without the knowledge of the priest . . . I also beat the widow Marfa and her son Kozma with a whip . . . because they kept in their tent a small stone idol, to whom they brought sacrifices . . . and I broke the said idol with an axe in front of an Ostyak gathering and threw the pieces in all directions.[27]

The same man, according to Khant petitions, charged one rouble for a Christian burial and five in hush-money for a traditional one. As priests were paid little or no official salary, such fees constituted their main source of income.

Improving native welfare was one of the aims of Speransky's reforms, which for the first time gave native Siberians rights in Russian law and a degree of official self-government. Settled tribes received the same legal status as state-owned serfs, and nomadic ones were enabled to elect elders, who were made responsible for tribute-collection and for administering customary law. At the regional level, councils of elders were to act as go-betweens with local government. More new legislation required that tribute and labour dues be defined precisely and ahead of time, banned preventative imprisonment and forced baptism, and set up annual fairs at which trading was to be carried on at fixed, equitable prices.

Again, these well-intentioned measures worked better in theory than in practice. Distinguishing between settled and nomadic peoples was often difficult, resulting in endless petitions for changes of status. The councils of elders worked well for the rich, sophisticated Buryat and Sakha, but less so for the hunter-gatherer peoples, who possessed no social units larger than the extended family. And as always, laws meant nothing without the cooperation of officials on the ground. Herzen deplored his colleagues' treatment of the 'poor, miserable, timid' Finno-Ugric peoples of Vyatka.[28] Whenever the local chief of police came by a fresh corpse he set off with it round the native villages, claimed in each to have just found it, and promised a murder trial unless paid off. Finally the villagers retaliated, locking him inside a hut and threatening to set it alight unless he accepted a 100-rouble bribe, which they preferred through the window on the end of a stick. The policeman demanded 200 roubles, and was burned to death.

Worst by far of all the ills Russian rule visited upon native Siberians – and one not even the best-intentioned, most efficient government could have prevented – were European diseases, especially smallpox, influenza and syphilis. The first epidemic – probably of smallpox – of which records survive broke out in 1630, and may have killed as many as half of all Khant, Mansi, Nenets and Ket. In the 1650s smallpox crossed the Yenisey, killing up to 80 per cent of the northern Evenk and Sakha, and nearly half the Yukagir. In the early 1700s it reached Kamchatka, cutting a swathe through the Itelmen and Koryak. Syphilis was a slower killer. Widespread among Russian settlers – no true *Sibiryak*, it was said, possessed a fully intact nose – it quickly spread to the indigenous peoples. 'One cannot view its effects,' wrote Gmelin of an Evenk village

> without a kind of horror . . . the only remedies in use are decoctions of poplar-bark and alum mixtures. They hasten many sufferers to their deaths, and it is hard to decide if those who die are not the happier. The people are destroyed little by little; those whom this cruel illness has not yet entirely consumed are incapable of work, and reduced to dying of poverty in a healthy, fertile land.[29]

Native Siberians attributed the plagues to the gods' displeasure, or to evil spirits. The Chukchi, the exile-turned-ethnographer Waldemar Bogoras recorded, visualised smallpox as a sliver of raw meat that burrowed under the skin, breaking out in sores and ulcers. In another version it was a gaunt, black-faced monster wearing garments of Russian broadcloth; in a third, a red-haired woman bearing a flaming torch, who galloped from camp to camp behind a team of scarlet sled-dogs, infecting all whom she touched. Syphilis was a tribe of tiny reindeer-herders, who pitched their tents on human limbs. To ward off disease-spirits, the Chukchi rattled snow-beaters at them or made them offerings of blood-soaked reindeer hide. More usefully, they knew to shun infected families, and drove away the pathetic survivors of decimated camps with shouts and brandishing of spears. They realised, too, that diseases came from the west, frequently asking Bogoras if all Russia was terrorised by such bad spirits, and why the Sun Chief did not fight and conquer them. One of Bogoras's assistants, an elderly former reindeer-herder and sufferer from what we would today call survivor's guilt, described the epidemic that killed his family:

> I had a dream. A cloud came from above, like darkness. It approached slowly, like a thick fog. I saw it approaching, and all grew dark around me. It was a black crowd, a gathering of men clad in black. In the bright midday they darkened the sun completely. I asked those nearest 'What have you come for?' They answered 'We have come to devour you!' 'Oh', I said, 'let me help you first.' I picked up a piece of wood from the ground, and suddenly I saw myself soaring upwards. Then I began moving to and fro, and struck with the stick

upon the top of all the tents of my camp. I struck down all the tents, but in reality it was the souls of my wife and children who I struck down. Thus I killed all of mine with my own hand. And from the time of that dream the disease was able to seize my whole family.[30]

About the government's attempts at disease prevention, Bogoras was scathing. The few doctors who could be persuaded to work in Kolyma, he wrote, were madmen, drunkards or quacks. Though Sredne Kolymsk had a hospital for Sakha syphilitics, its walls and floors were soaked with filth, and its warden stole the patients' food. When hungry, they 'would leave the hospital in a body and crawl round from house to house . . . Then the citizens would pay a ransom to keep them quiet.'[31] A government vaccination programme, in place since 1806, had proved worse than useless. Administered by barely trained 'vaccination-boys' equipped with worn-out, dirty syringes, it had probably caused more disease than it had prevented, and failed to ward off new smallpox epidemics in 1884 and 1889, which killed one in three of the entire Russian and native Kolyma population.

The first, because the first conquered and outnumbered, of the native Siberians to suffer the full effects of Russian rule were West Siberian peoples such as the Khant. From an early date, travellers remarked on the squalor and scarcity of their once rich and numerous settlements, and on their forgetfulness of their language and traditions. One who did so was the Prussian geographer Erman, who spent the winter of 1828–9 travelling among the Khant clans of the Ob. Hospitably welcomed into their one-room log-and-earth huts, he admired their embroidered nettle-cloth tunics, mighty bows, 'prettily carved' mammoth-ivory pipes, and the facility with which they calculated the date by the stars, a feat requiring intricate mental arithmetic. He also took a fancy to their intelligent, sharp-eared dogs, one of which he bought, christened Hector (shortened to Spotty by his driver) and taught, provoking universal hilarity, to ride in his sled. But he found a sad contrast between the reindeer-herding Khant on the relatively untouched lower Ob, and the fishing Khant on its heavily populated upper reaches. Whereas the northerners seemed healthy, well-grown and to have 'preserved the completeness of their domestic economy',

the southerners were visibly in decline. In some settlements the population was said to have fallen by seven-eighths over the previous fifty
years, thanks to famine, disease and Russian over-fishing. Alcoholism
was rife, as were eye and scalp diseases. When Erman's Cossack guide
pushed a crowd of drunks away from his surveying instruments, one
bitterly retorted ' "we are used to see you treating the Ostyaks like dogs,
while you are always praising the Russians!" ' They were aware, too,
that life was better the further away from Europeans one got:

> The settled Ostyak fishermen . . . asked us many questions respecting
> the condition of their northern fellow-countrymen; and with a ready
> ear and full hearts, they heard the praise of the land in which one
> could still wander with reindeer, and there was an abundance of soft
> furs for bed and clothing. And . . . they talked very seriously about a
> lost paradise; but it has been transferred to the north and beyond the
> polar circle.[32]

Sometimes – though not as often as the larger or remoter peoples –
the Western native Siberians fought back. The Time of Troubles saw
a rash of attacks on forts and tribute-collectors. Berezov, one of the
main tribute-collecting points on the lower Ob, twice almost fell,
first in 1595 and again in 1607, when a rising of 2,000 Khant and
Nenets was foiled with the help of an informer, who was rewarded
with ten roubles and two bales of cloth. There were similar attacks
on Pustozersk, on the western slopes of the Urals, and on Surgut,
another fort on the Ob.

The last big West Siberian native rising was the Nenets insurgency
of the 1820s and 30s, sparked by Speransky's reforms' unintentional
subjugation of the Nenets to their traditional enemies the Khant. Its
leader, chief Vavlo Nenyang, spent fourteen years raiding Russians,
Khant and rival Nenets alike before being captured and gaoled in
1839. Soon afterwards he escaped, rejoined 600 supporters in the
tundra, and threatened, claiming support from the White Tsar, to
march on the Russian settlement of Obdorsk unless granted tribute
forgiveness, food aid and freedom from oversight by a Khant puppet
chief. A year later he was recaptured, this time for good. A Polishwoman exiled to Berezov watched him being carted off to trial in
Tobolsk. 'I saw him in a waggon, surrounded by a strong escort of

Cossacks. His stature was robust; he was broad-shouldered, and had a bold, intrepid look.'[33] The blacksmith who had forged Nenyang's fetters told her that he had mixed their steel with horseshoe nails, proofing them against shamanic incantations. Mopping up Nenyang's followers nonetheless took another fifteen years.

The largest city in what used to be Khant territory is Tomsk, on the Tom river just above its confluence with the upper Ob. There in 1890, by which time it had a population of 31,000, Chekhov was dragged round the brothels by the local police chief, who cadged drinks, bored on about his divorce and declaimed a short story of his own composition. Tomsk was, Chekhov blearily concluded, even more vulgarly pretentious than Krasnoyarsk and Irkutsk: 'a pig in a skull-cap'. A few years later the first Englishwoman to take the Trans-Siberian Express, Annette Meakin, was given a tour by hospitable members of the local intelligentsia. As well as the university ('imposing though not beautiful'), with its unshaven, strike-prone students ('not prepossessing'), she was shown a prison, a music school, botanical gardens and fire-watch towers. What struck her most was the state of the streets:

> Every droshky raises a cloud of smoke-like dust. If you are within fifty yards of it, you get smothered. I found my 'khaki' blouses were invaluable; there is no material that bears dust and mud so well ... As soon as it began to rain there was mud, and after a wet night it was not unusual to find a pond several feet deep in the centre of one of the chief streets. Your driver never flinches, but takes his droshky through the shallows at a headlong gallop. We used to hold on to the sides and shut our eyes ...[34]

Her room at the Hotel Europe was inhabited by a bold and noisy mouse. When she complained, a waiter explained that although the hotel kept twelve cats, they seemed 'rather afraid of the mice themselves'.

In the spring of 1999 the city felt like the Soviet Union's last redoubt. On the trams, spotty conscripts in brown overalls shouldered wooden-handled shovels, off for *subbotnik* ('Saturdayer') duty clearing snow from parks and yards. Shops called Lavanda, Vernisazh, Gratsiya and, delightfully, Feniks, sold boxy suits and plastic shoes; the side-streets stank of newly thawed dog-shit, and the words 'Duty! Honour! Glory!' faded on a barracks wall. The October Hotel – ox-blood marble, dusty cacti, threadbare carpets – was having no truck with unaccredited foreigners. 'Do you have a letter of invitation?' the receptionist asked, eyeing my walking-boots. I hadn't. 'But you need one. This is the Party hotel – all right, the former Party hotel.' She would call a taxi and send me on to the Tomskaya. It had to be somewhere clean and quiet, I said, with no mafiosi. She sniffed: 'You're not in Moscow now. We don't have mafia in Siberia.'

From the Tomskaya, I went to look at the river. The ice was breaking, I had been told, and the whole city would be there to watch. Up and down the scabby quayside tall, green-eyed girls in film noir pan-stick sauntered, nibbling at sunflower seeds from cones of newspaper. Their husbands carried furled red roses, stiff in cellophane wrappers, and their children took rides on ponies with toast-rack ribs, or posed for photographs cuddling a muzzled bear-cub that dozed inside a cardboard box. There was even a camel, its hairy two-toed feet mournful in the slush. Near the bank, where the ice still held firm, fishermen hunched over drills and tackle-boxes. Further out ice menhirs and football fields slid and tumbled, all steady, implacable power. Back in my hotel room I switched on the television. The local station was broadcasting an anniversary gala. 'Town of our youth!', a plump couple wailed to shots of men in fur hats queuing at bus-stops. 'Where every building is a friendly face, our hearts are always with you!' The ads were for Barbie dolls – 'Make a good holiday for your child, at Prospekt Lenina 32!' – and for gimcrack wardrobes: 'European quality, Russian prices!'

The next morning I met two of Tomsk University's ethnolinguists: Olga Ossipova and her student Nadya Shalamova. An imposing old lady with a big dark apartment in one of Tomsk's collapsing wooden mansions, Olga had made it her life's mission to record the five Khant languages before they disappeared. Judging by those languages, she explained, the Khant saw the world in minutely observed physical detail, like a precise but perspectiveless scientific drawing. For example, they had no words that translated as 'bird' or 'fish', only words for specific species. Eighty per cent of their vocabulary consisted of verbs – there were different ones for 'sitting on a log', 'sitting on a stump' and 'sitting on the ground' – and they possessed an extraordinary range of terms to do with sound. 'The noise a bear makes walking through cranberry bushes' had its own word, as did 'the noise a duck makes landing quietly on water'. Abstract nouns were few. 'When I ask them how to translate "abundance",' Olga said, 'they come up with something like "many berries". "Happiness" is "my heart enjoys itself".' Naming European phenomena, they drew similes from nature. The word for 'photograph' literally translated as 'a pool of still water'; 'hat' as 'a wide-crowned tree that keeps off the rain'.

Today, Olga sighed, the Khant languages were dying. Back in the 1960s, when she did her fieldwork, it had been possible to find whole Khant-speaking villages. Now, only old people spoke the languages fluently. Middle-aged ones usually understood a few words, but the young knew none at all. To blame was the Soviets' removal of indigenous children to Russian-speaking boarding schools, and a mid-century influx of newcomers to the Ob basin: purge and collectivisation victims in the 1930s, oil and gas men after the war. The exiles took the Khant's best fishing-spots, and the oilmen polluted their rivers, sold them vodka and seduced their women: 'You won't find two children with the same patronymic – they've all got different fathers. There are hardly any pure Khant left.'

Although it is almost certainly too late to save their languages, for the Khant history is partially reversing itself. The oilmen are as numerous as ever: native rights groups are fighting to keep them out of the Ob's Big and Little Yugan tributaries, the only places left where Khant still wear traditional dress and openly practise shamanism. But Stalin's deportees and their descendants are leaving – not for European Russia, for they are Siberians now, but for cities like Tomsk.

One who had stayed behind was Kalyu Kallismaa. He was Estonian, and one of only fifteen people – ten of them Khant – left in Aypolovo, an old exile settlement near the source of an Ob tributary, the

Vasyugan. Nadya and I got a lift there with Sergey, a young Russian with a prematurely dissipated face who came once a month to help Kalyu with the farmwork, loved to smash the river's mirror in his overpowered dinghy, and holstered a battered old army revolver. We landed in floodwater, next to hand-chiselled canoes and a gibbet hung with fish. When Sergey switched off the engine, the silence was like a brick wall. Tall and gaunt, Kalyu splashed up to meet us. His small-holding – cowshed, sheep-run, vegetable patch – was Scandinavian-neat, his barn-like house a folk-museum of picturesque artefacts: birchbark knapsacks, wooden yokes, fish-traps, besoms, an enamel hip-bath. He and his wife might be in their seventies, he exclaimed, slapping his chest, but they were well able to live on their own. Only last birthday he had shot the bear – 'taller than me!' – that had killed their little horse. Nor were they bothered by the mosquitoes, smiling as I rubbed them in handfuls out of my eyes, mouth, nose and hair. 'By June,' said Kalyu, holding thumb and finger apart, 'they will be a thousand times bigger. Brrr! Like helicopters!' Later, the insects showed up as blurred hailstones in my snapshots, and drifted from the pages of my notebook like pressed flowers.

Behind Kalyu's robustness lay a family tragedy, one repeated millions of times in Stalin's Siberia. Up to the age of seventeen Kalyu lived with his lawyer father Konstantin, mother Marta and brothers Endel and Ilmar in Narva, a medieval river port on the Russian–Estonian frontier. They employed a maid and spent their holidays playing volleyball on Baltic beaches. At two o'clock in the morning of 14 June 1941, eight days before Germany's invasion of the Soviet Union, there came a knock on the door. 'It was a lieutenant of the NKVD' – Kalyu tapped his shoulder to indicate the epaulettes – 'and two Russian workers, with red armbands on. They gave us an hour to get packed. We piled everything into sheets. I wanted to take my bike, I remember, and my skis.' The family were taken to the railway station, where 'there was this long, long train – with cattle-trucks, not passenger wagons, I don't know how many. They started loading people in the evening, and kept going all night.' A five-week journey followed, first by rail, then on river-barges. Save for food they had brought with them, the deportees had nothing to eat. Starving, 'people went mad, crying and screaming, or throwing themselves into the gaps between the boats'. One woman slit her wrists and those of her two-year-old child. Once a day the barges halted to dump the dead.

The Khant fishing-camp of Aypolovo was the convoy's last stop. On its low banks, fenced by lightless, noiseless forest, 1,500 people were unloaded and put to work, with minimal tools, at erecting buildings and clearing trees for a collective farm. The first house to be built was the *komandatura*'s. 'That went up straight away, with proper logs. The rest of us lived in dugouts, covered with bark.' Rations were 500 grams of bread per person per day, and guards stood over the prisoners as they worked, shouting 'Are you waiting for Hitler? Get on and dig!' On 21 December Kalyu's mother committed suicide by poison. 'It was some drug she had brought with her from Estonia. I don't know what exactly – they didn't investigate how she'd done it.' Eight days later his nineteen-year-old brother Endel died also, of hunger and exhaustion. Endel was followed by eleven-year-old Ilmar, who had been sent to an orphanage downriver and contracted pneumonia after being driven out into the bogs to collect mushrooms. Death came quickest, Kalyu remembered, to 'women and the rich ones. There was this woman – she had had a five-storey house all to herself back in Narva, an *intelligent*. She went straight away.' His own weight dropped to thirty-seven kilos and his skin suppurated with scurvy sores, but he survived by trading his clothes for potatoes and by scavenging for nettles and rotten horseflesh.

Though he did not know it at the time, that winter Kalyu also lost his father Konstantin, who had been separated from the family at Narva. After Narva they met again only once, when their trains crossed in a shunting yard. 'I was on my way to get the slops, when suddenly there was my father looking out of a truck. I shouted to him "How's things?" And he shouted back "I'm longing for a smoke." So I threw him a packet of *papirosy*. Then the guard took my arm and dragged me away.' Forty-five years later Kalyu discovered that Konstantin had died soon afterwards in a labour camp near Sverdlovsk. He was not surprised. 'He was a town man, educated. He didn't know how to work with his hands.'

Kalyu had never been back to Estonia, not even since it regained independence. His daughters had married Russians, he said, so there was no need. What was more, he turned out to be a veteran Communist, as proven by the Party card, reverently wrapped in brittle polythene, which he pulled out from under his bed. He joined, it noted, in 1947, six years after the Soviets murdered his entire family.

I reeled. How could he do it?

'They said that if I didn't become a Party member I wouldn't be made head of my brigade. I had two children by then, I had to survive.'

He was unequivocally proud, moreover, of Aypolovo – or of Aypolovo as it was before the other exiles left and the government closed down its public services. Jackets pulled over our heads, we swished in soft, mosquito-filled rain through the long grass of what used to be its main street. This roofless building had been the school; that one there the generating-station. Of most, nothing was left save wooden foundations, floating like rafts among baby pines. Ten years ago, Kalyu said, 500 people lived here, in a 'very cultured way'. They had television, a kindergarten, a club. The *kolkhoz* had eighty cows – 'though I know that with you, just one farmer has more' – and the mushroom-station bottled an annual fifteen tonnes of wild fungi. 'Now it all just goes to waste, though lots of people would like to eat our mushrooms. Even in England perhaps.' Back indoors, he and Sergey sat down to get drunk. Sergey ended each joke with a slap on the old man's back, slurring, 'Look, he's not an Estonian any more! He's a proper Russian!' Kalyu's wife fluttered back and forth like a distressed bird, trying to hide the vodka bottles.

Almost every non-native I met in Western Siberia had a family history similar to Kalyu's. Nadya's grandparents had been Ukrainian peasant farmers. Like many others they were deported twice: first, when collectivisation began in 1929, from Ukraine to the Altai mountains, and again, during the purges of the 1930s, from the Altai to Western Siberia. During the barge journey up the Ob, Nadya's uncle Filip jumped and swam for shore. For half a century the family had no idea whether he had lived or died, until a cousin bumped into him in a post-office queue in the Kazakh capital of Alma-Ata. But these bare facts were all that Nadya knew. Why hadn't her grandparents told her more, I asked? Maybe it was too upsetting, she thought. Or perhaps they didn't want her to know too much, to get into trouble at school. She hadn't questioned them because exile wasn't very interesting; everybody's stories were the same. Similarly, when I pointed out that Belomorkanal was a strange name for a brand of cigarette, few grasped what I meant. Sixty thousand innocent people might have died digging the White Sea Canal, but that was not its primary association: it was an engineering feat, a geographical feature. Nobody baulked at vodka labelled Katorzhanka ('female hard-labour convict') and a waitress guilelessly described her home-town of Magadan – the Soviet Union's equivalent to Auschwitz – as 'all lights, like a fairy tale'.

Inured to the sufferings of their own parents and grandparents, it is not surprising that white Siberians have little in the way of liberal guilt left over for the native peoples. Back in Aypolovo, Kalyu had cited 'bossing about the Ostyaks' as one of the advantages of joining the Party. Though he claimed 'normal' relations with his Khant neighbours – and introduced us to some, chatting with them amicably – he also made it plain that he considered them a degraded, inferior breed. 'I'm the only person who grows flowers,' he said, pointing to a row of old tyres planted with the violas Russians call 'Anyuta's Eyes'. 'The Ostyaks don't grow anything; they just look for a bottle!' They stood and watched, he told us disgustedly, while the fox-farm burned down, and fought – 'with knives, forks, anything' – when drunk. 'We had this policeman, and he'd say, "Give those Ostyaks guns and a crate of vodka, then they'll all kill each other and we can put the last one in gaol!"' In the old village cemetery – its tangle of stars and crescents and four- and six-armed crosses a tribute to the inclusiveness of Stalin's terror – he showed us the graves of a Khant father and son. 'They were drinking, having a party, and the son hit the host. The next morning the host came round and shot them both. He got eight years and died in prison, of tuberculosis.' Gazing out from chipped ceramic medallions, the pair wore the same expression as the last of the Native-American chiefs in Edward Curtis's famous photographs: impassive, incalculable, staring the end of the world in the face.

Nadya's cousin Valentina, headmistress of the village school in

Staroyugino, a small town near the Vasyugan's confluence with the Ob, put her views more delicately than Kalyu, using the official term 'Small-Numbered Peoples' instead of 'Ostyaks'. But they came to much the same thing. Khant were mercurial, childlike, dirty, 'Africans'. She felt sorry for them, guilty even, but they had been made thriftless by government handouts, and it was scientific fact that they could not cope with alcohol. As for the boarding-schools that had deracinated their children and destroyed their languages, people 'were pleased to send their children there. They were given clothes for free. The girls got brown dresses, with a white apron for holidays and a black one for normal days. And they were fed four times a day, with sweets and everything.' Most of the crime in Staroyugino was down to its half dozen Khant families. They stole motors from boats, clothes from washing-lines, potatoes from potato-patches, hens from hen-coops. Since they didn't work, it was the only way they could raise the money to buy vodka. Nadya and I were well-meaning of course, but why didn't we want to interview Russians? She, Valentina, was a native person too. Her father had been exiled here in 1932.

Valentina's husband Andrey, a woodsman at the defunct local logging station, took us to meet one of their Khant neighbours. On the way, see-sawing over crashed boardwalks along streets that looked as if they had just hosted a tank battle, he quizzed me about England. What were our roads like? How many square metres of wood did it take to heat one of our houses through the winter? Did we – gesturing dismissively at a blue-green immensity of pines – have forests like this? No? So in that case, we had steppe? What threw him most of all was the information that my mother, despite living in a village, owned not a single cow. So where, he asked, stopping in his tracks, did she get her milk? Valentina and he had three cows: Blackie, Dochka and Mason, named after the lawyer in the soap opera *Santa Barbara*. Like his wife, he was discreetly sceptical of my ability to write anything useful about Siberia if this was my first visit, and half-amused, half-irritated at my interest in its indigenous peoples. This was where one of Staroyugino's last 'clean Ostyaks', Aunt Motya, lived, and if she wasn't drunk – snapping a finger against his neck – she might be willing to talk.

Aunt Motya was sober but a tricky interviewee – mischievous, theatrical and determined to get all the fun going out of the earnest foreigner crouching with her notebook. Round and pink, with brawny arms and a pug nose, she looked much like any Russian *babushka*. Typical too was her kitchen with its buckets of potatoes, washing hanging above the stove, eggs on a saucer and round-shouldered Okean fridge. Printed plastic carrier bags – one showing a puma, another Claudia Schiffer – were tacked to the walls for decoration, and through the window a wooden privy stood sentry over a sweep of snow.

Motya's accent, though, was not Russian at all, all pop and crackle in place of Slav sibilants. 'The tea's fresh! No worms! Take your coats off, we won't steal them!' She was seventy-four years old, she said, and her parents had been hunters. Each winter, they disappeared into the woods on skis, leaving their nine children to fend for themselves. When she was aged twelve, a man and a woman came in a boat and took all the village's children to a boarding-school 300 kilometres away: 'Our parents didn't want it, but they had no choice, they were frightened.' On arrival the children knew not a word of Russian, but the teachers still scolded them for speaking Khant: 'We were sort of second-class children. It was, "*Ostyachki*! Sit at the back!"' Aged fourteen, Motya was taken out of school and put to work in the *kolkhoz*, sawing up logs. Later she worked as a postwoman. The Russian children 'were always stealing my little horse's bell or tying a stick in my dog's mouth'. Now, she wished that Khant stuck up more for themselves: 'We're too timid to go somewhere, demand something, put our fists on the table. It's something we just don't do.'

As the anthropologists in Petersburg had predicted, what I could not get her to talk about was shamanism.

'We shouldn't discuss this.'

Why not?

'I don't know.'

But why not?

'Because. What do you want?'

I explained again that I was writing a book, recording what people like her remembered before it was too late. She tugged at her cardigan. 'You should have pitied us earlier. You should have thought about the Ostyaks before.' When she was young people used to tie scarves to the trees, but it was man's business, and she wasn't allowed to go and look. Newly arrived exiles, she remembered, used to steal the offerings. 'They messed everything up, broke everything. We'd ask, "Why did you do this? Why didn't you just walk past?" And they wouldn't even bother to reply.' Such sacrilege brought its just deserts: 'This Russian woman, this Fokina – I don't remember her first name – stole a piece of cloth from where we hung things on trees. She used it to make a new skirt for herself.' Motya pantomimed Fokina mincing along. 'The next day' – Motya thumped her thighs – 'she couldn't walk. My mother saw her and asked where she had got the cloth for her skirt. And Fokina said, "From a tree." So my mother told her, "Take it back and hang it up where it was before." She did, and the next day she stood on her legs again.'

Motya's children – by a Belarussian deportee – partially understood but did not speak Khant. Growing up, they had not wanted to learn the language, because Russians 'dirtied' it. 'The word "Ostyak" was an insult. People cried when it was written in their passports.'

Did she still speak Khant herself?

'Why shouldn't I speak it? It's my mother-tongue! You speak your language! There's just nobody left to speak it with!' That was enough questions; it was time for us to have some of her home-brewed vodka. Obediently I drank: one glass, two. A raw egg, Motya assured me with a glint in her eye, would be good for my health, so that went down also. By the third drink she was flourishing one of Nadya's cigarettes and swinging her hips to old torch songs: 'Like a sailboat, she's flying . . .', 'Far away, beyond the river . . .', and something about a 'harmonium that sings'. Out of the house, we swayed, singing, down wilderness-silent streets, past dungheaps, rickety fences, mongrels yawning from wooden doorsteps and chimney smoke that rose in perfect columns into the diamond-bright air. When Nadya and I got home, Andrey and Valentina laughed until they wept. We had wanted Khant, and now we had got them. Here was some noodle soup, and after that we were to go to the *banya*, which Andrey had heated up specially, and thwack each other with birch-twigs until we forgot our naive Western ideas.

The next day Andrey arranged a lift upriver for us in a gas-company helicopter to the village of Noviy Vasyugan. In the hold, we sat on metal benches either side of sacks of potatoes and somebody's new kitchen units. A teenager with a sore on her mouth hushed a newborn baby and a woman in a shell-suit and frayed white sandals hugged a bag marked 'In Transit to Afghanistan. Gift of Denmark'. Below, the helicopter's shadow spidered across acid-green larches and khaki pines, toppled like spillikins where loggers had been at work. As we landed, a calf cantered along a fence, and the downdraught whipped brown puddles into miniature tidal waves.

Waiting to meet us were Pyotr and Anisiya Milimors, Khant friends of Olga Ossipova. Small and russet-haired, with bright, puckish faces, the old couple were as active as the Kallismaas. They too chopped their own wood, drew their own water, dug their own vegetable-patch and caught their own fish, salt strips of which we chewed round their kitchen table. Anisiya, it turned out, was only half Khant, her mother having been one of the up to 1.2 million Poles deported to Siberia in 1939. But Pyotr's family had always lived on the Ob. In 1937, when he was five, their wholly Khant village was collectivised and renamed for Molotov, whose pact with Ribbentrop would soon partition Poland and banish Anisiya's mother east. Exiles-turned-agitators confiscated all the village's livestock, though Pyotr's parents managed to save one cow by bribing a vet to classify it as diseased. Four years later, when Hitler broke the Molotov–Ribbentrop Pact and attacked the Soviet Union, the village's men were conscripted into the Red Army. Most never returned; Pyotr's father died at the siege of Leningrad.

Primed, perhaps, by his interviews with Olga, Pyotr was happy to talk about shamanism. His great-grandfather, he said, had been a famous shaman, and he had inherited some of his duties. Two days' walk away – no we couldn't go there, the bogs were too wet – there was a sacred cedar, a 'beloved tree'. It was his responsibility, when he visited each summer, to hang offerings from its branches. 'I just say, "This is from so-and-so, he wants such-and-such," and I hang whatever it is up. You can give whatever you like – a scarf of course, or spectacles, a teacup, anything. But it has to be something shiny, something new.' When he was a child there was a shrine at the site. He hadn't rebuilt it because who would go there? 'The old people might, but the young ones, the ones who go away to study, they're not like that any more. We're the only ones left.'

Bear-feasts had died out before Pyotr was born, but his father told him about them. First, you had to look in the dead bear's stomach for a hairball. If you found one it meant that the bear had killed a man, and had immediately to be burned and buried. If there was no hairball you dressed the animal up – in men's clothes for a male bear, women's for a female – and the feast went ahead. A few months ago, Pyotr had killed a bear himself. 'There was milk in her teats, so I knew she had cubs. Then I heard a squeaking noise, "Pyu! Pyu! Pyu!", in the bushes, and there they were' – a scrabbling gesture – 'buried under the moss. She knew that she was going to be killed, so she tried to hide them.' When tracking a bear, you had to refer to it by 'a soft name – Little Brother, Little Father, something like that. Even if you're over here and he's over there, he knows that you're talking about him; he understands everything you say.'

I was done with questions; it was Nadya's turn. She set her dictaphone going and asked Pyotr to translate a list of Russian phrases into Khant. His answers were hesitant and her brows puckered with disappointment. He had forgotten many words, she told me later, and muddled his tenses. Before we left, the old couple insisted that we accept presents. Nadya received a handful of dried pike, light and scratchy as autumn leaves. I got a small metal disc. It was worn and pitted, but I could just make out the outline of a double-headed eagle. '5 kopecks,' it read, '1875. Russian copper currency.' As useless a means of exchange as the Khant's once pin-sharp language, it was probably the oldest object Pyotr and Anisiya Milimors possessed.

CHAPTER 3

THE BURYAT

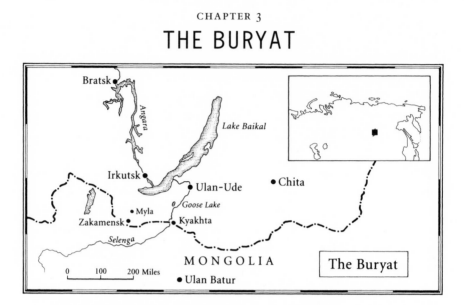

Russian to Buryat: 'Why have you got such bandy legs?'
Buryat to Russian: 'From Genghiz's time, when we sat on the Russians' necks.'

– Buryat joke, 1999

On the road out of Kyakhta a shabby metallic Lenin, canted forward as if into an ocean gale, extends a hand towards the fatigue-brown swell of Mongolia. Behind the border-crossing's gates a stationary line of canvas-covered trucks snakes away down hill to where roofs and chimneys shimmer along a thin gleam of river. The waiting drivers form a semicircle round a car bonnet, voices rising and falling to the soft slap of playing-cards. Presiding over all, grandly derelict, is a large nineteenth-century church. Its dome and belltowers are intact, but past the cows dozing in the shade of its portico the smells are of camp-fires and urine, and glass crunches underfoot. All that survives of its stucco ceiling is a single trunkless putto, whose wings echo a swirl of sparrows.

Once, Kyakhta was Russia's window on to China. Founded under the terms of a Russo–Chinese trade treaty in 1728, it was one of only two points on their long border at which trade was legal, making it, for about a century, one of the richest towns in the empire. From Kyakhta, Russia exported fur, leather, woollens, iron, glassware and hunting-dogs. In return came silk, spices, porcelain, lacquerware, tiger skins, rubies and, most of all, tea. In the 1780s a million tea-chests passed through the town each year. By the mid-1800s the quantity had almost doubled, and travellers cursed the mile-long tea-caravans hogging the road to Irkutsk.

To foreigners arriving from Mongolia, the resulting oasis of civ-ilisation in the middle of a waste of steppe came as a shock. The Italian journalist Luigi Barzini, perched on the jump-seat of Prince Scipione Borghese's Itala on the Peking to Paris automobile race of 1907, was dazzled:

> The first vision of that Siberian city had the fascination of a beautiful dream. We saw sharp spires, white houses with windows, roofs with chimney-pots, factories with tall chimneys; all of these most wonderful, incredible things ... It seemed as though Europe had come to meet us at the gate of Mongolia.[1]

For Russians, the town took on the fabulous status of a Las Vegas or Samarkand. 'Sandy Venice's' nabobs were said to have built themselves billiard-rooms and hot-houses, to buy their wives dresses from Worth, to fill their libraries with French novels and their stables with English thoroughbreds. They sent their daughters to study in Paris and imported Italians to build their churches, whose columns were of rock-crystal and whose silver doors glittered with precious stones. That all this was not entirely the product of fevered fancy (one of Kyakhta's daughters really did study sculpture under Rodin), is proved by the contents of its silent, dusty museum. Here, in hobble skirts and eyeglasses, are the staff of the Free Girls' Primary School; here a penny-farthing bicycle, 'brought from China', according to the fading label, 'in 1888 by Vasiliy Romanovich Lebedev, employee of the Hanko tea firm'. The 'typical merchant's house' room has an ormulu chest of drawers, bronze wall-sconces and watercolours of men in tight trousers romancing girls with camellias in their hair. Here, too, are the contents of Kyakhta's derelict churches. Where the sides of a glass case displaying 'cult attributes' do not quite join, visitors have slotted coins and notes through the cracks, so that they make a pile of offerings at the icons' feet.

Across the border from Kyakhta, divided from it by a strip of no-man's-land, was its Chinese twin town Maimaichen – in Mandarin, 'Buy-Sell'. 'One moment,' wrote the American journalist George Kennan in the 1880s,

> you are in a Russian provincial village with its characteristic shops, log houses, golden-domed churches, droshkies, soldiers, and familiar peasant faces; the next moment you pass behind the high screen that conceals the entrance to the Mongolian town and find yourself apparently in the middle of the Chinese Empire. You can hardly believe that you have not been suddenly transported on the magical carpet of the 'Arabian Nights' over a distance of a thousand miles.[2]

Its beaten-clay streets were exotic with shrines, tea-stands and paper-lanterns, and its merchants wore pigtails and close-fitting gowns of black silk, offering agate bowls, portable sundials and erotic woodcuts from open-fronted booths. Never before having encountered Chinese food, Kennan was nonplussed at a banquet given in his honour, listing its forty courses as 'prickly seaweed', 'lichens' and 'very slippery macaroni'. The Chinese were equally puzzled at him, fleeing when he unfolded his camera. For the Chinese government, he joked, the apparatus would come in useful as a means to quell riots.

With the construction of the Suez Canal and Trans-Siberian Railway, and the opening of Chinese treaty-ports after the Second Opium War, the caravan trade declined. Barzini saw empty streets and warehouses, and Kyakhta's few remaining merchants told him that they hoped for a trans-Mongolian railway line, or even for a road that would allow new-fangled automobiles to replace camels. Neither trains nor cars materialised, and the town crumbled. Maimaichen disappeared completely, burned to the ground during the Russian Civil War. Today, the only traces of it, as of Kyakhta's vanished wealth, are in the museum: hand-held weighing-scales, silk slippers and a pair of big bronze temple-bells, round whose scalloped mouths drift beetles, dragons and chrysanthemums.

The original inhabitants of this Russian-Mongolian borderland were a Mongol people, the Buryat. Nomadising over a Sweden-sized territory of mixed forest and steppe around the southern shores of Lake Baikal, they were closely related to the Khalkha and Dzungar Mongols to their south, in today's Mongolia. Possessors of a written language, firearms, metals, tribute-paying Ket and Nenets vassals, vast livestock herds and powerful clan leaders, they were the first for-midable nationality, after the Tatars, the Russians encountered on their march across Siberia.

Conquering them took Muscovy over thirty years, in a series of raids, counter-raids, ambushes and sieges collectively known as the Buryat wars. Cossacks built their first fort in Buryat territory, Bratsk on the river Angara, in 1631. Three years later the Buryat burned it down and massacred its garrison, and in 1638 and 1658 unsuccessfully besieged its replacement. The first fort on the upper Lena, Ver-kholensk, was founded in 1641 and continuously besieged for the next five years by Buryat armies up to 2,000 strong. In a typical despatch, its defenders pleaded for more mail and muskets:

> Sire, the Bratsk people [Buryat] have many mounted warriors, and they go into battle carrying metal shields and wear greaves on their forearms, and have spiked helmets; and we, Sire, your humble servants, are poorly outfitted, we have no armour, and our poor little guns cannot shoot through the shields of the Bratsk warriors . . .[3]

There were more revolts throughout Buryat territory from 1695-6, during which Irkutsk came under siege, and Bratsk's commander was still busy rounding up insurgents and uncovering arms caches when Gmelin and Müller passed through in the 1730s.

Towards the numerous, well-armed Buryat, Russia took the same conciliatory approach that had already subdued and assimilated the Tatars. In exchange for submission to the tsar, their clan leaders, or taishas, received titles, land grants and exemption from tribute. In 1762 they were allowed to raise regiments of 'native Cossacks', which guarded the border with Chinese-ruled Mongolia, and Speransky gave them salaries in return for exercising limited judicial powers.

By the 1800s the policy had produced peace, relative prosperity (from 1700 on the Buryat population, unlike most native Siberians', grew steadily), and a degree of Russification. To the west of Baikal especially, many Buryat converted to Orthodoxy, and gave up horses and cattle in favour of wheat and potatoes. Felt yurts mutated into octagonal wooden huts, then into rectangular cabins. Many of the changes were superficial and unattractive: governors complained about taishas who alienated their clansmen by over-eagerly abandoning Buryat customs for Russian ones, and travellers laughed at rich herders who built themselves Russian houses, full of hideous rugs and furniture, for show, but continued to live in yurts pitched out in the yard. Similarly the first two Buryat to arrive in Petersburg – a pair of scholars deputed, in 1817, to translate the gospels into Mongolian for the Russian Bible Society – failed to adapt. One accepted baptism and the Christian name Ivan only on his deathbed, weeping for his old name of Lotus, and the second returned to Buryatiya a lonely, violent old drunk.

Nonetheless, by the end of the century the Buryat had acquired a sizeable Europeanised middle class, complete with its own merchants, writers and increasingly, nationalists, who allied themselves with the Siberian regionalists, parried Petersburg's efforts to discourage nomadism, debated, furiously, the relative merits of the different Buryat dialects and turned out reams of poetry on the romance of the open steppe. A prime early example of the successful, hybridised Buryat was Pyotr Badmayev, a godson of Alexander III who represented Russia in the Mongolian capital of Urga (now Ulan Bator), briefly ran a Buddhist school in Petersburg and practised Tibetan medicine on the capital's faddish aristocracy. His successor as royal adviser on Asian affairs was Agvan Dorzhiyev, who for twenty years shuttled between Urga and Lhasa on behalf of Nicholas II and persuaded the tsar to allow the construction of a Buddhist temple in Petersburg's historic centre. Badmayev's pupil Tsyben Zhamtsarano lectured on ethnography at Petersburg University before moving to Urga, where he needled the conservative theocracy by opening a secular school, publishing an educational journal (its first issue covered everything from 'The earth, the continents, heat and cold' to 'The states of the world and their forms of government'), and by producing a one-kopeck translation of Tolstoy's life of Buddha, which argued that Tibetan Buddhism needed urgently to return to its vows of

chastity and austerity. A puzzled Russian colleague described Zhamtsarano as well educated 'but very superstitious. He believed in the
most impossible things: Amazons, dwarfs, man-eaters, dragons living
in wells, oxen living in lakes . . . When ill [he] would invite shamans,
quacks, lamas and Russian physicians, and simultaneously take all
their medicines . . .'[4] The photograph of a Mongolian delegation to
Petersburg of 1913, to which Zhamtsarano was attached as interpreter,
is telling. The Mongols face the camera apprehensively, unsure what
to do with their hands inside the wide cuffs of their silk robes. Their
Russian hosts – a Staff-Captain Gabrik in gold braid and Kitchener
moustache, and financial adviser Kozin in double-breasted overcoat
and wing-collar – look awkward too, embarrassed by the occasion's
Oriental splendour. The only person thoroughly at ease is the Buryat,
whose shaven scalp tops a three-piece suit and tie.

Zhamtsarano would have fitted in perfectly at a May Day opera gala
in Ulan-Ude, capital of present-day Buryatiya. Entirely Buryat and
entirely Russian-speaking, the audience oozed respectability: little
girls beribboned and obedient, old men bantam-proud behind serried
medals. Everyone seemed to know everyone else, and they all, as I
discovered when descended upon by kindly matrons during the
interval, worked either for the local government or for the university,
those being the only non-criminal, non-manual jobs that places like
Ulan-Ude have to offer. 'Ah! You know Khvorostovsky!', they cried
when I praised the famous young Russian-Siberian baritone. 'He's
from Krasnoyarsk. He's one of ours!' On the auditorium ceiling
happy Buryats threw garlands, blew trumpets and shouldered sheaves
of wheat beneath snow-capped mountains and a phalanx of fighter-
planes. At the triumph's centre monumental youths, one Slav the
other Asian, clasped fists at the summit of red-carpeted stairs.

The conductor raised his baton, and the curtain rose on the
Mongolian State Ballet and Opera Company, over from Ulan Bator.
A diva in sequins and a beehive gave us a song titled 'The Fate of
Man', followed by an Honoured Artist of Mongolia in a velvet
smoking jacket with 'Everlasting Glory to Mongolia' and 'Memories

of My Mother'. A tenor in stack heels and a beige morning-suit sang 'La donna è mobile', quite beautifully, in Russian, and then it was back to the beehive lady in a different dress with 'Friendship'. Three hours later Buryatiya's president, ex-First Party Secretary Leonid Potapov, took the stage. This was a celebration of national brotherhood, he announced, of pan-Mongol art and culture. Here was a framed certificate for the honoured head of the Ulan Bator opera collective, and a painting in a twirly plastic frame of Our Baikal. In return, he graciously accepted wilted carnations and a large rolled-up carpet. The Respected President thanked the Respected Deputy President, who thanked the Respected Mayor, who said a few words on behalf of the Respected Minister for Culture, who produced a very old Hero of Mongolian Labour, who thanked Our Dear Audience, until the chorus sidled off into the wings and Potapov was left on stage with his flowers and the rug.

There was a subtext to this display of pan-Mongol brotherhood, for in reality Mongolia's Khalkha and Dzungar Mongols bear a grudge against their Buryat relatives for acting as Russia's stooges during the Soviet takeover of Mongolia in the 1920s. For 150 years a feudal theocracy under Chinese suzerainty, Mongolia collapsed into chaos with the Manchu emperors' overthrow in 1911. In 1921 it was invaded by a Soviet army, which set up a brutal military government under Elbekdorji Rinchino, a Buryat Socialist Revolutionary. Buryat, also, were the regime's ministers of finance, trade, justice and education, its Comintern representative and its chief of police. Zhamtsarano headed a new Mongolian Scientific Committee.

In Mongolia on a painting trip in 1925, the Austrian artist Roland Strasser remembered an atmosphere of fear cloaked by bureaucracy. 'Urga,' he wrote, 'has become a Buryat city under Soviet domination ... The Buryat officials keep the Mongols in absolute terror.'[5] Shots rang out from the prison at night, the police followed him everywhere, and it took him months just to get permission to sketch. Religious dances had been replaced with propaganda plays in which

> Kaiser Wilhelm, Franz-Josef of Austria and the Tsar were buried in turn under the ruins of crumbling factories, and affluent factory-directors in sudden self-accusation caught up a stage pistol and blew out their brains at the harrowing sight of the hairy, sweating breast

of a worker ... Finally the curtain was lowered, usually in obstinate unmanageable jerks, to a loud chorus of the *International*.[6]

After several arrests and nearly a year's anxious wait for exit papers, Strasser got away with the help of a friendly Buryat official, who 'in his patent-leather shoes ... stood about at all corners and heard and knew most things ... He was a Mongolian-Russian half-caste, sufficiently related to both sides to keep his head well above these turbid waters.'[7] A well-connected American journalist, Marguerite Harrison, got an interview with Rinchino, who told her, in faultless Russian, that Buryat were in charge because Mongols were 'incorrigibly lazy, good-natured, indifferent and usually utterly devoid of personal ambition'. 'It was plain,' she thought, 'that if he had his way Mongolia would at that moment be a Soviet Republic.'[8]

Within little over a decade, most of the Buryat in charge of Soviet Mongolia had come to well-deserved bad ends. Rinchino was ordered to Moscow in 1928 and executed together with several colleagues in 1937. Zhamtsarano was arrested in 1937 and died in prison sometime between 1940 and 1945. Mongolians, though, neither forgave nor forgot. As Ivan Maysky, Soviet ambassador to London from 1932 to 1942, put it: 'The Mongols realise the cultural superiority of the Buryats, know that they could not do without them, but they do not like the Buryats, considering them traitors to the historical heritage of the Mongolian race ...'[9] As late as the 1960s, according to an American researcher, Mongolians suspected Buryat members of the Academy of Sciences of having advised Stalin on which of Mongolia's Buddhist monasteries to demolish, and 'laughed bitterly'[10] at the elimination of the word 'Mongol' from what until 1958 was Buryatiya's official title of 'Buryat-Mongol Autonomous Soviet Socialist Republic'.

Mongolians' reasons for distrusting Buryat lie in the past. But what about Buryat's feelings towards Russians, who are emphatically part of their present? Buryat might spend their Saturday nights listening to Verdi, but they were on the same longitude as Hanoi and Singapore. Surely they felt there was something odd about being ruled by Europeans, from a capital city 3,000 miles away?

I put these questions to Vladimir Khamutayev, leader of the national party Negedel or 'Unity'. A gauche, dishevelled man in his mid-thirties, he lowered his voice to a whisper as we bent over the giant, mutton-stuffed dim sum, which is Buryatiya's national dish, in the restaurant of my hotel. He had been inspired to enter politics, he said, while teaching in Irkutsk: 'I was always astonished at the seventh-grade books. In the *History of the USSR* there were only two paragraphs on the whole history of Buryatiya. It talked about the "first openers" of Siberia, about how they "joined a weak, undeveloped people". But really, the "first openers" were soldiers.' Independence, he nonetheless considered an impossibility. There were only 420,000 Buryat, they had been ruled by Russia for more than 300 years, and Slav in-migration and Stalin's gerrymandering of Buryatiya's borders meant that they were outnumbered three to one in their own republic. Probably only one in four spoke Buryat fluently and even they, it could be argued, did not speak the genuine language, since the Communists, fearing pan-Mongolism, had chosen as standard a minority dialect as dissimilar as possible from Khalkha Mongolian. What Khamutayev did hope for was some mild affirmative action and devolution: local control over more tax and spending, more Buryat-language education and a quota of ethnic-Buryat deputies in the republican parliament and Moscow Duma.

Moderate, practicable proposals, but doomed, it seemed, to failure. His compatriots, Khamutayev complained, suffered from 'redness of mind'. Though there were plenty of Buryat in the regional government, they were mostly lazy, self-interested ex-nomenklatura, beneficiaries of the old 'sandwich system' whereby if an organisation's top man was a Russian its number two was a Buryat, and vice versa. Ordinary Buryat couldn't be bothered to protest. Even in the heady late 1980s and early 1990s there had been no big pro-democracy demonstrations in Ulan-Ude, and since then people had lost faith in politics completely. An All-Buryat Congress had degenerated into 'jubilee speeches, hot air', and funding problems had reduced his own Negedel's staff from seven to one. Once, he said wistfully, he had had 'faxes, phones, all the equipment. But now the businessmen who used to support us are in difficulties themselves.' I began to understand why Buryatiya's leading opposition politician had been so reluctant to meet me in his office. It was probably his bedroom.

Another reason Khamutayev was doing badly was because he had no access to the media. Vyacheslav Dagayev, the young Buryat founder of *Inform-Polis*, Buryatiya's only privately owned newspaper, made it clear why. Who, I asked, would *Inform-Polis* be backing in the upcoming federal elections?

He spread his hands. 'My policy is – no politics!'

Why?

'Because I don't see anyone whom we can support. And because in our company charter it's written down that our aim is just to turn a profit.'

But wouldn't his readers appreciate his views?

'Look, there's danger in taking one side or the other. If we declare for, say, Luzhkov, it means we're against everyone else. And then they start making difficulties.'

What about local politics? Did any of Buryatiya's papers publish corruption stories, for example?

Tipping his chair back, he grinned and crossed his arms. 'Practically not. After experiencing how serious the actions of our president can be, we all go very carefully.' During regional elections the previous year a television news programme had been taken off the air when it criticised Potapov, and Dagayev himself had been threatened with legal action when he reprinted an article from the English-language *Moscow Times* on the police's violent break-up of an anti-government demonstration by Buddhist monks.

But did he agree with Khamutayev about the need for more autonomy?

'No, I don't. All this talk about pan-Mongolism, it's unreal. Even the Mongols wouldn't want us, because we've been too Russified. A Mongol can live in a yurt; we can't any more, we've changed physiologically. We'd die of disease, of cold!'

But didn't he think it an anachronism that Ulan-Ude was ruled from Moscow? Wasn't it the same as if Delhi were still ruled from London?

For the first time bitterness edged his voice. 'Well, maybe I do. But do you have any other suggestions? Shall we come to England?'

The Buryat were not about to launch an independence movement, but the better I got to know them, the less Russian they seemed. My interpreter Zoya, middle-aged manager of the European Union's Ulan-Ude office, was the perfect example. Bustling about on behalf of a Swedish water-resources expert, or deftly flirting in immaculate English with her Fauchon-provisioned French boss, her surface manner was that of an unusually chic and efficient Russian *intelligent*. But at home, as she explained over more gristly dim sum in Ulan-Ude's only café, she was enmeshed in a thoroughly Asian web of family rights and obligations.

Twenty years ago, she and her husband Sergey had been students together at an agricultural college. On a research trip, they happened to be passing near his home village, and he invited her to come and stay. Though they were no more than friends, his parents greeted them as if they were engaged: 'When we arrived, there was this formal banquet in progress. Everyone started to toast me, their new daughter-in-law, and to cover their vodka glasses with rouble notes. Sergey's father kept calling me his "golden Zoya", and his mother made up a bed for the two of us. I didn't want to make a scandal right there, but I tried to explain that it was a mistake. We did end up sharing the bed but we didn't sleep together – I said that if he didn't keep off I would hate him for ever and never marry him.'

Back home in Ulan-Ude, Zoya's mother said that if Sergey was serious, he would have to come and formally ask for her hand, bringing a proper bride-price. A few days later Sergey duly arrived at their flat with three car-loads of relatives, two sheep and twenty bottles of vodka. Making his request, he presented Zoya's father with an embroidered belt. Accepting it, Zoya's father gave Sergey a football shirt. Ever since, Zoya went on, she had held a privileged but responsible position within her husband's family. As she was the wife of an eldest son, even her oldest sisters-in-law addressed her using a special, respectful form, but she in turn was expected to help out all Sergey's relatives, one or other of whom usually shared their flat. It was another Buryat tradition for everyone to club together for big purchases. 'I've got four sisters, and we've got this one a new car and that one a fridge. The third one's going to study gynaecology in Moscow. It's a micro-credit system!' Russians, she said, took advantage of it: they would marry their son to a Buryat girl, let the girl's family buy the pair everything they needed to set up home, then look the other way when the boy waltzed off with someone else.

Zoya was also, it emerged over ice-cream, a convinced employer of shamans. Three had just been at work on her widowed father. 'They told me that after my mother died he lost his soul. And it was true – he didn't go anywhere, didn't even want to see his grand-children. Nadya Stepanova – she's a very strong shaman, she's on the telly – said that before she could get his soul back, she had to know who all his ancestors were. So I did some research and found them out, back four generations on his mother's side, five on his father's. And now he's much better; he even goes shopping.' For this useful service, Nadya had charged four dollars. She had been equally good value in repairing Zoya's sister's marriage, advising her to sprinkle her adulterous husband's clothes with vodka while he slept. Cleansed, he had broken off his affair with a nineteen-year-old, and the nine-teen-year-old had found a new lover, so now everybody was happy. Zoya's latest project was to persuade her boss to consult Nadya about his eyesight, which had become so bad that he missed the glass when pouring wine, and terrified his passengers from behind the wheel of the EU car. I could come too, for as head of the Shamans' Association Nadya was used to interviews.

Ringing at the reinforced door of a fifth-floor flat in one of Ulan-Ude's fly-blown apartment blocks, we caught Buryatiya's senior shaman in the act of changing out of a housecoat into a flowing purple tunic. She was sorry she was late, but the Turukhansk district committee had asked her to bless some fields, and we knew how these official things dragged on. While she freshened up, we could sit on the sofa and look at her photos. This was her outside St Mark's; Italian shamanists organised the conference last year. And here she was on the Pont Alexandre III, from when she lectured at the Sorbonne. The old man with the tattooed chin was a Maori, a very famous shaman; and that, the one in spectacles, was the Dalai Lama. Nadya had met him twice.

How much, I asked, did Nadya's shamanism resemble the

traditional sort, as described by nineteenth-century anthropologists? Were the rituals she used the same?

Her imperial bulk shifted, and her plucked eyebrows rose: 'You in the West can look in all those books, you can read about what we used to do. But here we've never had anything; it was thought harmful. We've been oppressed by everybody – the Christians, the Buddhists, the Communists!'

So how did she know that what she was doing was genuine?

'Of course it's genuine! The spirits tell me what to do directly! In England, you've lost your Druids, your Celts, your deep knowledge; the spirits can't reach you any more.'

Clearing away the coffee cups, Nadya spread out architectural drawings for a new shamanism centre, for which she had already acquired a prime site next to my hotel. Equipped with a giant circular mirror, solar panels and a 'healing hall', it looked like a cross between a flying saucer and a yurt. Where, I asked, nerving myself for a request for a donation, would she get the money? I need not have worried. She tapped the logo on one of her brochures with a vermilion nail: 'Baikal Bank. Our sponsors.'

Purbozhap, commonly known as Valeriy, Tsydenov was a very different sort of shaman – parish priest to Nadya's conference-circuit cardinal. I met him on the side of a hill above Zoya's husband's home village of Myla, amid what the travel writer Peter Fleming aptly called the 'operatic passes' south of Baikal. In the evening light, the peaks and valleys had the improbable loveliness of a film-set, as if one could cross from one cobalt ridge to another in a couple of strides, or push out a hand and make the crenellated horizon wobble.

Valeriy was there to ask the blessing of the mountain's guardian spirit ('landlord' in Russian) on a young Buryat couple who had driven up with their children from the nearby town of Zakamensk. Self-conscious as communicants, they laid offerings of sweets, biscuits and vodka on the grass. Telling the woman to cover her head, Valeriy poured tea from a Thermos and started spinning in circles, spilling the steaming liquid as he went. His chant was a quick, soft, monotone: 'This family have brought you a gift of white food. They ask for your protection. They ask that their children work easily and be wise at school, that you watch over them from above and support them from below, that disease and misfortune pass them by ...' Tea gone, he motioned the man to stand in front of him, gripped his head between his hands and blew into his ears with a sharp spitting noise. 'I am asking you to give this man energy through my ten fingers, to protect his house, his barns, his cattle, to make him clean, to take away all his troubles ...' Over by the couple's van, their children were playing with a squeaky hand-held computer-game. Valeriy lit a match, blew it out and clapped twice. The ceremony was over. The couple discreetly proffered a few notes, scolded their children into the back seat and slalomed away between windfall branches into a sunset of MGM gold.

Stumbling in their wake, I asked Valeriy how he found his vocation. His account – mystery illness, resistance, acceptance, catharsis – could have come straight from a pre-revolutionary anthropologist's field-notes, or an analyst's casebook. Born in Myla, he went to art school in Novosibirsk, and worked for a while in a shop selling artist's materials, then as a painter-decorator. Always sickly – headachey, prone to vomiting – he started to suffer ghastly dreams in his early thirties. In some, he heard a whispering sound, and spat to frighten it away. 'But the spit came round and landed on my stomach again. It was horrible!' Others were so terrifying that his 'heart stopped. I saw these black, black arms, here and here. And I felt as if a severed head had fallen on my legs, slimy, gelatinous, like in a horror movie. Dogs ran round the house all night, barking and barking.' He was plagued by ladders, madmen and portentous cows, became afraid to sleep at night and awoke each morning bathed in tears. Eventually his wife took him to see an elderly shaman in Zakamensk, who said that the spirits would leave him in peace only when he became a shaman too. To start with, Valeriy thought the whole thing nonsense, but in the end he followed the shaman's advice and had felt fine ever since.

Did the older shaman show him what to do, tell him what words to use?

'No, there were no lessons. And the words depend on me. One day I can say one thing, another day another. It just comes.'

Did he go on soul-journeys?

A laugh. 'No – that's for very strong shamans. I only manage a trance when I'm drunk!'

In a clearing Zoya's in-laws Viktor and Svetlana were grilling kebabs. As we sucked burned fingers and waved cigarettes about to keep the mosquitoes off, Valeriy told me more. Most of his work, he said, was for private individuals – handicapped children, infertile women, men with venereal disease ('They never say, but I can always tell'). Once a year, he presided over community ceremonies at this sacred mountain and two others, asking their guardians for a good harvest and for protection against wolves for the newborn lambs and calves. At the top of each hill Myla's mayor, *kolkhoz* chairman and oldest men made libations of milk and vodka, while the younger men, women and children gathered below, roasting sheep. In dry years Valeriy led the whole village to a sacred lake, in which even Russians knew better than to swim, and stirred coins into it with a copper ladle. Afterwards, it always rained. Recently, he had performed a special ceremony on behalf of the village school, which needed logs for a new sports hall. 'Normally we wouldn't take timber from a sacred hill. But times are so hard – no transport, no fuel – that the administration decided to ask the guardian for permission. I prayed, and gave some cloth and coins and grain. Because of that, when we cut down the trees there weren't any accidents, nobody was injured. If you don't make offerings something always goes wrong.' Viktor, a boyhood friend of Valeriy and the school's headmaster, nodded approvingly. He was thinking of ordering another ceremony to keep his pupils off drugs.

The sun and the mosquitoes had disappeared, and it was getting cold. Viktor led the toasts: 'May you blossom like a flower. May you be rich in friends. May your table always be full. May your children grow as easily as the grass.' He had, it turned out, a sweet tenor voice. One song was about a man's love for his beautiful horse, another about a boy dead in the wars, a third about a girl in a car who tells a boy on a pony that she will marry him if he can gallop fast enough to catch her. I had to sing too, and clumsily chose 'Dear Lord and Father of Mankind', provoking an awkward silence. 'A hymn?' asked Zoya. 'Yes?' 'The Bonny Earl of Moray' – secular, mournful, highland – went down better. Tomorrow, Valeriy said, he would take me to see a newly restored Buddhist temple for which he had designed the decorations.

So he was a Buddhist as well as a shaman?

'Of course.'

What about Orthodoxy?

He laughed, pulled a crucifix from under his shirt and pointed at the sky. 'Oh yes, we've all been baptised. It's all one God.'

Believing in several different things at once is something Buryat are good at. Buddhist missionaries from Tibet first arrived among them in the early 1700s, and absorbed rather than extirpated shamanism. Old gods shouldered their way into the Buddhist pantheon, and old sacred sites turned into nominally lamaist obos, fluttery with rags on the shores of every lake and crest of every mountain. Cautiously encouraged by the tsars, who approved the preaching of pacifism, the hybrid religion flourished. By 1917 Buryatiya had thirty-seven Buddhist monasteries and 15,000 lamas – at one in five of the adult male population, far too many for Western observers, who thought the monks lazy parasites and Buddhism's spread a Chinese ploy to neuter a previously warlike race.

Among Buryat Buddhism's critics was an obscurely heroic band of Congregationalist missionaries: a 24-year-old minister's son, Edward Stallybrass, newly married to a tallow-chandler's daughter, Sarah; a self-educated Glaswegian weaver, Robert Yuille, and his wife, Martha; and a former actuary for the Scottish Widows' Fund, William Swan. Financed by the London Missionary Society and approved by the biblically inclined Alexander I, they embarked for Russia in May 1818 with grand ambitions, reasoning that since the Buryat were recent and apparently half-hearted Buddhists they would prove ripe for conversion, and might even serve as a bridgehead into Mongolia and China. After eighteen months in Petersburg and Irkutsk learning Russian and Mongolian, they built themselves a mission-station – dubbed Stepney after Sarah's home parish – in Selenginsk, a moribund, sand-blown village on the scenic but remote banks of the Selenga.

At first, things seemed to go well. The Buryat, Stallybrass wrote, were a 'harmless, inoffensive sort of people'[11] and almost embarrassingly hospitable, killing sheep in his honour almost before he stepped inside their yurts. Sarah and Martha taught Buryat girls needlework, spinning and basket-weaving, and Stallybrass, relying on his copy of *Buchan's Domestic Medicine*, attracted custom from miles around as a doctor; so much so that he wrote home for a similar manual on surgery.

In the summer of 1820 the missionaries began touring the lamaseries, preaching, distributing tracts and scotching superstition with the aid of a pair of globes and a microscope. The monks were polite but unreceptive. Rather than enter into argument, Stallybrass complained, they pretended that they could not read, or that his ideas were 'too much for their minds'.[12] Since Buddha's language was Buryat, one lama declared, it was right for Buryat to worship him, just as it was right for Europeans to worship Jesus because he spoke Russian. Most infuriating of all was their mild but immovable insistence that Buddhism and Congregationalism amounted to much the same thing:

> The Lama ... either from politeness or stupidity, pretended that he saw no reason why their religion and ours might not be both true; and he evidently wished to let the matter pass, and suffer my statements to remain uncontradicted, rather than risk a discussion. I urged him, and all present, however, to hear and examine the doctrine of Christ, saying that we did not shrink from any investigation of our system, for it was THE TRUTH, and they would sooner or later find it to be so.[13]

Seven years later, even the monks' patience was wearing thin. Most, Stallybrass lamented,

> now decline as much as possible all discussion, and indeed all but unavoidable intercourse with us. They are generally speaking unwilling to hear us when we would make known to them the way of salvation, and even avoid speaking in favour of their own tenets ... One of them, the chief Lama of a temple, lately closed a discussion with me to this effect: 'I am an old man; my system of faith I have held too long to change it now. It is therefore in vain for you to argue with me ...'[14]

Evangelising among Buryat laymen proved equally difficult, since the short months when they were not busy with their livestock they spent getting tipsy on fermented mares' milk, and it was impossible to command attention in the confusion of children and animals filling their yurts. The apathetic few who attended Sunday services were mostly outcasts, scroungers or keen-to-please mission employees. Saving the Buryat, Yuille pithily concluded, was 'like drawing a Cow out of the Mud'.[15]

Undaunted, the missionaries fell back on linguistic work. Painstakingly annotating reams of sutras, cosmologies and handbooks of divination, Stallybrass and Swan compiled not only a Mongolian–English but a Mongolian–Tibetan dictionary, before embarking on a translation into Mongolian of the Bible. The Old Testament took them ten years, and they had just finished the New when the London Missionary Society finally cut its losses and recalled them home. In twenty-three years they had converted four Buryat. Martha and Sarah had died of typhus and dysentery, as had Stallybrass's second wife and five of the mission's thirteen children. During all that time Stallybrass and Swan had been back to England once, to raise funds, and Yuille not at all. A generation later travellers unearthed the odd greybeard who had been taught his letters at the mission school and since forgotten them again, and discovered that local legend had turned the missionaries' dead families into ghouls. Stallybrass's dictionaries and Mongol-language schoolbooks gathered dust in the library of London's Royal Asiatic Society, unpublished and unread.

The head of the Buryat church, or Khamba Lama, was headquartered at Goose Lake monastery, seventy miles south-west of Ulan-Ude. Founded in 1741 and extended throughout the 1800s, by the end of the century it possessed several temples, 900 staff, a school, a printshop and a library. The American journalist Kennan was ushered into a freezing reception room furnished with a Paisley carpet, heavy Russian tables and chairs, life-size silk-scroll portraits of eminent lamas, and crude coloured lithographs of Alexander III and Kaiser Wilhelm. Half an hour later the Khamba Lama – 'about sixty years of age, of middle height and erect figure, with a beardless, somewhat wrinkled, but strong and kindly face' – appeared, regally attired:

He wore a striking and gorgeous costume, consisting of a superb long gown of orange silk shot through with gold thread, bordered with purple velvet, and turned back and faced at the wrists with ultramarine-blue satin ... Over this beautiful yellow gown was thrown a splendid red silk scarf a yard wide and five yards long, hanging in soft folds from the left shoulder and gathered up about the waist. On his head he wore a high, pointed, brimless hat of orange felt, the extended sides of which fell down over his shoulders ... and were lined with heavy gold-thread embroidery.[16]

After tea Kennan attended a service in the monastery's biggest temple, whose gods, gongs, banners and butter-lamps he found almost too much to take in — 'so crowded with peculiar details that one could not reduce one's observations to anything like order'.[17] The ceremony was stranger and more impressive than he had expected, though fifteen minutes of cacophony from cymbals, drums, rattles and eight-foot trumpets was 'quite long enough'.[18] Over fruit and madeira with the Khamba Lama, he was amazed to discover that his dignified and learned host had never heard of America, and believed the world to be flat:

'You have been in many countries,' he said to me through the interpreter, 'and have talked with the wise men of the West; what is your opinion with regard to the shape of the earth?'

'I think,' I replied, 'that it is shaped like a great ball.'

'I have heard so before,' said the Great Lama, looking thoughtfully away into vacancy. 'The Russian officers whom I have met have told me that the world is round. Such a belief is contrary to the teachings of our old Thibetan books, but I have observed that the Russian wise men predict eclipses accurately ... Why do you think the world is round?'

'I have many reasons for thinking so,' I answered; 'but perhaps the best and strongest reason is that I have been around it.'

By the meal's end 'the Grand Lama seemed to be partly or wholly convinced of the truth ... and said, with a sigh "It is not in accordance with the teachings of our books; but the Russians must be right".'[19]

I drove to Goose Lake with Oleg, a young cousin of Zoya blessed with a tiresome line in anti-Semitic jokes and inexhaustible curiosity

Evenk reindeer-herders, from an early nineteenth-century travel book.

Above: A Sakha bride in her wedding clothes, in front of a *balagan*.

Below: Eskimo tents, photographed by the Polish revolutionary-turned-ethnographer Waldemar Bogoras. The inflated seal-skins were used as whaling floats.

Koryak hour-glass houses. In summer, they were entered by a side-door, in winter, via the smoke-hole in the roof. 'They are pervaded', wrote a traveller, 'by a smell of rancid oil and decaying fish; their logs are black as jet and greasy with smoke, and their earthen floors an indescribable mixture of reindeer hairs and filth trodden hard. They have no furniture except wooden bowls of seal-oil, in which burn fragments of moss, and black wooden troughs which are alternately used as dishes and seats.'

A Tuvan yurt.

An Evenk 'Shaman or Devil-Priest', from a seventeenth-century Dutch travel book. Note his furry feet.

'Siberian Shamans
performing a Ritual'

Irgit Kalzan–ham, photographed on his arrest in 1938. Six decades later his daughter was able to recover the picture from the archives of Kyzyl's KGB.

Ivolginsk near Ulan–Ude, in Soviet times one of only two Buddhist temples allowed to operate in Buryatiya.

A modern shaman re-consecrating a
disused sacred site; southern Tuva, 1999.

Yermak's Cossacks fire on Khan
Kuchum's Tatars, in Vasiliy Surikov's
painting of 1895.

Yermak advertises agricultural machinery
for an Omsk manufacturer, 1909.

as to Western consumer-goods prices and rates of pay. On the road out of Ulan-Ude, someone had tried to Russify the landscape by planting birches, as incongruous in the parched steppe as the funereal spruces that front every former Party building from Uzbek deserts to the azure Black Sea. Soon the birches petered out. Then so did the telegraph poles, the fences and the stubble-fields, until the view had distilled to a vast hazy beigeness, so minimalist that we might as well have already crossed the border into Mongolia. Brown buzzards wheeled over brown cows, and sometimes in the far distance a horseman floated, riding always at a walk, never at a trot or canter. Whenever we breasted the brow of a hill Oleg wound down his window and threw out a pinch of corn from a bag tucked under his gearstick. Everyone, he explained to the patter of grains against the bodywork, gave to the gods in this way. The other week he hadn't bothered to stop at a big obo on the road to Selenginsk. A few miles on his car broke down, and he had to walk all the way back to give the gods cigarettes. On his return, it started again straight away. A friend of his was once stupid enough to steal money from an obo. The next day the gods sent him through the ice of a frozen river, and he was lucky to escape with his life.

Goose Lake was dominated by a large power station. We admired the view from a designated beauty spot, its trodden earth cobbled with cigarette butts and pistachio shells. 'It provides electricity for the whole of Buryatiya!' said Oleg, pointing at the chimneys. 'For Tuva and Chita too!' Down on the lakeshore, a slum of a village straggled, all crazy shacks and drifting refuse. I pushed open a pair of gates and there, in a big bare enclosure, were Goose Lake monastery's three surviving temples, bells clinking in the wind from tip-tilted eaves. The largest was boarded up, but another buzzed with loud, rapid chanting. Inside, shaven-headed boys swayed over prayer-scrips, cross-legged on a raised dais. From the back wall, through spirals of incense, paintbox-bright Buddhas smiled and gestured, and dragons ramped up crimson pillars to a ceiling hung with seven-tiered windsocks stitched together from a dozen different curtain fabrics. Glass-fronted cabinets burst with butter-sculptures, peacock feathers and plastic flowers. In one, I spotted a bottle of Stolichnaya and a Twix. A notice near the door told new converts what to do:

On entering the temple remove your hat.
Do not step on the door frame.
Do not put your hands in your pockets, or sit with your arms or legs
    crossed.
Having entered the temple, proceed in the direction of the sun.
Go to the altar and pray.
Put any gifts you have brought with you on the table.
To order a prayer come to the cash desk.

We found the head lama in a cabin in the temple grounds, hiding
from his mother, girlfriend and infant sons behind a newspaper. The
wall above his bed was decorated with 3-D posters, one of kittens in
a basket, another of a table laid with Ben Nevis whisky and tomatoes
sliced to look like flowers. Was it hard, I asked, to get people brought
up on atheism believing in Buddha again? The monk sighed and
scratched. 'In the first years of perestroika it was easy. Everyone came
because it was something new. Now there are fewer of them, but they
are much more serious.' The revival of shamanism did not bother
him. 'We're good friends, brothers. People are always asking us to do
ceremonies together – obos, funerals, sanctifying houses.' Baptist
and Moonie missionaries were another matter. 'They're aggressive,
scandalous! They don't preach to people, they just grab them!' All
the money for restoring Goose Lake had been raised locally, which
was why the big temple wasn't done yet. 'The government hasn't
given us a kopeck! If you interview those big pine cones in Ulan-
Ude, you tell them they're killing Buddhism in Buryatiya!'

Given Buryatiya's fate under Stalin, Goose Lake is lucky to have
survived at all. On news of Nicholas II's abdication in March 1917,
politically prominent Buryat, including Dorzhiyev, Zhamtsarano and
Rinchino, converged on Chita, in eastern Buryatiya, and formed a
Buryat National Committee, or BurNatsKom. Short-lived and fissile,
it never had a clear programme, but its leaders (at that stage still
centrist or centre-left) broadly stood for what a congress called 'bourgeois national autonomy' – meaning a regional parliament, Buryat-
language education and mild pan-Mongolism. In elections to a local

Constituent Assembly in November, BurNatsKom and an allied Buryat party came second to the Socialist Revolutionaries, with a combined 30 per cent of the vote. The Bolsheviks came a poor fourth, with 8 per cent.

When the Russian Civil War broke out in early 1918, Buryatiya descended into chaos. Fourteen different governments, wielding half a dozen different armies, claimed to control the region over the next four years.[20] Czechs taken prisoner during the First World War took up arms when Trotsky tried to halt their evacuation along the Trans-Siberian Railway, and briefly held Irkutsk and Ulan-Ude. The Buryat–Mongolian border was laid waste by the original Mad Baron, Roman von Ungern-Sternberg, a wild-eyed Baltic-German who loathed Jews and commissars, believed himself to be a reincarnation of Genghiz and reputedly soaked his battle standards at his captives' slit throats and upholstered his saddles with human skin. BurNatsKom supported Grigoriy Semyonov, a half-Buryat former officer in one of the 'native Cossack' regiments, who raised a 2,000-strong army with Japanese help, stormed up and down the Trans-Siberian in the armoured locomotives 'Merciless' and 'Destroyer', and executed 1,800 prisoners in five days near Kyakhta. His troops' rapes and massacres are detailed in the memoirs of William Graves, the general in charge of American support for the Whites in Siberia.[21] To his extreme frustration, Graves was obliged to ignore the atrocities, since Semyonov was anti-Bolshevik. The high point of Semyonov's career was his formation, in February 1919, of a pan-Mongol 'Dauria Government', complete with constitution and representatives at the Paris Peace Conference. The following year Japan disowned him and his leading followers were captured by the Bolsheviks.

Emerging victorious from the war in Buryatiya towards the end of 1921, the Bolsheviks turned to Nicholas II's old envoy to Tibet, Dorzhiyev. Made Khamba Lama, Dorzhiyev attempted a reconciliation between Communism and Buddhism, arguing that they preached the same virtues, and that since Buddhism did not assert the existence of a universal God it was a 'religion of atheism'. Some of his supporters went even further, suggesting that Lenin was Buddha's latest reincarnation. The compromise did not hold, for by 1928, as the Leningrad Academy of Science's leading Mongolist, Nikolay

Poppe, discovered on a field-trip, Buryat already held the new government in fear and dislike:

> For the first few days after my arrival the Buryats were mistrustful and obviously afraid that I might report on them if they said anything against the regime. They therefore tried to convince me what loyal Soviet citizens they were by telling me how happy they were, and how much they owed to the Soviets for their happiness. Soon, however, they showed me old photographs in which they appeared in their best garments: the women in silk robes with golden coins sewed along the hems, and wearing precious necklaces. They said: 'Formerly we used to wear beautiful garments, but we have hidden them so nobody can see them, and now we try to look as poor as possible, and wear only the worst garments we have.' These, then, were their true feelings![22]

For Stalin – by 1928 already Party General Secretary for six years – the non-Russian nationalities, especially those who possessed no industrial proletariat and had fought against the Bolsheviks during the Civil War, were anathema, and he set out to destroy their societies and cultures even more completely than those of the almost equally unfortunate Russians. In the Buryat's case that meant eliminating their taishas, who still commanded allegiance within their clans, dispensed justice and owned vast herds, and their lamaseries, centres of the national faith and of learning.

Stalin's anti-Buryat campaign began in 1929 and peaked in the late 1930s, though lamaseries were still being demolished in the 1940s and 1950s. Historical research on the topic is only just beginning and, much of the information given here came from a doctoral student in Ulan-Ude, Dandar Dorzhiyev, who had been granted access to local KGB archives. Collectivisation – the confiscation of all privately owned livestock, agricultural stores and land, accompanied by the deportation or execution of recalcitrants – began Union-wide in 1929. In Buryatiya it took place in two main stages. A decree of 1929 confiscated 780 square miles of land, and from November 1929 to February 1930 around 1,000 herders and farmers, both Buryat and Slav, were executed, and another 19,000 deported or imprisoned. Another 20,000 or so were 'dekulakised' from 1931 to 1934, though here Dandar had no execution/deportation/imprisonment split.

Resistance was disorganised but widespread. Dandar had found records of five separate risings, each involving about 150 people. They started in the spring of 1930 among Russian Cossacks and Old Believers and quickly spread to the eastern Tungka district, home to the big Buryat cattle herds. The risings' leaders and targets tended, ironically, to be similar sorts of people: soviet chairmen, collective-farm bosses, Komsomol leaders and policemen. Victims were abducted, convicted at informal trials of 'using Soviet power against the peasants' and summarily executed. At least 1,000 Soviet officials had been killed by 1934. When the Tungka rising failed the participants fled south with their families to Mongolia, pursued by GPU troops and artillery. When the GPU caught up with them they turned to fight, armed only with old rifles and hunting knives, and all but three out of 200 were shot to pieces. The commonest form of protest was the despairing slaughter of livestock. Together with the general unrest and loss of the country's most successful herders, it cut Buryatiya's cattle numbers by more than half, giving rise to a serious – and again completely unresearched – famine. Between 1926 and 1939, according to government censuses, Buryatiya's population fell from 237,500 to 224,700 – a decrease unexplained save by terror and starvation. Poppe, in Ulan-Ude for a conference in 1939, was told that he should cash in his ration-card at the Party dining-hall, since no food was to be had anywhere in the city. Returning to his hotel with a loaf of bread under his arm, he was pursued by a respectable-looking woman who told him her children had not eaten for two days and fell to her knees when he handed it over.

Simultaneously, the Party launched its attack on Buddhism. From 1926 lamaseries had been heavily taxed, and lamas deprived of the right to vote, travel or take non-manual jobs. In 1929 anti-religious propaganda intensified. Stalin personally pronounced Agvan Dor-zhiyev's Buddhism-equals-Communism theory to be 'absurd',[23] and monks were excoriated as 'sworn enemies of socialist reconstruction', 'lama-aggressors', 'lama-criminals' and 'lama-thieves'. Selling them food or giving them shelter became a criminal offence punishable with prison. Local Party organs were encouraged to compete in the monasteries' physical destruction, and sent teams of activists, backed by militia, to loot their temples and libraries. Teachers brought their classes along to join in. 'Nobody refused, we were like sheep,' a schoolboy who participated told me sixty-five years later. 'It was a shame, a shame, to throw away all those beautiful things. But if I had said no, I would have been taken to prison.' As it was, his father was arrested and never seen again – 'not a noise, not a breath' – and he and his mother spent six years in a labour camp. Monasteries that were not demolished outright were turned into soviet headquarters or tractor-repair shops. Closed in 1929, Goose Lake was first used as a transit prison for lamas on their way to the Gulag, then as a hospital, a dormitory for railwaymen, a saw-mill and a chicken farm.

Left to mourn the destruction was Poppe. Lost from Egetuyev lamasery, he wrote, was a tenth-century Chinese statue of Buddha, carved from a single piece of sandalwood and sent to Buryatiya for safekeeping during the Boxer Rebellion. From the great Aga monastery at Chita disappeared an ancient Tibetan and Mongolian library, a printing-press with hundreds of unique woodblocks and a filigree and enamel model of the Buddhist paradise Devazhin, including dozens of delicately worked temples, trees, flowers and animals. Shortly before Aga was demolished, the great Russian film director Vsevolod Pudovkin used it as a set for his absurdly propagandistic but visually gorgeous film *Genghiz's Heir*:

> In one scene some lamas were required to form a procession coming out of the monastery, carrying volumes of the Kanjur, a collection of Buddhist works, on their heads. This procession walked around the monastery and here the scene ended. The books were then thrown into a ditch by the road, and the actors started on the next scene. What books were not destroyed then were later sent to paper-mills for recycling.[24]

Poppe applied for permission to retrieve some of Aga's treasures for the Academy of Sciences, but was for three years denied travel papers, by which time only 'pitiful relics'[25] remained. In Ulan-Ude for another conference in 1936 he found himself seated next to Buryatiya's ethnic-Buryat Party boss, Mikhail Yerbanov, and took the opportunity to plead for at least one monastery to be conserved as a museum. 'I disagree, professor,' Yerbanov jocularly replied. 'I'm sure you would also wish to preserve a few lamas, and I can assure you that we are keeping them in labour camps where they are being so well looked after that you need not worry about them.'[26]

The lamas Yerbanov and his colleagues were looking after so well were attacked, like the herders, in two main stages. From 1929 to 1934 1,162 were shot, imprisoned or sent to camps. The pace quickened again from 1937 to 1938, when roughly another 600 were shot, 400 gaoled locally and 1,000 sent to camps. Typical charges against them were 'anti-Soviet agitation', 'counter-revolutionary pan-Mongol espionage', 'spreading of offensive rumours about the fall of Soviet power' or 'listening to anti-Soviet conversations'. Practitioners of Tibetan medicine were accused of 'charlatanism' or 'poisoning Soviet people'. Instructed by their religion not to use violence, the monks resisted with rituals for the destruction of the Soviet state. At Aga they built a new shrine, burying inside it 100,000 needles which they prayed would arise as a steely army to fight the destroyers of the faith.

One notable victim was the eighty-three-year-old Khamba Lama, who died in prison two months after his arrest in 1937. Ulan-Ude's KGB archive includes a three-page handwritten note on his interrogation. In it, Dorzhiyev admits hating the government for its destruction of Buddhism, at which point the interview ends – as a note in a different hand at the bottom of the page puts it, 'because of illness'.[27] The Leningrad temple for which he had lobbied Nicholas II so hard turned into a Building Workers' Union gym, then a military radio station, then a zoological laboratory.

Until perestroika, all the above was a taboo subject. Soviet writers referred to the execution, imprisonment, deportation or starvation of a sizeable proportion of Buryatiya's population, as well as the demolition of nearly all its historic buildings, as the 'forced reduction of Lamas' and 'liquidation of kulaks as a class'. Western Communists – wittingly or unwittingly – went along with the euphemisms. A travel book titled *Dawn in Siberia*, written by one G. D. R. Philips and published in 1942, is a prime example. Filled with photographs of wolfram mines, veterinary students and cheerful multi-ethnic school-children, it blames, without a hint of sarcasm, 'wreckers' at the Institute of Culture for livestock losses, and praises the Party purges of the late 1930s for uncovering a Japanese plot to establish a regime 'where the chief puppets would be feudal khans and abbots; where the herdsman would be tied to his lord as a serf'. Thanks to Moscow's vigilance, readers are assured, Buryatiya is now flourishing:

> Its people, one-time nomads, reach out and take for themselves the soap and the Shakespeare, the gramophone and fresh fruit that Western Europe has long known. More and more of the things which make life broader and fuller, more pleasant and more inspiring, become available to this little people in the heart of Asia as they go on from Socialism towards the full Communism which they still only dimly appreciate.[28]

'It is a pleasure,' Philips concludes, 'to find the political and economic doctrines to which one has pinned one's faith justified in their practical application.'[29]

Unblinded by faith was Poppe. Having seen forty out of ninety colleagues at the Leningrad Academy of Science's Oriental Studies Department, as well as most of his learned Buryat acquaintance, shot or gaoled, he departed the Soviet Union with the Wehrmacht in 1943. From an academic post in America, his bitter footnote was as follows:

> In Asia Minor and Greece the ruins of ancient temples are extant, and the ancient culture of Hellas is there to be studied. Nothing has been left of the Buddhist temples in Buryat-Mongolia ... The fate of Lamaism in the USSR is a tragic example of the complete and wilful eradication of a religion and serves as a warning that Communism is out to crush mercilessly whatever stands in the way of its path to the enslavement of mankind.[30]

After the war, Buddhism, like Orthodoxy and Islam, was granted strictly limited official sanction again, allowing the reopening of two Buryat monasteries. Their handful of Party-approved monks were as craven as Dorzhiyev in the 1920s, preaching plan fulfilment, international nuclear disarmament and the breeding, in the words of a 1969 address by the Khamba Lama, of 'worthy builders of Communist society'.[31] Buddha's sayings became a 'song to the greatness of labour'.

Outside these limits, the government punished religious activity as ruthlessly as ever, as witnessed by the career of the Buryat guru Bidya

Dandaron. Born out of wedlock in 1914, at the age of seven he was declared heir to a prominent lama. Aged twenty-two he moved to Leningrad, officially to study aeronautical engineering, unofficially to attend lectures at Poppe's Oriental Department. The following year, the Leningrad purges being at their height, he was arrested and sentenced to ten years in the Gulag. In 1944 he was released and returned to Buryatiya, only to be rearrested and sent back to the camps three years later. In the Gulag, however, he met numerous lamas, with whom he was able secretly to pursue his Buddhist training. By the 50s he had won his own religious following: a measure of his charisma is that in one prison his disciples included a NKVD colonel, a Gestapo officer, a German journalist and two Ukrainian Jews. Released in 1955, he got a job at a sociology institute in Ulan-Ude, and continued discreetly to teach a widening circle of enthusiasts, many of them Muscovites and Balts. By 1972 the authorities were sufficiently rattled to arrest him yet again, and put him on stage-managed trial in Ulan-Ude. Newspapers and the official Buddhist church accused him of organising ritual sex orgies, of beating his wife and son, of rape, alcoholism and of spying for the Japanese. Sentenced to five years' corrective labour, he died in prison two years later. After bad publicity in the West, it was decided not to arrange a show trial for four of his followers. Instead they were declared insane and incarcerated in psychiatric hospitals. The KGB archives on the whole episode remain firmly closed.

I found the surviving contents of Buryatiya's destroyed Buddhist monasteries, inappropriately enough, in Ulan-Ude's eighteenth-century Holy Trinity Cathedral. Tussling with a padlock, a curator let me in. The lights weren't working, she apologised, because her institute couldn't afford to pay the electricity bill. In the porch we tripped over a stuffed fish, a wooden saddle and two newly cast bells in bubble-wrap, ready to be hung when the cathedral was reconsecrated and handed back to the Church. Inside, the building had been sliced into cubicles, each of which gleamed floor to ceiling with a junk-shop medley of silk, brass, celadon and lacquer. The curator wondered what would interest me. I should look at this drinking-vessel hollowed from a human skull, and at this ritual whistle carved from a virgin's thigh-bone. The papier-mâché masks were for the Tsum dance; the oblong books with wooden bindings the 110 volumes of the Kanjur, illuminated with inks ground from seven different precious stones. The Bodhisattvas were so many that even she could not identify them all. The pale, effete one with lilies sprouting from his elbows was Maitreya, a future incarnation of Buddha. The one with fiery hair and a necklace of scalps was some sort of protector saint, and the one with ten heads looking in ten different directions compassionate Avalokitesvara, who watched all the sufferings of the world, weeping green tears for men, white for women.

The last cubicle housed the relics of the latest Buryat religion to get the push. From every surface, in every conceivable medium, shiny-pated Lenins and hirsute Stalins exhorted, pondered, hunched over desks. The curator pointed at a picture of Stalin embracing a buck-toothed girl in a sailor suit. Once, she said, it hung in every schoolroom, under the caption 'We Thank Our Dear Comrade Stalin For Our Happy Childhood'. It was even made into a statue for Moscow's Stalinskaya metro station. The original photograph was taken in 1936 at a reception for Buryat shock workers, and the girl was Gelya Markizova, four-year-old daughter of a Buryat Party chief. Two years later Gelya's father and fifty-three of his colleagues were executed, and her mother was sent to the Gulag. Gelya went to an orphanage, under a new name.

Just as everyone in Tomsk was a descendant of deportees, every Buryat seemed to have at least one relative who had been imprisoned or executed under Stalin. The great-uncle of one of the matrons at the opera gala had been shot for being Yerbanov's chauffeur. Finding people who could remember Stalinism at first hand was harder, but in Myla, Viktor introduced me to Dolgor Dymbrilova, still in her right mind at ninety-seven, and the oldest person in the village.

Tiny inside her armchair, Dolgor was nervous in front of a for-eigner. Her milky eyes could no longer see, but she turned her head this way and that at my questions and Zoya's translations, dabbing at baggy stockings with hands like sloughed snakeskins. Her ancestors, she said, were 'sky-dwellers', meaning that they had come from Mongolia. She only knew the names of seven generations, but her father had been able to go back more than thirty. During the repressions he wrote them all down in a book which he hid in a cave. Later, Dolgor went back to find it, but 'the mice had made a picnic. Where there used to be all those ancestors, there were just bits of paper blowing about in the wind.'

How much, I asked, did she remember of the 1930s? Her trickle of a voice flowed faster: 'They were terrible times, terrible! We just sat in our houses, waiting to be arrested. We didn't even pray.' Her older brother was sent 'somewhere in the north' for ten years; her younger one, a student monk, was taken to Ulan-Ude and shot. Her uncle 'was a lama, an old old man. They took him to prison and put him under a bench. He said, "Let me go, I can't breathe!" And they kicked his eye out. It was his own nephew who did it! He'd joined the Komsomol.' Collectivisation was enforced by Buryat Komsomol leaders from Irkutsk: 'We were like servants to them – we saddled their horses, did whatever they asked. People were terrified of them. They took all our animals and we didn't say a word. They could beat you or send you to prison for no reason, just because they wanted to. They weren't afraid of anything, not even the devil!'

Through it all, Dolgor never lost faith in Buddhism. Plucking at her cardigan, she drew out a locket. Her daughter Rinchin-Handa – 'it means Glorious Pearl, but usually I'm just called Margarita' – prised it open to show us the Sanskrit hieroglyph 'Om', first word of the famous mantra *Om mani padme hum* ('Jewel in the Lotus'). When she was a child, she explained, her mother had never dared instruct her in religion, though she did say that the gods existed, up in the sky. Rinchin-Handa's own locket contained two grains of wheat. 'The lama gives you one. You put it in a bottle with cotton wool, and if you're a good person, if you pray a lot, it multiplies.' Her other miraculous treasure was a piece of cloth blessed by the Dalai Lama. 'When he came to Ulan-Ude in 1994 I couldn't go and see him because of the children. But when I went outside to pray there was this wonderful smell, and pictures in the clouds.'

The day I left Myla, peaceful in its ring of green mountains, Viktor showed me an exhibition hall attached to his school. The walls were hung with the usual photographs: the first Buryat *traktoristka*, singing groups in national dress, delegates to an All-Union Agricultural Symposium. Viktor's pupils had been busy crafting exhibits: a pom-pom dog, a cross-stitch sampler of the Kremlin, a cardboard model of a yurt. In the centre of the room they had improvised a miniature war memorial, decorated with two colour posters. The first was of 'Zhukov, General of Victory', the second of 'Generalissimo Stalin'. Above, illuminated from within so as to do duty as an eternal flame, was a child's plastic football.

CHAPTER 4

THE TUVANS

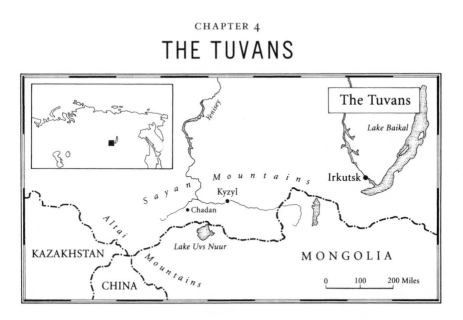

'A Russian is not a man.'
– Tuvan proverb, 1926

Four hundred miles to the west of Myla, the spring grass floated above the ground like green mist. In front, dun hills rose in gentle bell-curves to a high, round, roof-of-the-world sky. Behind, the ranges turned blue, and in the far distance, slate-grey. Our ponies flushed out cuckoos and hoopoes, and a buzzard planed so low that I could see the gleam of his eyes. Even on a wooden saddle, riding felt like flying.

The man I was with, Baibek Sat, was a throat-singer, throat-singing being a vocal technique that allows the production of up to three notes at once, and the Tuvan national art form. To persuade him to demonstrate I had to sing in return, and after each 'And Did Those Feet' or 'Thank You for the Music' he slapped his boots and breathed 'Was that a LOVE song?' His own contributions, all fluting radio signals and dense, crunchy harmonics, sounded as if they came from outer space or the depths of the ocean. In the old days, he said, 'every song had to include a *Komsomolyets*, an agitator, a tractor-driver. It had to be, I'm proud of my country, the USSR; I sing to the glory of my country, the USSR. If we sang them now, everyone would laugh.' The previous week he had entered a throat-singing competition at the local Kinoteatr 'Forty Years of Soviet Tuva' and been awarded two sheep.

Back at the Sat family's yurt, Baibek's veterinary brother Ayas had arrived with his children to castrate the goats. His daughter Elchey ('Everlasting Happiness') tipped the first animal on to its back and dragged it over. Ayas did swift, horrible things with a knife; the goat screamed and rolled its golden eyes. Arzhaan ('Healing Spring') and Eres ('Nimble and Courageous') swung on a fence, crowing with laughter as it stumbled away again, bleating and stupefied.

When it was all over we ducked indoors to drink salted tea. The smells were of woodsmoke, horse and lanolin, the talk of cattle-rustlers from across the Mongolian border and the shocking frequency of forest fires now that the fire-fighting service had broken down. Hearing the title of my book, Baibek told a story about a local shaman. 'It was at the time of the repressions. She was arrested and put in gaol. But she opened the door and set off home. She was resting on top of a mountain when the *militsiya* came to get her. She put out her hand, like this, and they flew backwards. They tried twice more, and the same thing happened each time, so they gave up and went back to town. When they got there, it's said, they all died. So did the *babka*.'

Why her too?

'Of course she died! She couldn't heal people, so what sort of life was it going to be for her? She was a strong shaman, very strong. There aren't such shamans now; they were all killed. Maybe in a few generations we'll have strong ones again.'

Ayas was more interested in the here and now; specifically, in the fact that the *kolkhoz* didn't pay him a salary any more. I asked him why, since its livestock were now privately owned, herders didn't pay him individually. He chuckled: 'They're all my relatives! They give me a drink, then it's bye-bye!' In England, he was sure, life was much better. How much did a cow cost with us, or a horse? In Tuva, a good horse was worth fifteen cows; an old one, fit only for meat, just one. As in Khant country, there was bafflement when I admitted that my mother, though she lived in a village, owned no cows at all. Perhaps, Baibek suggested, they had been eaten by bears?

'In England, we don't have bears.'

'No bears! What about wolves?'

'We don't have wolves either. But we do have foxes.'

'What sort of foxes?'

'Red ones.'

'Only red ones! No black? No silver?'

Anxious to uphold the honour of British fauna, I got out my dictionary and looked up the word for badger. It was no good. Tuva had badgers too.

The hallway of Everlasting Happiness's school was decorated with a mural. Top left, sinister Orientals gazed hungrily at snow-capped mountains. Top right, they thrashed a cowering youth with knotted whips. Bottom left and right, soldiers strode forward under scarlet banners, a teacher pointed at a blackboard, and a boy and girl clasped hands under a hammer-and-sickle and an aeroplane. The young couple were, naturally, happy Soviet Tuvans. The evil Orientals were the Manchu Chinese, who ruled them from the 1750s until 1911. Before that – an era the mural omitted – the Turkic Tuvans were led by Mongol khans.

Until the late 1800s, Russians had little contact with Tuva, and what they did have verged on farce. The first to scout the region, in 1616, were the Cossacks Vasiliy Tumenets and Ivan Petrov. Expecting simple tribesmen, they took with them the sort of trade goods popular with the Nenets and Khant: tin plates, buttons, kettles and knives. Tuva's Altan ('Golden') Khan Sholoi Ubashi, whom they found camped by Lake Uvs Nuur just over the present-day Russo–Mongol border, came as a surprise. A courtly, clean-shaven sixty-year-old, he received them robed in yellow satin, throned on a carpeted dais in a tent furnished with lacquerware, ivory and silver. The bemused Cossacks took him for a Muslim, admiring his 'lofty felt mosque' and attendant lamas, who wore robes 'like those of the Greeks, without arms, and merely thrown over the shoulders'.[1] Hastily putting away the buttons and kettles, they presented the khan with seven silk gowns with gold fastenings, in return for which he agreed an alliance, and gave the Russians horses, sheep, sable-trimmed cloaks, a sickly slave-girl and some heavy hints about the sort of gifts he expected in the future. Tsar Mikhail, the Cossacks advised on their return, 'might be gracious enough to send him ... say three silver vessels, and a pearl, and about twenty muskets, and two good swords; but cloth, tin and copper he need not send'.[2]

Three years later one of Ubashi's lamas arrived in Moscow with an updated present list. As well as gold, silver, jewels and armour, the khan now wanted gunsmiths, a Turkmen racehorse and 'a dwarf to look at'. Mikhail's reply was polite (Ubashi's name was inscribed throughout in gold), but distant. Though most of the requested items were on their way, no racehorse would survive the journey. 'As to the dwarf,' he apologised, 'there is none in our empire at present. One was brought here, indeed, from abroad, but he is dead; we breed no such people in our country, nor do those imported live long.'[3] Disappointed, Ubashi took out reprisals against Muscovy's Kirghiz tributaries, prompting Mikhail to instruct the governor of Tomsk to have nothing more to do with the Tuvans, since 'our empire has received no benefits from them up to now – only demands'.[4]

With the ascent to the throne of a new Altan Khan, Ombo Erdene, Russian–Tuvan relations resumed – with no more success than before. In 1634 Erdene stripped the envoy Yakov Tukhachevsky of twelve horse-loads of gifts, made Tukhachevsky take an oath of allegiance to him rather than vice versa, and put in demands for a bell, telescope, striking clock, doctor, silversmith, tanner, Russian–Mongol inter-preter and 'a monk who has been to Jerusalem'.[5] Tukhachevsky's secretary, he added, should be flogged in the tsar's presence, for rudeness and for stealing a pot of mutton stew. A fourth group of envoys were fleeced of all their belongings down to the collars off their jackets, and a fifth was kept waiting three weeks for an audience, then packed off home without horses or a guard. In 1667 Erdene's successor was taken prisoner by a Dzungar rival, at which point the Golden Khans, responsible for some of the most ridiculous passages in the annals of Russian diplomacy, exit, waving present lists, recorded history.

While Tuva's rulers thought up new ways to infuriate Muscovy, the Mongols to their south, divided into Khalkha in the east and Dzungars in the west, fought each other, making themselves increasingly vulnerable to the aggressive Manchus. In 1688 the Dzungars captured the great Khalkha lamasery at Erdeni Juu, and the Khalkhas submitted to the Manchus for protection. The Dzungars held out for another seventy years, only to be annihilated following an abortive Khalkha anti-Manchu rising.

With the Dzungars' defeat the whole of Mongolia, including Tuva, was incorporated into the Chinese empire. The Manchus exacted crippling tribute – the equivalent of 3,000 sable per year – but otherwise left the country alone, banning Chinese peasant settlers, restricting traders and deputing local government to the local Mongol aristocracy. As a result, Mongolian society hardly changed for over a century, remaining genuinely feudal well into the 1900s. Nobles and monasteries continued to exact labour dues from the non-noble laity, who in turn exploited a large slave class. There being no generally accepted currency, taxes were paid and bargains struck in sheep, eagles' feathers and blocks of brick tea. In the prison at Urga, horrified visitors reported, criminals lived in stacked wooden boxes four feet long and two feet deep, with holes just big enough for their manacled hands. Following Buddhist custom, corpses were dumped on open hillsides, so that the country's few permanent settlements were terrorised by packs of savage, flesh-eating dogs.

Equally anachronistic were Mongolia's heads of the state and of the church, the Khutuktus. Reincarnations of Buddha, they were in reality Chinese puppets. At least one was secretly assassinated, several died mysteriously as children, and so as further to reduce their power, rules were introduced excluding reincarnations born outside Tibet. The eighth and last Khutuktu, Jebtsundamba, was a joke figure: a drunk, blind, promiscuous syphilitic whose principal mistress, the wife of a wrestler, ran off with her hairdresser, and whose chief catamite paid for infidelity by being buried alive. When Jebtsundamba died in 1925 the sale of his possessions included everything from Ming vases to watches, musical boxes and a large stock of Czech felt hats, garlanded with paper roses.

The best-known description of pre-revolutionary Tuva is from the English explorer and naturalist Alexander Carruthers, who spent eleven months there from 1910 to 1911, accompanied by the big-game hunter John Miller, whose photographs of large dead animals illustrate Carruthers's sporting chapters, and Morgan Philips Price, a botanist and 'well-known figure with the Ledbury Hunt'.[6] Having bought horses and supplies on the Russian border, they took five weeks to cross the Sayan mountains bounding Tuva to the north, slowed to a rate of five miles a day by fallen trees, 'a torment' of mosquitoes and rivers that failed to appear on their maps. The forests were monotonous, wet and silent – 'a hundred miles of desolate sand-waste', Carruthers grumbled, 'is not so repulsive'[7] – and their only inhabitants were an aboriginal tribe of reindeer-herders, who traded milk for needles and exhibited no sign of outside influence save for the occasional iron cooking-pot. In comparison the sunny grasslands of Tuva proper seemed like paradise. The only disappointment were the Tuvans themselves, who had fecklessly failed to learn weaving, pottery, boat-building or even the simplest sort of agriculture. Instead they wasted time 'imitating the bagpipes'[8] and loafing around their lamaseries, breeding-grounds for nameless vice and disease.

What would buck Tuva up, Carruthers decided, was European colonisation. 'The whole country', he wrote, 'appeared to be awaiting ... a more virile and progressive people',[9] who would exploit its natural riches and turn the Tuvans into 'a more useful and more capable race'.[10] The nearest available Europeans were the Russians, who had begun to appear in the region in the 1860s, under an agreement with the Manchus that allowed in traders if they lived in boats or tents. From 1881 they were permitted permanent buildings, and by Carruthers's time were a small but established presence, reminding him of 'the best type' of Boer or Canadian. The most prominent of them gave the explorers a tour of his ranch, where he was experimenting with different strains of corn and fruit-tree, and improving horse stocks with the aid of a stallion sired by the great Galtee More, winner of the Derby, St Leger and 2000 Guineas.

The settlers' legal affairs, Carruthers noted, were in de facto charge of a Russian official from over the border, who settled disputes and checked on the Tuvan chiefs just as if Tuva were already a Russian colony. Add to this the fact that Tuva's rivers flowed north, and the certainty, in Carruthers's mind at least, that 'Russian protection would be welcomed by the natives',[11] and the country's proper place seemed to be within the Russian empire. 'I realised,' Carruthers concluded in what became a famous passage, 'that this region, although within the limits of the Chinese Empire, is essentially Siberian in character. It is an integral part of Siberia, its drainage flows to Siberia and the Arctic ... Physically, politically, and economically the basin should belong to Russia, and not to Mongolia.'[12]

Petersburg agreed. A few months after Carruthers left Tuva, China's Manchu dynasty collapsed and Mongol nobles declared Mongolia an independent state under Russian protection. Khutuktu Jebtsundamba became its first and last king, expanding his title from 'Holy Enlightened One' to 'Venerable Incarnation, Sainted and Brightest Emperor'. Preoccupied with the coming war in Europe and unwilling to antagonise Japan, Russia handed Mongolia back to China under Sino–Russian treaties of 1913 and 1915. Tuva, however, Russia kept for herself. In 1912 Nicholas II sent in troops to protect Russian settlers, whose ranches the Tuvans were burning down, and in 1914 he annexed the region outright, founding the town of Belotsarsk or 'White Tsar', now the Tuvan capital of Kyzyl.

Three years later, Russia was swept into a revolution of her own. At least five different armies marched across Tuva: Reds, Whites, Chinese warlords, the Mongol Revolutionary People's Army and the bizarre Burkhanists, followers of a pan-Turkic liberationist cult from the Altai mountains. In January 1920, as the Mongolian Revolutionary People's Army entered Tuva, the chairman of the Military-Revolutionary Committee of the Tomsk-based Fifth Red Army sent a telegram to Lenin and Trotsky:

The Mongols have entered the province and ejected our peasants

from the villages. These peasants fought against [the White leader]
Kolchak and were independent of him. The Soyoty [Tuvans] are a
nomadic tribe oppressed by both Mongols and Russians. Do you
consider it necessary to allow the Mongols possession of the Urianghai [Tuva], or to take it by force of arms, or to organise an
Urianghai Soviet Republic on the Bashkir pattern? Let me know.[13]

By summer 1921 the Bolsheviks were secure enough to carry out the
third suggestion, and erect a Tuvan puppet-state. On 14 August a
small group of Tuvan Bolsheviks, backed by Russians and Buryat,
declared a People's Republic of Tannu-Tuva. Working out its precise
official status took a few more years: the Soviet Union's diplomatic
list of 1924 subordinated the Russian representative in Kyzyl to the
Russian consul in Urga, and 1925's put him under the consul in
Peking. In 1926 a Russo–Mongol treaty confirmed Tuva's independence – to the continued apparent bafflement of senior Tuvans.
An American Communist played host to a Tuvan embassy to Moscow.
The envoys entered the Kremlin's Red Hall, he remembered, in
shepherds' coats and hats, harangued him about horse diseases and
plainly cared less for the proletariat than for disinherited younger
sons. When he showed them pictures of New York they declared,
after deliberating with their translator, that they could not be tricked
into believing such buildings existed, for they would surely fill with
clouds or impale the moon.

One of the very few Westerners to visit inter-war Tuva, in 1929, was
Otto Mänchen-Helfen, an Austrian social-democrat Sinologist who
headed the ethnography department of Moscow's Marx-Engels Institute. He found it possessed of a population of fewer than 100,000,
three cars and no roads. Kyzyl consisted of two streets of wooden
huts. 'Over there,' he wrote, 'is a blockhouse (the Foreign Ministry);
here is another (the Mongolian legation). Then comes a yurt, then
nothing for a long stretch, then another cabin. It seems more like a
lost Russian village than a capital.'[14] The town's one newspaper was
written in Mongolian, which almost nobody (Tuvan being a Turkic
language) understood, and in the evenings the electricity stayed on
only when there was a film showing at the cinema. Pudovkin's newly
released *Mother* was a hit:

The film broke at least twenty times that night, but that only made the viewers happy. So much the better! Now the fairy-tale would last that much longer! They could not understand anything, not the slightest bit. No Tuvan ever saw a railroad or a factory in his life; no Tuvan knows what a strike is. They could never have guessed what was going on. The subtitles were in Russian; they could not read them, but their pleasure was nevertheless unending ... When horses appeared, the whole room went crazy. They jumped up, screaming, and drove the horses with wild cries of 'Caa! Caa!'[15]

During close-ups they shouted, 'We paid full price! We want to see a whole person!'

Tuva's initial post-revolutionary government, though never truly sovereign, had been allowed to run its domestic affairs more or less as it wished. Its first prime minister, the young pan-Mongolist Donduk Kuular, was able to maintain close relations with Buryatiya and Mongolia, proclaim Buddhism the state religion and restrict atheist propaganda and Russian settlement. The country had its own currency and its own, triangular, stamps (one of which, ignoring Tuva's complete lack of railways, featured a train racing a camel). Mänchen-Helfen's trip coincided with a crackdown at the hands of hardline cadres trained at Moscow's Communist University of Toilers of the East, or KUTV – a manufactory, as he put it, for 'human bombs':

Hundreds of young Orientals – Yakuts, Mongols, Tuvans, Uzbeks, Koreans, Afghans and Persians – are trained there to explode the old ways in their homelands. In three years shamanists are turned into atheists, worshippers of Buddha into worshippers of tractors. Equipped with soap, toothbrushes, and meager Russian, these fine fellows – crammed with catchwords and slogans and fanaticised, as missionaries surely must be if they are to accomplish anything – have the mission of pushing their countrymen straight into the twenty-first century.[16]

Appointed 'commissars extraordinary', five young KUTV graduates purged Tuva's Communist Party of one in three of its members in twelve months. Donduk was sacked, and later executed as a 'rightist-opportunist'. As in Mongolia, many of the stooges who took over in their stead were Buryat, including the heads of the Comintern and secret police. The latter, Mänchen-Helfen noted, had been educated in a lamasery but was now a devoted Communist. Fat, tousled and brilliantly voluble, he loved amateur photography and 'did his odious work with downright devotion'. Buryat also staffed Kyzyl's new Party school, preaching agitprop even cruder than its Russian counterpart: 'Their world falls into Soviet Russia (the Realm of Light) and the remaining countries (the Realms of Darkness). What the Russians do is always good; what the others do is always bad.'[17] None of the government officials Mänchen-Helfen interviewed would tell him anything about Tuvan folklore, since they were 'ashamed of it: it was stupid drivel prattled merely by old men and women no longer of entirely sound mind'.[18] Pigtails and spicy Chinese tobacco were disappearing, and pointy silk hats giving way to sailor's caps from the State Trading Office. Riots had broken out, he was told, on rumours that Tuvan women were to be forced to bob their hair.

Tuvan independence, Mänchen-Helfen concluded, was a sham. 'I believe,' he wrote, 'that Tuva does not deserve to be called anything other than a Soviet colony. Politically, it is subject to Russia. Economically, it is subject to Russia ... Intellectually, it is subject to Russia.' The Tuvan parliament took its orders from the Tuvan People's Revolutionary Party, which took them from Moscow, and left to themselves, the Tuvans would 'rejoin Mongolia straight away'.[19] Wisely, he kept these views to himself in the anodyne article he wrote for the *Moskauer Rundschau* on his return to the capital. He published his real feelings from Berlin in 1931, provoking a furious review, again in the *Rundschau*, from Dr Karl Schmückle, a German Communist who had dogged his steps round Tuva. Mänchen-Helfen, Schmückle raved, was a twister of facts, a hack specialising in anti-Soviet smear campaigns, a 'pathetic disciple of the right wing of the Second International' and worst of all, a supporter of the sort of fake socialism espoused by the British Labour Party.[20] In 1938, shortly after the Anschluss, Mänchen-Helfen demonstrated his political astuteness once again by leaving Austria for America. Slavish Schmückle, who stayed on in Moscow, had meanwhile been arrested, charged with counter-revolution and shot.

Mänchen-Helfen met two lamas in Tuva, interviewing them in a yurt in the grounds of their monastery. The first, Mongus Lopsan-Cinmit, had invented the Tuvan language's first alphabet. A lanky man in his fifties, he seemed friendly but ill at ease, ducking questions and eye-contact, and fiddling nervously with his rosary. Though his private shrine included a picture of the Dalai Lama, he abruptly denied having any contact with Lhasa. A second lama, Kara-Sal Samdanobic Erencin, turned up with a thermos of tea. A 'jolly, high-spirited, worldly old man', he was happy to discuss Chinese politics, but 'spoke exceedingly cautiously about Russia'[21] and professed to atheism. The monks were right to be apprehensive, for Stalin destroyed Buddhism in nominally independent Tuva as ruthlessly as in long-colonised Buryatiya. In 1929, Tuva had twenty-five lamaseries and some 4,000 lamas. Two years later it had one lamasery with fifteen lamas, and by the end of the 1940s, none at all. Erencin was shot in 1938, Lopsan-Cinmit in 1941.

Sixty years later I drove 125 miles west of Kyzyl to meet Dembik Oorzhak, one of the ever fewer Tuvans old enough to have witnessed the destruction at first hand. Parked for the summer above a broad green valley, her yurt was smarter than Baibek's, sporting a decorative floral lining and chests of drawers stencilled with Mongol curlicues. Opposite the door, in place of a shrine, cardboard suitcases formed a plinth for a gleaming mechanical sewing machine. Though in her late seventies and the mother of ten children, Dembik flitted about with the agility of a child, shaking sheepskins and plumping bolsters. Almost before I had put down my rucksack she began to load me with gifts: a jar of sour cream; a pair of socks knitted from the wool of her own sheep; the home-cured skins, soft as cashmere and flexible as suede, of two newborn goats. In return, I presented her with an encyclopaedia-sized brick of strawy local tea and a tin in the shape of a London bus. Money flustered her, and she refused to take any at all.

In Carruthers's day, Dembik's valley was the site of Chadan, one of the biggest monasteries in Tuva. His photograph of its chief temple shows a tall, square, white building with windowless, inward-sloping walls, carved pillars and a deep verandah. By the time Dembik took me there, all that was left of it were eroded adobe walls, shapeless as termites' nests in willow-fringed water meadows. Characteristically,

Carruthers was critical: the temple's monks, he complained, were an impudent, ill-kempt mob, and its contents mostly gaudy rubbish. But Dembik remembered it as a magical place. 'It was spiritual, beautiful,' she said, fluttering her hands. 'Chinese masters built it, all in cedar-wood, without using a nail! The gods' – jabbing her stick at lovers' initials – 'were here. They shone all over, with real gold, so bright that I was scared to go inside. During services you could hear the trumpets three kilometres away!' Then soldiers came from Kyzyl. 'They pulled everything down, spoiled it, set fire to it! All the lovely silks too! Even the lamas joined in! If they didn't like the temple, why didn't they just close it? Everyone has their history, but they have to go and burn ours!' The people who did it, 'the ones who rubbed the gods' faces in the ashes, they went blind afterwards, or mad'.

Next, Dembik remembered, came collectivisation. 'That was the very worst time. The Reds came and took all our cows, just drove them away. They wanted us to grow wheat, but we hadn't got any tools so we had to scratch up the ground with our hands. They took people too. Anyone who was against them, they just took them and shot them.' One of those arrested was Dembik's father, who spent four years in gaol in Kyzyl. A few days after his release his wife died, leaving him with eleven children. Bravely, he still refused to join the *kolkhoz* or to send his children to the Red Yurt propaganda-station set up on Chadan's ruins. 'In the end they just gave us a plan, "You give us so many kilograms of wheat, and you can stay in your yurt."'

Where Chadan's Buddhas used to stand, someone had set up a table for offerings. A chipped saucer contained coins, safety-pins and a waterlogged cigarette. Dembik had brought juniper twigs. I held open my coat so that she could set light to them out of the wind. She wafted the sweet smoke into my face, turned to the table and bowed, muttering a prayer. When she straightened up her cheeks were running with tears.

'*Dochka*, little daughter, will people in England really want to read about all this?'

'I hope so.'

'It is good, little daughter, very good.'

As with Buddhism, so with shamanism. When Mänchen-Helfen

visited, shamans were still an accepted part of public life. He met several, finding them 'infinitely more likeable, sincere, and humane' than the 'good-for-nothing'[22] lamas. Every yurt, including those belonging to government officials, contained shamanist fetishes alongside Buddhist butter-lamps and silk-scroll paintings, and he was delighted to be presented with a shaman's drum by the head of the secret police.

Where the drum came from, Mänchen-Helfen does not seem to have enquired. Its owner was presumably an early victim of the shootings, gaolings and deportations that all but destroyed shamanism throughout Siberia in the 1930s. Since shamans were charged (with extortion and 'charlatanism') under the ordinary criminal code rather than under anti-religious laws, estimating their total victim numbers is difficult. In 1931, a census put the number of practising shamans in Tuva at 725. By the end of the decade, in public at least, there were none left.

I heard one shaman's story from my landlady in Kyzyl, a tiny, birdlike woman who stuffed me with pancakes, wore floral housecoats that fell open revealing her knickers, rummaged in my makeup bag and scolded whenever I trespassed on to the hospital-shiny floors of her flat without first remembering to take off my shoes. Perched geisha-graceful by the television, she told stories by the hour. Did she, I asked, believe in *albysy*, the shapechangers that crowd Tuvan folktales? Certainly she did. In her childhood village there had been 'this Russian woman, an *albys*. Once we found a pig running about, and we knew it was her so we cut off one of its ears. Then we went to her house and there she was, lying on the stove, going "Ai ai ai" and holding her head!' People still changed shape. David Copperfield did it; she had seen him on the telly.

Her own connection with shamanism emerged from a photograph album. Among the pigtail-pert schoolgirls and honeymoon couples bashful in front of St Basil's, a gaunt, middle-aged man stood out. Gazing expressionlessly away from the camera, he wore a sheepskin coat and held two shiny metal discs. He was Irgit Kalzan-ham, my landlady's late husband's father, and the discs were mirrors, attributes of his vocation as a shaman. The photograph had been taken by the NKVD, when they arrested him in 1938. Two years later he died in prison. The female shaman with whom he had shared a cell escaped by changing herself into a dog. As she was running home to see her children a hunter shot at her twice, but each time she made the bullet swerve away. Afterwards the man apologised, explaining that he had not known she was a *shamanka*.

Had my landlady's husband been a shaman too?

'Oh no! He was a Communist! He never talked about his father, not even to me.'

And indeed, in the photographs he did not resemble his father at all. In one, he looked important at an engineering conference. Another showed him laid out in his coffin, pillowed by official wreaths. My landlady patted the funeral picture affectionately: 'That was him. Such a handsome man. Just like a Japanese.'

Stalin ended the charade of Tuvan independence in 1944. On 16 August a rump Tuvan parliament, or 'Little Khural', unanimously declared the following:

> The Tuvan people has experienced the whole 23-year period of free revolutionary development with the great Soviet people.
>
> The Soviet State has become mightier under the sun of the Soviet Constitution, and attained a flowering of the material and spiritual strengths of large and small peoples in a unified socialist family.
>
> To live and work in this family is the solemn desire of the whole Tuvan people. There is no other route for us than the route of the Soviet Union. Fulfilling the undeviating will and burning desire of the whole Tuvan people, the Extraordinary Seventh Session of the Little Khural of the Workers of the Tuvan People's Republic resolves:
>
> To request the Supreme Soviet of the USSR to take the Tuvan People's Republic into the USSR.[23]

Two months later the request was granted, and the Tuvan People's Republic became the Tuvan Autonomous Region of the Soviet Union. Though Soviet sources claim that Tuvans approved the move in a plebiscite, no such vote ever took place. Historians debate why the annexation, a curtain-raiser for the post-war subjugation of Poland, Hungary and Czechoslovakia, happened when it did. Stalin may have wanted to secure newly discovered uranium deposits, to warn Chiang Kai-shek off Mongolia, or to present the Allies with a *fait accompli* at Yalta. If the latter theory is correct the strategy worked, for the Allies raised no objection to Russia swallowing a country five times the size of Belgium. Possibly they did not realise that the annexation had happened at all, since news of it was initially published only in *Tuvinskaya Pravda*. When it was finally announced on foreign radio in 1948, the only complaint came from Chiang Kai-shek's Kuomintang, which still regarded Tuva as part of Mongolia, and Mongolia as part of China.

From 1932 until 1973 the Kremlin's Tuvan satrap was Solchak Toka, one of the five KUTV graduates who overthrew Donduk in 1929. His first job was as Minister of Culture, in which capacity he launched the campaigns against Buddhism and shamanism. In 1932 he became General Secretary of the Tuvan People's Revolutionary Party, and in 1944, having survived the purges that did away with many of his colleagues, was confirmed as First Secretary of the new Tuvan Communist Party. Post-annexation, he led a second collectivisation drive against Tuva's herders, turning them from independent and often prosperous cattle-breeders into ill-paid labourers on inefficient, autocratically run state farms. Though the resulting famine was not as severe as Buryatiya's, between 1944 and 1955 livestock numbers dropped somewhere between a third and two-thirds.

For these achievements Toka was made a Hero of Socialist Labour and an alternate member of the all-Union Central Committee, a rare honour for an indigenous Siberian. In 1951 he won the Stalin Prize for Literature for works including a play titled *Three Years as a Cell Secretary* and an autobiography depicting himself as a barefoot orphan who lived by begging scraps from villainous nobles before being rescued by fatherly partisans. Despite loading Toka with dignities, Moscow was also careful to buttress him with reliable Slavs. A list of Tuvan officials from 1949 reveals that the Second Secretary and propaganda chief, as well as the heads of the local branches of the interior, education and agriculture ministries, the NKVD and the prosecutor's office, were all Russians or Ukrainians.

Dina Oyun grew up in the 1970s, before Toka's Tuva began to crack. During our interview in her Kyzyl flat she kept up what amounted in Tuvan terms to a fashionable whirl, dashing from door to phone and back again with flicks of her hennaed hair and artfully distressed clothing. The flat, and her fluent English, were inheritances from her father, a senior KGB officer. But even for a privileged KGB child, Tuvan-ness had entailed a sense of inferiority. In kindergarten, she remembered, 'the teachers would say, "Children, we have such an international group here – Russians, Tatars, a Tuvinka!" And I would shout, "I'm not a Tuvinka!", and burst into tears.' Rural relatives were an embarrassment. 'They drank too much, didn't wash, made lots of noise. I didn't want to be Tuvan, because it meant being like them.'

The first time Dina heard the race issue aired in public was at a Komsomol conference in the late 1980s. 'Usually all the speeches were prepared beforehand. You knew exactly who was going to say what. But this time, a boy jumped on stage and told us that we were covering up the fact that Tuvans hated Russians and Russians hated Tuvans, called them devils. It was a bombshell. Everyone fell silent and he was asked to leave. For me it was an enormous shock. I hadn't thought about racism, hadn't felt it. But he said it existed, and afterwards I began to notice things, to see that he was right.'

In 1990 the dam broke completely. In February the Tuvan Democratic Movement, led by a philologist at Kyzyl University, Kaadyrool Bicheldei, held its founding congress, and began peacefully to campaign for more Tuvan-language education, better jobs and housing, and all-Union republic status for Tuva within the USSR. Spring and summer saw a wave of violence against Russians and Russian-owned property, resulting in at least eighty-eight deaths. A deputy interior minister sent from Moscow to supervise the situation was briefly taken hostage, and troops had to be sent in to quell protests at the arrest of Tuvan arsonists. In December the Tuvan parliament followed other ethnic regions by declaring 'sovereignty'.

By August 1991, when Moscow hardliners attempted their coup, Tuva had quietened again. At the time, Dina was working as a presenter on local state-run television. 'We were pursuing all the high-ups with microphones,' she remembered, 'but their position was not to say anything, just to wait.' *Tuvinskaya Pravda* was backing the junta and her bosses playing safe with piano recitals, but the local businessman who possessed one of Tuva's two fax machines passed her transcriptions of Yeltsin's speeches from outside Moscow's White House, which she and her friends photocopied and posted around Kyzyl. On the second day of the coup the city soviet came out for Yeltsin, announcing a pro-democracy demonstration for the following morning. The conservative regional soviet chose the same moment to put vodka on sale for the first time in a month, with the result that only a few hundred people attended. But the city had picked the winning side, and a fortnight later the regional soviet chairman quietly resigned. So low-key was the whole episode, according to an American observer, that its only visible result was a rearrangement of the white stones overlooking a road out of Kyzyl. Where before they had read 'Glory to October!', they now spelled 'Glory to Tuva!'

In March 1992 a sixty-year-old collective farm head turned Party boss, Sherig-ool Oorzhak, won elections to the new Tuvan presidency, and in October 1993 parliament adopted a constitution giving Tuva the right to secede from the Russian Federation if the move were approved in a referendum. Coinciding with other regions' demands for decentralisation, the move fuelled speculation that the Federation was about to go the way of the Soviet Union and split into its constituent parts. Since 1944, as an American defence analyst put it, Tuva had been Russia's Tibet. Was it now about to become Russia's Lithuania?[24]

The answer, it soon became apparent, was No. Like Potapov in Buryatiya, Oorzhak swiftly turned his republic into a personal fiefdom, suppressing, by bureaucratic rather than violent means, independent journalists, politicians and businessmen. By the time I met Dina she had lost, thanks to her insistence on giving airtime to Bicheldei, her job presenting the television news, and been sidelined into features on border guards and camel-breeding. Tuva's first and only privately owned television station had just been closed down by Oorzhak's broadcast licensing committee. Its founder, a former actor, wore a look of amused fatalism on his handsome, nicotine-furrowed face. The official pretext for closure, he explained, was 'lack of necessary documents. I ask, "What documents, exactly?" And there's silence, nothing, they just don't reply.'

Wasn't this illegal? Couldn't he appeal to Moscow?

A shrug. 'The devil knows!'

Like every Russian I met in Tuva, he thought the republic's pretensions to autonomy a joke. 'All our government does is go to Moscow and beg for money. The president flies out, he flies in again, and at the airport he gives a press conference saying, "Look, comrades, I've got you another seven million." We're a tiny place – 300,000 people – and there are all these bureaucrats sitting in their offices doing absolutely nothing. What's the "economics ministry" for? We don't have an economy at all!'

The next person I interviewed was Bicheldei, then leader of a minority faction in the Tuvan parliament. A neat, donnish man, he apologised for having kept me waiting, explaining that he had been in court, defending himself against charges of subversion. To judge by the weariness with which he waved away questions – 'not a drama, just stupidity' – this was as routine an annoyance as the photocopier breaking down. Why, I asked, was Tuva still ruled by Moscow? It had been independent – in theory at least – between the wars, and two-thirds of its population were ethnic-Tuvan, making it the only region of Siberia whose indigenous people were in a majority. Most bits of the former Soviet Union in the same position – and several, like Ukraine, that had never before been independent at all – were now genuinely sovereign states. Didn't historical logic dictate that Tuva followed?

Bicheldei sighed and shook the dregs of his coffee. Tuvans, he said, weren't like Chechens. 'We're pragmatic, Asian. We know that we're too small to go our own way, that we'll always be dependent on somebody. If we leave Russia we'll just be under China. So the question is, Who's better, who's worse?' As for the old pan-Mongol ideal, 'A union with Mongolia to share poverty? Where's the sense in that?' The clause in Tuva's constitution giving it the right to secede was a useful lever for squeezing subsidies out of Moscow, but more of a moral statement than a political one. As I left he presented me with a sheaf of brightly coloured triangular postage stamps. Like the issues of the 1920s they featured traditional symbols of Tuvan identity: throat-singers, wrestlers, camels. Bicheldei was pleased with them; they had been printed in Austria, he said. Unfortunately, they could not be used actually to post a letter. Moscow had not agreed.

Though politically Kyzyl was back in the Kremlin's grip, culturally its Russian veneer was flaking away. The first shamans' clinic I visited operated out of a lopsided shack next to the central bazaar. The shaman on duty was busy throwing out a pair of drunks. From his guileless, weatherbeaten face, I guessed that he came from the countryside, and so it transpired. His mother and grandmother had been shamans, he said, and until recently he had practised the same profession in his home village, before moving to Kyzyl in hope of better pay. Wanting to see him at work, I pretended to have a stiff back. He sat me down in a chair, massaged my head with rough, rimy hands, sucked – like a singer breathing in before a big solo – my illness out of my ears and blew it out of the window, gabbling prayers. Being forced to sit still and say nothing for ten minutes was calming, and close to he smelt very human and not unpleasant, of sweat and cigarette smoke, dirt and rain.

As I counted out my fifty cents' worth of roubles, he confided that the last time Westerners called he sent them on to Nine Heavens, the new clinic whose adverts I might have seen on television. Housed in newly converted offices off a leafy central boulevard, it was indeed a swanky outfit. In the waiting-room, distantly busy with the muffled ting of bells and rattle of maracas, a notice declared it dedicated to the 'teaching, study and development of the shamanist religion in the social life of citizens'. Next to photographs, the resident practitioners listed their specialisms: cures for kidney complaints, stomachache and 'sounds in the head due to alcoholism'; purification ceremonies, fortune-telling with stones, 'moral encouragement against melancholy' and *bio-massazh*. A door opened and a head popped out, crowned with gold ribbon, scallop shells and the dried wings and claws of a large bird of prey. It was the practice's senior partner, and he was happy for me to watch him treat a teenager suffering from nightmares. In bra and knickers, the girl lay on a couch. Donning a patchwork coat hung with windchimes and wooden fish, the shaman danced, drummed and sang with great vigour and panache for a good thirty minutes. As he towelled himself dry, he explained that before receiving his religious calling he had been a professional throat-singer, and before that, director of folkloric events at a provincial House of Culture. Pocketing my fee – eight dollars this time – he gave me something suspiciously close to a wink.

The following evening the Dalai Lama's envoy to Moscow held a service in Kyzyl's municipal theatre. Waiting for the doors to open a crowd of two or three thousand shoved and shouted. The frenzy subsided inside the auditorium, where the envoy sat cross-legged on stage surrounded by bowls of fruit and robed boy-lamas. Conducted in English and Tibetan via a Russian interpreter, the service lasted three hours. The boys wriggled and the interpreter fiddled with his microphone, but the Tuvans were rapt, earnestly following the prayers in smudgily Xeroxed translation. By repeating each syllable after him, the lama told them, they were becoming 'real Buddhists. A white light comes out of my mouth, enters your mouth, and stays in your heart.' The first lesson Buddha taught was to help others, for 'trying to catch happiness with a selfish mind is like trying to catch your shadow. It looks as though you have almost caught it, but however hard you run, it runs faster.' The second was not to kill any living thing – especially not in sacrifice to the guardians of lakes and mountains. Converting all at once was hard he knew, so if they preferred they could kill nothing but cockroaches. The line got a laugh.

Service over, the congregation queued up to be blessed. They carried photographs and holy books, and the turquoise scarves they presented as offerings grew to a gossamer pile at the front of the stage. Hoping for an interview, I waited in the wings with a young policeman. People were going round twice, he said, even three times. Come his turn, how should he hold his hands? With palms flat together, like this, or with them slightly apart? When he joined the end of the line I could not see what he had decided, for my view was blocked by a cloud of kingfisher silk.

Siberia's coat of arms. A pair of sable are flanked by a *Sibiryak*, holding an anchor symbolising Russia's river-borne conquest of the continent; a Tatar with bowcase and quiver; a Nenets and a Khant, both proffering furs.

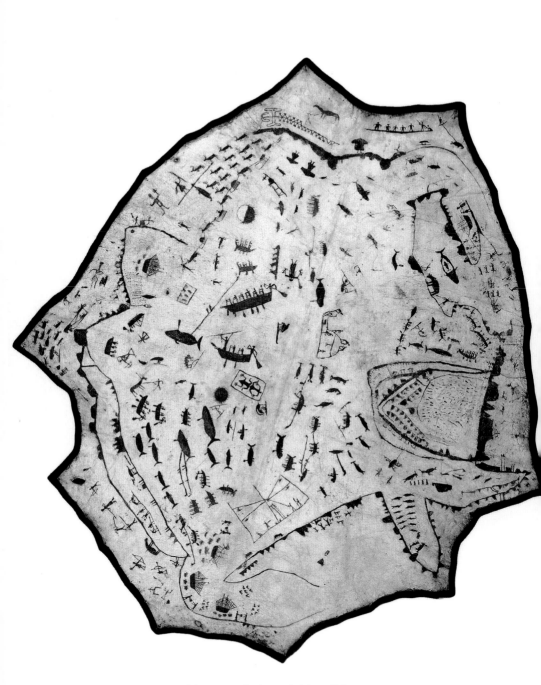

A pictogram on sealskin records the activities of the
Chukchi year: whaling and walrus-hunting, reindeer-
herding and trading with visiting ships. The sketch's
outline corresponds to the Chukotkan coastline.

A colonial official in his office; Markovo, Chukotka, 1901.

Cultural assimilation went both ways, as demonstrated by a Russian priest and (overleaf) a Sakha mother and daughter.

The Triumph of Enlightenment over Superstition, formerly an exhibit in Leningrad's Museum of the History of Religion and Atheism.

A poster of 1931. The slogan reads 'Elect the worker to the native soviet. Don't let in the shaman and the kulak'.

Stalin with the daughter of a Buryat Party chief. Two years after this once-popular propaganda photograph was taken her father was shot and her mother sent to a labour camp.

zaq
z | a | q

zaq

Zz

Oḥlagu p'suḏra.

Maṭki-oḥla	ŋəŋk-zuḏra.
Umgu-oḥla	ŋəḥs-ṭuḏra.
Utku-oḥla	təmk-zuḏra.

Oḥla-men imŋ-əri p'suinəḏ.
Oḥlagu plakat-rajuḏ.

Tət ozr, təmk-zuja,
ŋəḥs-ṭuja, ŋəŋk-zuja!

Z Z Z zom zaq

A Nivkh-language reading primer published in 1936. The highlighted couplet reads: 'When you get up in the morning, wash your hands, wash your ears, wash your face!'

Top: The road to New Chaplino

Above: Dembik Oorzhak's yurt

Left: Provideniya

Viktor Innokentiyev

Rita Buldakova

Baibek Sat, with throat-
singing prize.

Mikhail Ettyn

CHAPTER 5

THE SAKHA

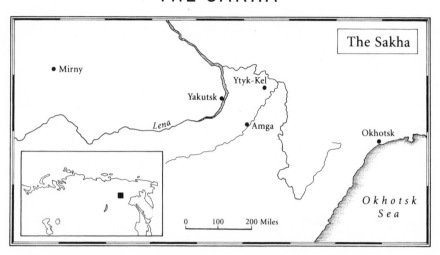

My last year's love has no straps on her moccasins
And this year's love wears horseskin moccasins
About you, my love, there is much talk.
Can it be, my love, that the tale is true?
She betrayed me for a low Yakut
And the low Yakut captured my love.

— Cossack song, 1880s

Build a helter-skelter three-quarters of a mile high and half a mile across, turn it upside down and sink it into the ground, and you have Mirny's 'Peace' open-cast diamond mine. From a viewing platform at its lip the lake at its base shrinks to a puddle, and the dumper-trucks spiralling up its circumference to children's toys. The trucks drop their loads at Processing Plant Number 3, where the ore is reduced from boulders to gravel by a Vorticist maelstrom of rusty machinery. Here and there homely flotsam has washed up among the drums and conveyor-belts: a kettle, a jam-jar of tea, a newspaper folded open at the horoscopes. 'He who does not work,' proclaims a sign, 'does not eat.'

The factory's manager takes me to a back room where we do not have to shout. The biggest crushers, he says, are American, imported when the plant was built in the 1970s. In those days everything to do with diamonds was so secret that the government wouldn't let Americans into Russia to help install them. Instead the Russian and American engineers met in Japan, where the machines were assembled, demonstrated and dismantled before shipment on to Mirny. 'We must have put them together again right,' the manager says, 'because they're still going.' He has been to London once, for a conference. 'I thought' – crooking an arm as if carrying an umbrella – 'that you would be stiff, like this. But in fact you were quite friendly, quite normal.' What did the English think of Russians? I scour my brain for something combining truth and courtesy: 'We think you are poets, philosophers. That you have a lot of soul.' The manager wonders if I know the Englishman Mike Smith. He is a mining engineer, an important *spetsialist*, and he lives in a city called Kent. Perhaps I could pass on a letter and this enamelled badge. Here's one for me too, a souvenir from Processing Plant Number 3.

Mirny ('peaceful' in Russian) started life in the 1950s as a row of geologists' tents. By the late 1960s a visiting Canadian, the Inuit-rights campaigner Farley Mowat, was able to describe it as 'one of the avant-garde cities of the USSR'. It had theatres, cinemas, 'young, vigorous, athletic' residents, and the most up-to-date hospital he had ever seen.[1] Today it is hard not to believe that he was either blind or lying. Outside my hotel, mongrels squirm in dustbowls, and grass grows out of cracks in the steps up to the town hall, the other side of a blistered Lenin statue ringed by parched orange marigolds. On the street corner, a teenage mother negotiates her pram round a kiosk stocked with faux-Parisian colognes: 'Million Dollars', 'Orgasm', 'Hooligan', 'Sheriff' and 'Despot'. The breeze brings a whiff of hydrogen sulphide, and at the end of each short procession of five-storey apartment blocks – their lopsidedness the result of building directly on permafrost – the forest broods dark and low. The only way to get here is by plane or river-boat, so there are no cars.

I am chaperoned round by Mikhail, Mirny's twenty-something press officer. By the end of a day of us interviewing drab, defensive men in drab, dead offices he has given up pretending that it is a happening place to live. To blame, he explains, is the state-owned mining monopoly Almazy Rossiy-Sakha, or AlRoSa, which owns the whole city – hospital, schools and television station as well as the mines – but refuses to spend any money on it. The elected city council, budget-less and packed with ex-ALRoSa men, has no power at all. We stop at a kiosk to load up with Admiral Kolchak beer and dried fish, and go to visit his sister Vera, who lives with her husband and two daughters in a wooden barrack originally designed as unmarried shiftworkers' housing. The family's entire living space is perhaps twelve feet square, forcing them to share a fold-out bed and to hang their most intimate belongings on the walls. Downstairs, a single bath and three stinking toilets serve fifty people. None of this seems to daunt Vera, who smokes like a navvy and slaps at her little girls: 'Go and get your mother a drink! What do you think you were born for!'

What does she do when it's minus forty outside and the children want to run around?

'We hang them out of the window for a bit. Then while they're defrosting they're quiet!' Compared to most, she says, she's lucky. Her husband has a job as a truck-driver – though it doesn't pay enough to buy a flat, especially not now that the schools charge fees. Mikhail wants out. 'I'm not going to waste my young life here. I'm looking at Yakutsk, maybe even Moscow.' He says it defiantly, blushing, as though confessing to dreams of Hollywood.

Until the mid-1600s all eastern Siberia – all Asia east of Baikal and north of the old silk road – was as unknown to Europeans as the reverse of the moon. In his great atlas of 1570, the *Theatrum orbis terrarum*, the Antwerp geographer Abraham Ortelius gave it the kingdoms of St Thomas and Prester John, a Great Cham in a tasselled jousting tent, an Island of Falcons and a freshwater Scythian Ocean, complete with pot-bellied ship and grinning leviathan. The stories the fur-traders who had started nudging east along the Arctic coast brought home were equally fantastic. William Pursglove, an English merchant who spent the winter of 1611–12 buying pelts from the

Nenets, was told of rivers whose beds glittered with precious stones, of 'Mountaynes of Christall', and of men who ate snakes, worshipped golden idols and kept great stores of 'Corne, Beefes, Horses, Sheepe, and Goates'.[2]

The following year a 26-year-old Haarlem silk-trader living in Moscow, Isaac Massa, published a second-hand account of one of the first encounters with eastern Siberia's indigenous peoples. A few years previously Siberian Cossacks had sent Evenk allies on a tribute-collecting expedition east of the Yenisey. To their surprise, the Evenk arrived at a large and previously unknown river. Its water was so salty that objects thrown into it bounced back to land, and the locals made strange booming noises which the Evenk took to indicate thunder on the opposite bank, or a town with bells. 'Departing,' Massa goes on, 'they took some of these people with them, but they all died on the way, either through fear, anxiety, or change of climate; for which the Tingoesy [Evenk] ... felt very sorry, for at their return they affirmed they were fine fellows, well built, having small eyes and flat faces...'[3]

The river was the Lena and its people the Sakha. The Russians copied the Evenk in calling them Yakut, or 'horse people'. In appearance they resembled the Japanese, with smooth, pale, oval faces and straight, jet-black hair. But despite living in pine forests on permafrost they spoke a Turkic language, herded horses rather than reindeer, and told each other proverbs about leopards and camels, animals never seen in the north. The paradise of their cosmology was a southern steppe, with valleys like green silk and birches shiny as hammered tin, where the grass grew taller than a colt, the sun never set and the cuckoos never stopped cuckooing. Folktales describing wars with the Evenk confirm that the Sakha originally came from Central Asia, pushed out, perhaps, in the twelfth century, during the upheavals caused by the rise of Genghiz Khan. Though technologically relatively advanced – their mud-walled crofts had chimneys, and they knew how to smelt iron and make clay pots – they were illiterate and entirely shamanist. Their most remarkable cultural products were *olonholar*, epic poems tens of thousands of verses long, performed from memory by specialist bards.

Muscovy's conquest of the Sakha began in the spring of 1632, when the seasoned Buryat-fighter Pyotr Beketov arrived on the upper Lena under the usual orders to 'collect the Sovereign's tribute and explore new lands'. One of his first encounters was with the Sakha chief Shor. As he reported to Tsar Mikhail, Shor's men 'did not want to come under the Sovereign's mighty hand, or pay tribute . . . Instead they argued, and tried to kill the servitors, hoping to receive help from their unholy gods.' The Russians killed Shor and five other Sakha warriors, but failed to collect any furs. They did better in August, coming away from a fight with a chief Shurenyak with 105 sable and Shurenyak's son and nephew as hostages. In September and October they won two more skirmishes, killing twenty Sakha and capturing another 170 sable. Their bloodiest encounter, the following March, was with chief Ospek of Dubunsk, who had gathered his followers in a single settlement and fortified it with logs and boulders. When Beketov appeared demanding tribute they replied with arrows. The Cossacks stormed one hut, killing twenty Sakha. But 'they could not take any of the others by assault, so they set fire to them with all the Yakut people inside . . . Only three women managed to escape, and the servitors captured them.' Beketov concluded his account of the campaign with an inventory of furs taken – 2,471 sable pelts, 25 sable cloaks, eight fox and two beaver – and a plea that Mikhail grant him largesse, since in the tsar's service he and his men had shed their blood, 'suffered every privation, starved, eaten every unclean thing, and defiled our souls . . .'[4]

Though Russian histories often credit Beketov with conquering the Sakha once and for all, in reality fighting continued nearly until the end of the century. The fort – later the city of Yakutsk – that Beketov built on the Lena's great curve north towards the Arctic Ocean immediately came under a four-year siege, and subsequent reports list dozens of tribute-collectors killed and blockhouses abandoned. Especially bloody was the reign of fort commander Pyotr Golovin, who arrived with 395 Cossacks in 1640. In 1642 his brutality provoked a general rising, during which forty-two tribute-collectors were killed and Yakutsk was besieged for a second time. Furious, Golovin took revenge on his own men as well as upon the Sakha, flogging, burning, blinding and impaling to such an extent that the Cossacks themselves pleaded to Moscow for rescue:

He has tortured us ... and our wives ... He ordered 150 blows of the knout at a time, burned us over bonfires, dislocated limbs, poured icy water over heads, pulled at veins and navel with hot pliers ... broke ribs, scattered hot ashes on backs, drove needles under finger-nails ... and ordered that men be placed on a hot frying-pan.[5]

Golovin was duly recalled and punished, but his replacements were little better, typically provoking needless unrest before their own disgraced dismissals. So unpopular did they become that during the last big rebellion of the period, of 1681–2, the Sakha chief Dzhenik of the Kangalas was able to recruit to his side exiled Russian schismatics and Cossacks who had taken Sakha wives. Routed, Dzhenik was brought to Yakutsk and flayed alive. Two hundred years later, according to an exiled revolutionary, Sakha told each other tales of how the executioners wrapped his new-born child in his still-warm skin:

To this day, in the farthest north-east of Siberia, you will hear in some dark hut, lighted only by the fire, the story of the dreadful death of Djennik, told in monotonous recitative by an old blind woman ... The old woman describes in minute detail the terrible operation of flaying, and what kind of knives are used; and on the seats by the wall listen Yakuts; with pale, terrified faces, too frightened to utter a word.[6]

Other Sakha stories of the time had the Russians defeating them by trickery. In one, they crush to death the hero Dygyn by luring him inside a tower and dropping a log on him. In another, they found Yakutsk as the Carthaginians did Carthage, by agreeing with the Sakha to take only as much ground as can be circumscribed by an ox-hide, then cutting the hide into strips so as to circle enough land for a city. 'Stony-eyed' and 'ice-eyed' were standard Sakha insults. European beards were 'dog-like', and those who wore them unimaginably old.

All that was left of Cossack Yakutsk by the time I got there was a timber watchtower, parked amid willowherb and pustular asphalt next

to the city museum. A notice said that the museum was closed by order of the fire department, but its front door was open so I wandered through shuttered corridors to the back offices, where the director was sitting at her desk, eating cake. No, she said, she couldn't open up for me; no, she couldn't let me view the archives; and no, her assistant couldn't do these things either, because she had gone to her dacha. What I could look at was a decrepit whale skeleton, imprisoned behind chain-link fencing out in the yard. Yakutsk's other tourist attraction, the Permafrost Institute, had its own big sad animal: a concrete mammoth, trunk and forefoot martially upraised on a plinth in the middle of a dried-up fountain. A pair of Sakha newly-weds were posing in front of it for their wedding video. The bride sulked in ruched acetate and lace gloves; the groom pulled on a cigarette. The doll tied to the radiator of their beribboned car was a platinum blonde. I told my taxi-driver to head home, and we lurched along streets that made no distinction between roadway and pavement, past buildings either half-built or half-derelict, to my hotel, where archipelagos of plaster had fallen off the walls and the bathroom resembled a punishment cell. 'Yakutsk,' I scribbled in my notebook, 'a total dump.'

Nobody else liked it either. Overwintering there in 1736, the German naturalist Gmelin complained that the stars appeared at 2.30 in the afternoon, and that the inhabitants spent most of their time asleep. 'They have hardly eaten,' he wrote, 'before they return to bed, and if the day is dark, they often don't get up at all.'[7] The town was the scene of the worst disaster of his ten-year-expedition, when one of its frequent fires destroyed his entire stock of money, clothes, notes and collections. The fact that he discovered permafrost in Yakutsk was no consolation, since when he got home nobody believed him, preferring to stick with the theory that the earth got hotter the deeper you dug. Eighty-five years later, the forthright Scottish explorer Cochrane thought it one of the 'most dreary-looking places' he had ever seen.[8] Most of its few Russian inhabitants were not on speaking terms, and when they did socialise the men drank themselves insensible at one end of the room while the women sat in silence at the other, nibbling sugar lumps. This did not preclude a comic parade of rank: visitors had to kiss the hand of the governor's wife, who sat

'motionless upon the sofa, without making the least acknow-
ledgement of such a condescension'.[9] Even at the end of the century,
Yakutsk had no hotel, and it was unsafe to go out at night without a
revolver.

Despite its crudity, Yakutsk was a powerful city. Jumping-off point
for the conquest of Kamchatka and the Amur, it became the administrative capital of a territory the size of India, an empire within an
empire. To the Sakha, Russian rule brought all the usual ills. Heinrich
von Füch, exiled to Yakutsk from 1735 to 1744, detailed them in an
impassioned petition, written at the behest of Sakha friends, to
Empress Elizabeth. In eleven years, he wrote, he had come across one
honest colonial official. The rest extorted at least twice the legal
tribute from the natives for personal gain, and confiscated the goods,
wives and children of recalcitrants. Hardly a Cossack did not have
native slaves. When natives tried to present complaints to investigators
sent from Petersburg, local officials waylaid the petitioners on their
way to Yakutsk, bought them off and sent them home again. Spread by
travelling tribute-collectors, European diseases were causing outlying
Sakha to die like flies, and putting an intolerable tribute burden on
survivors:

> I saw one nomadic settlement where only two out of ten men
> survived; the survivors had to pay the arrears for all those who had
> died ... I personally knew several wealthy Iakuts who had to pay for
> all their dead relatives. They were so impoverished that before I left
> they had had to forfeit all their livestock and horses, and sometimes
> pawn their wives and children. Some hang or drown themselves.[10]

Füch reserved especial ire for the Sakha's labour obligations, which
included conveying officials and supplies across 500 miles of bog
and mountain from Yakutsk to Okhotsk, embarkation point for
Kamchatka. Sakha called the trail the 'weeping road', because it lost
them so many horses. When Cochrane made the journey in the
summer of 1822 only one out of his thirteen animals survived. 'I
mention the circumstance,' he wrote, 'that my readers may be fully
aware what a terrible undertaking it is for the traveller, and what a
cruel one upon the unhappy Yakut and his still more unhappy horse.'[11]

An equally splendid eccentric, the Evangelical nurse Kate Marsden, was less perceptive. Equipped with Bovril, a deerstalker and 'good solid old-English plum puddings',[12] she spent the summer of 1891 touring leper colonies in the forests west of Yakutsk. In a memoir titled *On Sledge and Horseback to Outcast Siberian Lepers*, she attributed her safe return 'to abstinence, and also to Jaeger clothing'.[13] She owed it too to fifteen Sakha porters, who cut a path for her through hundreds of miles of swamp and forest, marking the way with poles and blazes. They undertook the task, according to Marsden, out of pity for the lepers, 'readily and lovingly ... of their own will and without remuneration, though to accomplish it they had to lay aside their summer work in the fields ...'[14] Without remuneration, yes. Readily and lovingly, perhaps not.

Subject to extortion, disease and forced labour, the Sakha population initially fell drastically, perhaps by as much as 70 per cent in the fifty years following Beketov's arrival. But around 1700 it started to recover, and by the end of the 1800s, when received opinion was that the smaller northern peoples were nearing extinction, it had grown to about 227,000. The 1989 census puts it at 382,000, making the Sakha the most numerous native Siberian people after the Buryat.

Sakha and Buryat were the only indigenous Siberians to do this well under colonial rule, probably because in both cases the Russians were forced to delegate local government to native leaders. Buryat's taishas were too powerful to be overlooked and Sakha outnumbered Russians too heavily, for even by 1926 they still made up 90 per cent of the Yakutsk region's population. From 1667 Sakha chiefs were exempted from tribute and given judicial powers. Later they were given the right to imprison, to administer corporal punishment and to distribute land. The measures effectively enserfed Sakha to their own nobility, but also created a self-confident Sakha ruling class. In 1767 Sakha chiefs attended Catherine's Great Legislative Commission, an opinion-canvassing venture whose first session opened in the Kremlin's Palace of Facets with the announcement 'Russia is a European country'. One of the chiefs, a prince Arzhakov, is said personally to have buttonholed the Empress with a request for extended privileges, prompting the rebuke, 'Where are you standing?'

His reply, as he shook handfuls of soil from his boots, was 'On Sakha land.'

Among Russians, Sakha acquired a reputation for enterprise, industry and brains. Strip a Sakha naked and dump him in the forest, it was said, and a year later you would find him in a comfortable house, surrounded by barns and cattle. In 1786 the governor of Irkutsk told the American adventurer Ledyard that the Sakha were the most 'sensible' of the native peoples, had 'good natural parts and genius', and were 'capable of any kind of learning'.[15] Ledyard had ample opportunity to confirm this in person, since it was in Yakutsk that he spent a winter under arrest before being deported all the way back to Poland. The Sakha, he wrote, were dignified, 'uniformly tranquil and cheerful', and 'laconic in thought, word and action'.[16] Cochrane, who preferred his natives wild and warlike, compared them unfavourably with the nomadic, deer-herding Evenk. They had 'more regular and pleasing features' than the Evenk. They were also 'more hospitable, good tempered and orderly'. But they had 'a servility, a tameness, and a want of character ... The more a Yakut is beaten, the more he will work; touch a Tungoose [Evenk], and no work will be got from him.'[17]

Nearly a century later, the stereotypes were still going strong. The Socialist Revolutionary Vladimir Zenzinov, exiled to a remote settlement in the early 1900s, noticed, disapprovingly, that Sakha dominated local trade and had turned their language into a *lingua franca*:

> Undoubtedly, the Yakuts are the most cultured and vital people here ... They are shrewd and crafty, and adapt themselves to new conditions ... Compared with the Yakuts, the other races seem naive savages. Wherever the Yakuts penetrate, the other natives are forced out: the Tunguses and Yukagirs flee from them.[18]

The Evenk, in contrast, were 'unusually hospitable, simple-minded and trustworthy', preserving 'the best features of the savage races'.[19]

Additional proof of Sakha success was Yakutisation. The Prussian geographer Erman noticed that Russian peasants settled along the Lena smoked Sakha pipes and wore soft, horse-skin Sakha boots, whose upturned toes they bound to their legs with thongs. They spoke Sakha among themselves, especially when they did not want outsiders to understand them, and their Russian was larded with Sakha words. They were distinguishable from 'real Yakutish Yakuts',[20] Erman concluded, only by their fairer complexions and poorer clothing. All this disgusted his Cossack driver, who accused the peasants of having abandoned every Christian custom, stuck righteously to his Lenten fast, fell ill and had to be sent home. By the end of the century intermarriage meant that even physical differences – though not race consciousness – had largely disappeared. 'The Russian drivers in some villages,' an exile observed, 'have become almost entirely like the Yakuts amongst whom they live. They have narrow, slanting eyes, broad cheekbones, and hairless faces; and of Russian they know only a few words.

'But ask your driver if he is a Yakut.

' "No, I am Russian," he will reply, with offended dignity.'[21]

In the villages Russians were turning Sakha. But in Yakutsk bourgeois Sakha were copying the Russians. Watch-chained and astrakhan-collared, parasolled and bombazine-bosomed, they are there in nostalgic sepia in the city archive, posed with bentwood jardinières in front of sketchy Alpine peaks or classical ruins. The group portraits of local dignitaries – taken, with monster pine or stucco front as backdrop, to commemorate royal births or jubilees – are reminiscent of the Raj, juxtaposing embroidered robes and white summer uniforms, sloe eyes and mutton-chop whiskers.

From these prosperous, Europeanised families there emerged, as among the Buryat, a national intelligentsia. Self-awareness was boosted by education, particularly at the new universities of Tomsk and Irkutsk, and by contact with political exiles, who arrived in Sakha in large numbers in the late 1800s and early 1900s. Confined to remote native settlements for years at a time, the exiles got to know the indigenous peoples uniquely well, coming to play an odd dual role as prisoners and aid-workers, criminals and carriers of culture. In the words of one:

When the inhabitants learned that I was Polish, they came to me for solutions to all their problems; they brought their broken guns, asked for advice on smoking fish, demanded that I cure the blind, that I heal their sick women, and wouldn't believe that I wasn't capable of doing all of this. 'But you're Polish!' Yukagirs and Yakuts would say, surprised and hurt by my refusal. For them, a Pole was a man with 'golden fingers', who knew everything and could do everything.[22]

They also passed on education and, discreetly, political know-how. The region's junior officials, wrote Zenzinov, were 'mostly natives, of no education, limited in their views, in a word, petty bureaucrats serving for the purpose of eventually retiring with a pension'. But given the job of guarding exiles they learned to value their wards, hired them to tutor their children and 'would occasionally display a certain liberalism, so long as it did not interfere with their careers'.[23] Often, exiles found themselves acting as native ombudsmen, presenting requests to the authorities on their behalf and taking their part in disputes and misunderstandings.

Short of educated manpower, the Russian authorities were equally loath to let exiles go to waste. Arriving in Yakutsk in 1910, having already escaped from exile twice, Zenzinov was summoned for an absurd interview by the regional governor, who told him that he was being sent to the Arctic fishing-village of Russkoye Ustye, and that it would be interesting, since no qualified observer had been there before, to hear what it was like. Should Zenzinov be willing to take meteorological readings, the government would be happy to provide thermometers and barometers. In Russkoye Ustye Zenzinov was received by the village's headman, to whom he read out, as the only literate person available, the governor's orders respecting his own imprisonment. They cannot have been harsh, for he was subsequently able to pass his time recording the inhabitants' customs and stories, dosing them against tapeworm, teaching their children the alphabet, reading Plato and Kant, keeping a journal and taming a fox pup, a pair of linnets and a 'very naughty and quarrelsome' teal.[24] Escape attempts – one involving attaching messages to migrating geese, the second disguising himself as an itinerant member of the Academy of Sciences and bribing Chukchi nomads to take him across the Bering Strait – came to nothing. But in 1914 his term of exile ended and he returned to European Russia, where he became a member of the Petrograd Soviet, of the abortive Constituent Assembly and of the even shorter-lived Government of the Urals, before emigrating to America.

Sympathy between political exiles and the nascent Sakha intelligentsia blossomed during the 1905 revolution. On news of Nicholas II's October Manifesto granting an elected Duma, exiles joined forces with the Sakha lawyer and playwright Vasiliy Nikiforov to form a Yakut Union, which lobbied for lower taxes and for restrictions on the police and on Russian settlement. Backed by a labourers' strike, it forced the resignation of the Yakutsk city council and won, despite the brief arrest of its leaders, representation in the first Duma.

The movement found its voice in the poet Aleksey Kulakovsky, a Sakha teacher who wrote under the pen-name Oksokoolekh, or Eagle-Man. His Sakha-language poem *The Shaman's Dream*, of 1910, uses the style of the old *olonholar* to thunder against overpopulation, industrialisation, militarism and colonialism – prudently targeting 'leering' America, 'ingenious' Japan and 'artful' Britain rather than imperial Russia. Very soon, the shaman of the title presciently warns, the world will erupt into war and revolution.

Fourteen years later, when his prophecy had come all too true, Kulakovsky added some extra verses. 'Fermenting like mare's milk', the people have indeed arisen and tried to found a new order. But 'The ideas of ten people went in ten directions/The opinions of a hundred people went in a hundred directions', so that now 'No one knows who struggles with whom/No one knows what this struggle is for'. Things cannot improve until the new regime 'restrains its wrath and ardour/Finds wisdom, and fills the gaps in its knowledge/Drops its clumsy style and steps back a little'. The poem closes with a lament for the Sakha nation, swamped by land-grabbing Russians:

> They will make the best of us their hard-working slaves
> They will make the bravest of us their prompt slaves
> The youngest of us will be their efficient slaves
> The old women will be their milkmaids
> The young women will be their cooks . . .

In one hundred years no one will see the smoke of our hearths,
No one will open the doors of our dwellings
No one will find the places of our settlements
Our dwellings will disappear
Our fires will die out
Our names will be forgotten.[25]

Kulakovsky had reason to be bitter, for since the revolution Sakha had suffered near-continuous violence and seen their leadership split and destroyed. On news of Nicholas's resignation in March 1917 the old Russian revolutionary–Sakha intelligentsia alliance temporarily reformed. Representatives from fifteen different political, professional and national groups, including even Yakutsk's handful of Tatars and Jews, formed a Yakutsk Committee for Public Safety, or YaKOB. Though in practice YaKOB did little more than keep the peace in Yakutsk, in theory it stood for racial equality, a democratic and genuinely federal Russia, and encouragement for Sakha language and culture. Nikiforov and Kulakovsky created Sakha Aimakh or 'Sakha Clan', a cultural society that during its brief life laid on lectures and literacy classes, published a reading-primer and put on three plays.

Having refused to recognise October's Bolshevik coup, in July 1918 YaKOB was overthrown by a Red Army unit sent from Irkutsk. The following month the Whites threw out the Reds, but in December 1919 two more putsches in quick succession put the Bolsheviks back in power. Leadership of the new government went to two young Sakha Bolsheviks: the teacher Maksim Ammosov and the folklorist Platon Sleptsov, better known by the pseudonym Oyunsky, from the Sakha word for 'shaman'.

The next eight years saw three anti-Bolshevik risings in the region. The first, of 1921–3, involved a mixture of Socialist Revolutionaries and Sakha nationalists, led by a Tatar merchant Yusup Galibarov. They occupied several towns north and east of Yakutsk, but never captured the capital, which was defended by a mixed Russian and Sakha Bolshevik force. In late 1922 they were joined by a 700-strong detachment under the White general Anatoliy Pepelyayev, who sailed from Vladivostok to the Okhotsk coast, marched inland towards

Yakutsk, taking the town of Amga on the way, and declared a Provisional Yakut People's Government. In the summer of 1923 the Red Army drove him out of Amga again, and his followers fled to Hokkaido or into the forest.

The following spring Galibarov and Mikhail Artemyev, a Sakha teacher who had been on Pepelyayev's staff, mobilised rural Sakha and Evenk into a 500-strong force that retook Amga and most of the coast. Again, their gains were short-lived, and the following summer Artemyev abandoned Galibarov and negotiated peace with Yakutsk. The rising's aims, Artemyev (prudently) told a commission sent from Moscow to confirm the armistice, had been as much economic as political. To avoid further unrest, he advised, the government should release its political prisoners and cease to abduct opponents. It should also appoint officials who spoke the native languages and understood native customs, give subsidies and tax holidays to native villages, and build better roads to Yakutsk, so that herders could more easily drive their deer to market.

Two years later Artemyev went out to the villages again to raise support for a Young Yakut National Soviet Socialist Party of the Middle and Poor Peasants, which would stand for 'Socialism without Communism' and genuine autonomy. Sixty-four Young Yakuts were promptly shot, and another fifty-seven sent to the White Sea island death-camp of Solovki. Ten years later, during Stalin's Party purges, it was the Sakha Bolsheviks' own turn for the chop. Sleptsov-Oyunsky died in prison in Moscow in 1937. Ammosov, who had gone on to become First Party Secretary of Kirgiziya, met the same fate a year later.

My interpreter in Yakutsk was Sonya, a 29-year-old Sakha lecturer at the city university. Blessed with lunar calm and self-possession, she made me feel, until I got to know her, large and loud, gauche and puppyish. When I asked her questions the silences span out so long that I began to worry that I had offended her, or that she had not heard. Her answers, when they came, were as the judgements of Solomon.

If I wanted to see traditional Sakha life, Sonya said, we should go to Ytyk-Kel, a country town 125 miles to the east, on the other side of the Lena. Though the Lena is still 900 miles away from the ocean at Yakutsk, it is already four miles wide, and the ferry-ride through its shifting channels took an hour. On the opposite bank, we teetered down a plank on to a beach and squatted on our heels with the other passengers waiting for the trucks that might, or might not, take them on to their villages. Here, for the first time, I heard Sakha spoken, a lilting, syncopated tongue that a nineteenth-century American likened to a mixture between Irish and Italian. Our van, when it came, could have been a piece of installation art; its interior an extravagant collage of scratched metal, crazed glass and bursting foam. The roads were so bad that I sat with one hand braced against the roof and the other across my chest, cursing myself for not having put on a sports bra. Through the window, loaf-shaped ricks stood upside-down in looking-glass lakes, and cumulus clouds tea-clippered across a dome of trade-wind blue. 'The sky,' I remembered a Polishwoman who had been among the hundreds of thousands deported here in 1939 telling me, 'was our escape.' Ponies jostled out of the way and haymakers paused and squinted, pitchforks at the vertical. Twice, we passed concrete gravestones with steering wheels attached.

Our first halt was at a ring of wooden posts, connected by lengths of rope. Shaggy with wisps of cloth and horsehair, they marked a sacred place, and the driver added coins to a metal stand proffering an eraser, a pen-knife and a fuse. Our second, third and fourth stops were for punctures, and Sonya and I passed the time sitting on the verge in a buzz of crickets, talking English Lit. The writers she knew best were an odd, dated bunch: Galsworthy, O. Henry, Theodore Dreiser, Jack London, Somerset Maugham. Her favourite was Jane Austen, and she had been overjoyed to find a bootleg copy of the BBC's *Pride and Prejudice* on a Yakutsk video stall. She had never been to England, and was unlikely to do so any time soon, even if the British consulate gave her a visa. From Yakutsk, the round-trip flight to Moscow cost $480, ten times her monthly salary. When I described how shocked I had been at the housing in Mirny she allowed her eyes discreetly to twinkle with amusement. Growing up in Yakutsk, she had lived with her family in just such a one-room flat. When they moved her father was able to load all their belongings on to a single sled, and pull it across town himself.

Ytyk-Kel was more of an overgrown village than a town. Save for a few government offices all its buildings were of wood, and cows grazed the dirt streets, which petered out into woods bright with orange haws and brimstone aspen. We stayed with Ludmilla Ignateva, a bustling middle-aged Sakha woman with whom we had got chatting on the ferry. Her husband was away haymaking, but two of her daughters were at home: Vasilisa, the quiet, wifely one, and little Nastinka, the joker. Their house was large and immaculate, with empty Nescafé tins stacked in pyramids on top of the cupboards for prettiness, and strips of horsehide nailed round the doors to keep out the draught. One whole room was devoted to an entirely symbolic new sink unit. The actual water supply, Ludmilla admitted, consisted of ice cut from a nearby lake, stored in a pit in the yard and melted in a barrel as needed. Woodlice crept in and out of the moss caulking the walls, which smelt of resin and wept amber tears.

Over supper – bread and a bowl of cream mixed with berries – I asked Ludmilla questions. When she was growing up, she said, there had been no bakery here and no television. She rode to school on a bullock, with her inkpot tucked under her arm to keep it from freezing. Marriage rules were strict: girls had to marry outside their clan, and God forbid you fell in love with a Russian. Nowadays people didn't mind so much, though the women's committee, the *Zhenkom*, still organised match-making dances with neighbouring villages, and it was fashionable again to compile family trees. Children weren't given secret names to hide them from evil spirits any more either, though if a girl fell ill one might disguise her by cropping her hair. Nastinka's was cut short for that very reason: 'It makes her look different. It means nothing bad will happen to her.'

The other thing Ludmilla did for the spirits was to smear *salamat*, a roux of flour and butter, on the walls of the cowshed when her cow was about to calve, so that the calf might be healthy and a heifer. Afterwards, she used the cow's first milk to make special patties, and left them on the cowshed's rafters. I should take a look at the shed, because it was originally her grandparents' *balagan*, *balagannar* being the mud crofts which Sakha used to share with their animals through the winter. Ludmilla's neighbours had built themselves a new one for entertaining, taking the design from Sieroszewski's book. I didn't know it? Sieroszewski was a Pole, an exile from before the revolution, and he wrote down all the old Sakha traditions. Ludmilla, though, was happy to use her *balagan* as a shed. They had been horrible to live in, she remembered; dark and low and smelly. No wonder that all but three of her grandmother's twenty-two children had died in infancy.

After supper we squatted outside on the porch, sipping tea and watching Nastinka chase chickens and strike poses. Ludmilla's brother-in-law Ivan turned up, a melancholy half-Russian doctor who chain-smoked and looked even sadder when I asked about alcoholism. Drink, he said, was 'the problem of problems', and Sakha were even more susceptible than Russians. 'We're less controlled when we drink, because our history of drinking is much shorter. When I came here in '77 not one Sakha knew how to make moonshine. And now, thanks to Gorbachev, everyone's got their own still. They come to the clinic drunk. We treat them, clean them up, and then they go out and start drinking again.'

Did he have competition from shamanism? There used to be one genuine shaman in Ytyk-Kel, he thought – Foma Chashkin at Kirovskaya 30. He hadn't called himself a shaman, just a healer, which kept him out of gaol, despite often being in trouble with the *militsiya*. Once he was arrested for stealing. The policeman put him in a cell, locked the door and went outside. And there was Foma, sitting on a bench in the sun. The policeman rearrested him, but when he went back out there was Foma again, on his bench with his pipe. Eventually the policeman gave up and let him go. Ivan didn't believe in shamanism himself, but nonetheless considered Foma to have been a 'good' shaman. 'He knew what he could heal and what he couldn't. Fractures and so on he sent to us – I took out his grandson's appendix. What's bad are these people who've come along since perestroika. They don't care what they do as long as they get paid.'

Ludmilla had used Foma to ease her father's epilepsy – legacy of his *tankist* days during the Great Fatherland War – and to help her oldest daughter recover from a divorce: 'He told her to put this piece of birchbark on her chest every night. Nobody but him knew what the shape meant, but it looked quite like an M, and her husband's name was Mikhail.' The new breed of so-called shamans who performed at folkloric events she thought artificial, sacrilegious even: 'Real shamans don't make an exhibition of themselves. Putting on a shaman's coat like that, just for show, can do harm. People don't like it; it scares them a little.'

By the Brezhnev era, Sakha had long since ceased to be a politically active place. As in Buryatiya, Communist elites shared out limited powers behind closed doors, Sakha dominating the local soviet and administration, Russians the mines. The majority toiled voicelessly, Sakha in fields, Russians in new-built factories. The title Autonomous Soviet Socialist Republic meant nothing: you could not put up a lamp-post, people joked, without orders from Moscow. No dissident movement emerged, and though Sakha outnumbered Russians until the late 1950s, certainly no separatist one.

Brotherhood of Peoples, however, did not rule. Chaperoned round by Sakha members of the Yakut Writers' Union, even the uncritical Mowat sensed unease. His guides, he noticed, were uncomfortable among Mirny's Russian mining engineers, whom they considered 'good Soviet citizens', but 'not *quite* like us'.[26] The engineers were patronising in return, reminding Mowat of white Canadians' attitude to the Inuit. When he asked them why they had no Sakha colleagues, they replied that Sakha were 'only a few generations away from the Stone Age, and most of them don't take kindly to city and factory life, perhaps because they are not ready for it yet'.[27] A Ukrainian dissident exiled to Sakha in the late 1970s noted frequent ethnic brawling (most towns and villages, he observed, contained no-go areas for Slavs), and racist graffiti. Insults included 'monkeys', 'woodchips' and 'slit-eyes'.[28] Having been several times threatened by drunken Sakha youths, he declared himself a victim of 'local internationality tensions' and asked for a transfer elsewhere. The fighting that broke out, after a shooting incident, between young Russians and Sakha on the streets of Yakutsk in June 1979 was serious enough to warrant the use of troops – and went completely unreported in the press. Summer 1986 saw more riots, and anti-government demonstrations by Sakha university students. The Party duly accused the students of 'improper, nationalist' behaviour and imprisoned their leaders, some of whom were not released until 1990.

Everyone I talked to in Yakutsk had their own theory about the 1986 riots. One was that they began as a scuffle between rowdy students and the police, who subsequently put an ethnic spin on events so as to divert attention from their own incompetence. Another was that they were provoked by the KGB, to discredit perestroika. What nobody seemed to want to believe was that they were about race. I met Itar-Tass's Yakutsk correspondent, a young man called Oleg, who claimed to be Sakha but looked Slav as stuffed cabbage and borscht, in a café. He was nervous with the subject, glancing over his shoulder and tapping non-stop at his cigarette. When the fighting broke out he was holidaying with friends at a campsite out of town. One night car-loads of drunken Sakha turned up armed with sticks and iron bars. Shouting 'Kill Russians!' they tore open some of the tents, dragged the campers out and beat them up. One man was beaten to death. Nevertheless, Oleg insisted, 'it wasn't really a national riot, just criminal groups. Somebody stirred it up artificially. The authorities could have stopped it straight away if they'd wanted to.' So he didn't think that there was any ethnic tension in Sakha at all? At school, he admitted, his class had always divided into two teams, Sakha and Russian, to fight for a sledging hill. But the division had not been to do with nationality – 'it was just so as to make it easier to tell the teams apart'.

A Sakha deputy to the regional parliament was no more forthcoming. Westerners, she complained, had race on the brain. 'You come here and talk and talk, and it seems as though you're trying to find a black cat in a dark room.' My questions on rates of racial crime and inter-marriage were meaningless. The government didn't collect such statistics; they were 'political symbolism, the flutterings of a flag on a ship'.

What about language? Wasn't that a hot topic?

'According to the law, all our textbooks are supposed to have been translated into Sakha. But everyone prefers to study in Russian. At university, if you can't speak Russian you can't compete.'

So what about all the rural Sakha moving to Yakutsk to look for work? Before, Yakutsk had been a Slav city. Didn't Russians resent the change?

'In the past Sakha and Russians fought each other. Now, Sakha just fight among themselves.'

And the economy?

'I have a Russian neighbour. She lives just as badly as I do.'

Elsewhere I fared better. A sociologist at Yakutsk University reminded me of Zoya's fastidious distaste for the factory hands at Ulan-Ude's locomotive plant. When she was growing up, she said, the only Russians in her village had been construction-workers: 'I thought that all Russians drank vodka every day, swore, stank of drink. When my father went to Moscow for his postgraduate degree – I was about six, I suppose – I was really surprised. I saw that they didn't smell, they didn't fight. I couldn't believe they were Russians!'

In Ytyk-Kel, Ludmilla cackled when I asked how many Slavs were left in town. 'Not many! When perestroika came they all sprouted wings and flew away!' The few left behind were long-time residents who spoke Sakha perfectly. Twenty years ago there had been regular Saturday-night fights with a neighbouring Russian village. Now these were rare, though neither she nor her daughter had any close Russian friends. Ivan chipped in with a story about his parents' interracial marriage. When his Sakha father first visited his Russian mother's family in Tambov, they regarded him as a freak. 'His mother-in-law felt his head, like this. And he said, "What are you looking for? Horns?" And it turned out he was right!' Sonya smiled ruefully. In her grandparents' time, she said, ambitious Sakha men tended to marry Russian women, because they were better educated. In the 60s and 70s educational opportunities evened, so there were more Sakha–Sakha marriages. Today, there was a shortage of eligible Sakha men, so ambitious Sakha women found themselves Russian husbands. Among her students she saw 'these girls – very simple, straight from the village. And in a year or two they're fine. They know how to dress, how to do their makeup properly, how to talk to people. But the boys don't change; I don't know why.' Who she herself would marry, she had no idea. Most of her friends had moved to Moscow or abroad, and Yakutsk's remaining menfolk were not much interested in Jane Austen.

If Russia were to break apart in the same way as the Soviet Union, Sakha, in theory at least, is one of the places where it might start to happen. It is rich: the $1.5 billion of diamonds it produces each year make it one of the few republics that puts more into the federal budget than it takes out. And at close to 40 per cent, the Sakha proportion of its population is high and rising, partly because the offspring of mixed marriages are redefining themselves as Sakha, partly because Russians are leaving. Even shorn of its Pacific seaboard – the Bolsheviks redrew the maps in 1922 – it is eleven times bigger than Britain.

In practice, Sakha independence is hard to envision, even if, as is currently unimaginable, Moscow were to consent to it. Russians, though no longer in a majority, are still Sakha's largest single ethnic group. Another 1–2 per cent of the population is made up of non-Sakha native peoples – Evenk, Even, Yukagir and Chukchi. Were the Sakha to edge towards real autonomy they would spark 'matrioshka nationalism', with each nationality making its own, similar demands. There has already been talk, among radical Russian nationalists, of the heavily Russian-populated south of the republic joining neighbouring Khabarovsk region, and Evenk in particular resent the Sakha's past collaboration with Russian rule, accusing them of Yakutisation in the same way that Sakha accuse Russians of Russification. Sakha's mineral wealth is less significant than it seems too, since the republic depends on Russia for imports of food and consumer goods. Its only non-Russian border is along the barely navigable coast of the Arctic Ocean.

Most of all, as with the bulk of the ex-Soviet Union, Sakha has not gone through a genuine democratic revolution. In the late 1980s dozens of small political parties emerged, collecting under the umbrella-groups Sakha Omuk ('Sakha Nation'), led by a theatre director, and Sakha Keskile ('Sakha Perspective'), led by a professor of linguistics. In tune with the times the republic soviet declared 'sovereignty', and renamed the Yakut Soviet Socialist Republic first the 'Yakut-Sakha Soviet Socialist Republic', then the 'Sakha Republic (Yakutiya)'. August 1991's attempted coup in Moscow exposed the movement's fragility. As in Buryatiya and Tuva, a brave few turned out in support of Yeltsin and democracy, but the vast majority kept their heads down and waited to see what would happen next. At the time Itar-Tass correspondent Oleg was deputy-editor of a small weekly paper. The day after the putsch Yakutsk's mayor called him into his office and told him not to publish anything inflammatory. Oleg's response was to typeset his bland leading article so that the first letters of each paragraph spelt out the word *svolochi* ('scum') and go duck-shooting with friends.

Wasn't it an odd time for a journalist to take a holiday?

'Honestly, we just wanted to get drunk and forget about it. The next day we heard that Yeltsin had won. And we thought, in this country we can't even get a coup right!'

December's elections handed the presidency to Mikhail Nikolayev, the middle-aged, half-Sakha Party boss who had used a watered-down national-democrat platform – 'state sovereignty' for Sakha within Russia and mild economic reform – to win chairmanship of the local soviet and a seat in Gorbachev's semi-democratic 1990 parliament. Like many regional leaders, he swiftly turned himself into a petty local autocrat. Thanks to his stranglehold on local media, public criticism of his leadership has been muted, and mysteries such as who paid for his son to study in Britain remain unsolved. Because privatisation has not happened and new businesses are strangled by corruption-breeding tax and licensing laws, the president also has patronage over what is left of the local economy. The national opposition parties have been split, sidelined or suborned, and Soviet-style travel restrictions discourage criticism from abroad: a decree of 1997 forces foreigners to get entry permits from the Sakha 'ministry of the interior'. More stamps, I discovered, were needed simply to change hotels.

The opposition was disarmed, too, by Nikolayev's show of regionalist muscle. In September 1992 he encouraged the Sakha parliament to enact a constitution declaring that Sakha had the right to leave the Russian Federation, that it could form its own army, that its natural resources belonged 'to the Sakha population', that republican law took precedence over federal law and that Sakha had joint 'state language' status with Russian. More concretely, in March of the same year he negotiated an agreement with Yeltsin whereby the republic was permitted to retain 20 per cent (later raised to 25 per cent) of its diamond and 11.5 per cent (later raised to 30 per cent) of its gold profits, and to export a percentage of its gem-quality diamonds directly, independently of Moscow's agreement with de Beers. In a blatant piece of quid pro quo, Nikolayev signed the deal on the same day that he signed Yeltsin's Federal Treaty giving a new legal basis to post-Soviet Russia. The following year Sakha joined a wave of regional tax strikes, winning permission to pay for federal programmes on its territory directly, rather than through Moscow.

Other native Siberians envy these gains. Buryat cite them as an example of the kind of arrangement they would like for themselves. They have sparked talk of 'asymmetric federalism' – the idea that Russia will turn into a motley patchwork of loosely connected states, each with its own separate relationship to the centre. But in reality, they add up to rather little. Even before Vladimir Putin began his drive to bring the regions back to heel, disputes with Moscow were resolved via back-room negotiation rather than the courts, consigning Sakha's grandiose constitution to irrelevance. By spring 2001 the Sakha parliament had surrendered the clause on its right to form an army, though it was still holding out on the 'sovereignty' declaration and diamond deal. In December of that year Nikolayev bowed out of the race for a third term in office, and handed over to Moscow's favoured candidate, the head of AlRoSa. As for Sakha's diamond profits, their only visible fruit are a few absurdly sumptuous government buildings in Yakutsk, their ox-blood marble and mirror glass as incongruous among the rotting tower-blocks and haywire cabins as Gulf States airports amid Bedouin tents. Since they were built by the same Swiss construction firms accused of paying $29 million in bribes to Pavel Borodin, manager of the Kremlin's property portfolio from 1996 to 2000 and previously mayor of Yakutsk, much of the rest of the money can be taken to have disappeared into private bank accounts overseas.

On our last day in Ytyk-Kel, Ludmilla arranged for one of her sons-in-law to drive us to an architectural park. Rambling about boggy magenta meadows, we inspected fortified Cossack grainstores, wooden yurts and *balagannar*. Exiles' crofts featured prominently, memorial plaques flaking to the trill of skylarks and sweetness of camomile. The biggest building in the collection was an Orthodox church. Converted into an exhibition hall, it contained pails, ploughs, peasant costumes and photographs of the Sakha Bolsheviks of the 1920s. The attendant left off watering the tomato-plants crowding a windowsill and hurried over. Why did the labels tell us about Ammosov's and Oyunsky's books and birthplaces, I asked, but fail to mention that Stalin had them both shot? She shuffled. 'We haven't got any money to renew the exhibits. But you can see that Oyunsky's bust is black, and that the velvet underneath is red, like blood. It implies that he was killed . . .' The whole park, it turned out, was the brainchild of a local Sakha apparatchik, now aged ninety-three and still a devoted Party member. But as well as Communism he had loved, rather guiltily, old buildings, endlessly lobbying that they be moved rather than demolished, and meticulously photographing those that he failed to save. Nobody could persuade him to retire, so until he died everything would stay just as it was.

CHAPTER 6

THE AINU, NIVKH AND UILTA

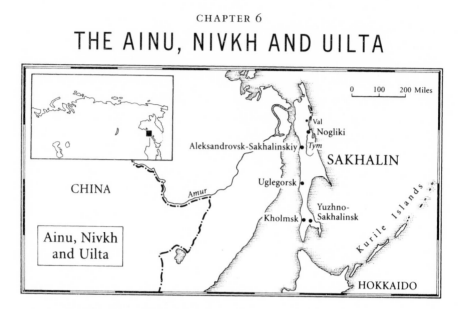

In our village we have a reading hut.
Every evening men and women visit the reading hut.
They read books. They listen to the radio.
Does your village have a reading hut?

What is a kulak?
A kulak is someone who lives off someone else's labour.
A kulak gets rich by taking orphans, enslaving them, and selling the
  orphan girls.
Does your village have a kulak?

— Nivkh-language reading primer, 1932

On 7 April 1855, twelve months into the Crimean War, the frigate
HMS *Sibylle*, accompanied by the steam corvette *Hornet* and the brig
Bittern, set sail from Hong Kong, northwards towards Russia's Pacific
coast. Commanded by Commodore Charles Elliot, the squadron's
aim was to avenge a humiliating defeat at the hands of the Russian
frigate *Aurora*, which the year before had fought off, against heavy
odds, a Franco-British attack on the port of Petropavlovsk.

Captain Bernard Whittingham of the Royal Engineers had shipped aboard the *Sibylle* as a visitor. Pleased to be escaping the typhoon season, he recorded events in his diary. On 12 May, having rounded the Korean peninsula and passed the Japanese island of Honshu, the squadron sighted the snow-capped hills of Sakhalin, an unexplored Siberian peninsula, according to the chart, just to the north of Hokkaido. Along its western shore wooden huts on stilts came into view, clustered round the mouths of streams. The first village the sailors investigated was deserted, but the inhabitants of the second came to meet them, led by 'a magnificent savage: tall, lithe, straight and strong, with hair, beard and moustaches never desecrated by the touch of scissors' – 'far nobler', Whittingham thought, 'than the Red Indian, who I had always fancied was the pride of wild men'.[1] Noticing a bear in a log corral, he asked the villagers by means of sign language whether he might be permitted to shoot and skin it. The proposal 'met with looks of horror ... The natives gradually made us understand that if any accident happened to the bear, they would instantly fall ill ...'[2] They were more helpful on the subject of the *Aurora*, indicating via scratches in the sand that ships had run north up the coast five days earlier.

With the Siberian mainland to its left and Sakhalin to its right, the squadron pressed on northwards in pursuit. On 20 May, just after prayers, a lookout reported 'a sail under the land'. Ahead lay three wooded islands, in the gut of what appeared to be an elongated bay. In their shelter, six vessels lay at anchor, fluttering the blue and white of the Russian ensign. The squadron had caught up with the *Aurora* at last. *Sibylle*'s decks were cleared for action, shot and shell were brought up from below, and the officers strapped on swords and pistols. Elliot transferred to the *Hornet*, which steamed cautiously forwards to within 2,000 yards of the nearest Russian corvette. It being too near nightfall to launch a serious attack, he 'gratified the eagerness of the boyish crew by giving orders to hoist the red ensign and to try the range of the long thirty-two-pound gun in the bow'. The shot fell short. The Russians cheered and fired back. A second, better-directed exchange forced the *Hornet* to retreat.

For the next two days, the *Sibylle* sailed back and forth just out of range of the *Aurora*'s guns, hoping to tempt her into leaving her position. When the Russians refused to budge, Elliot had the choice of attacking immediately, before they had time to move their artillery on to the surrounding hills, or sending for reinforcements. Seeing that he had the Russian ships trapped against land, but boasted only sixty-nine guns to their 106, he opted for caution, and ordered the *Bittern* away with a request for more firepower. Four days' fog-bound blockade later, the *Sibylle* approached the *Aurora* for a second time. 'As we skirted the well-known bluff,' wrote Whittingham,

> every glass was turned towards the bay, and long before it was possible to see them, masts were descried by anxious and eager eyes. A nearer approach revealed that the Russian ships had evidently changed their positions, though where they had moved to could not be discovered; and slowly and disagreeably the conviction came into every mind that the enemy's squadron had escaped.[3]

On shore it was obvious that the Russians had decamped in a hurry, leaving behind cordage, uniforms, half-read books and loaves still warm in an oven. Under cover of fog and using a brief flaw in the wind, mortified Elliot concluded, they must have slipped past his lookouts and out of the bay. Three weeks later, from the same 'magnificent savages' of a month before, he discovered the truth. 'One of the most intelligent,' Whittingham wrote, 'began to comprehend our signs, and to answer them by similar pantomime. By pointing to each shore, and tracing their outlines on the sands, they were incited to complete them towards the north, which they did at once vociferously and unanimously, by almost joining the two shores then expanding them ...'[4] Sakhalin was not a peninsula but an island, and the Russians had escaped not to the south out of a bay, but to the north, through a shallow but navigable strait. Two dispiriting months of 'wet fogs and cheerless cold days' failed to discover them again, and in August *Sibylle* and her escorts 'silently and dully'[5] turned for home.

Elliot's faulty chart was based on one compiled in 1787 by the French navigator Jean François Galoup de La Pérouse. Approaching, like Elliot, from the south, he got about halfway through the Sakhalin straits before deciding that sandbars made them impassable, and that

Sakhalin was probably joined to the mainland by an isthmus. Ten years later an Englishman, William Broughton, pushed fifteen miles further north, but reached the same conclusion. The first Russian survey of Sakhalin was carried out in 1805 by Adam Johann von Krusenstern, the Baltic-German commander of a government-sponsored circumnavigation. A cautious, painstaking man, he filled his journal of the voyage with dry technical notes, congratulating himself in his final entry for not having mislaid 'a mast or a yard, nor even an anchor or a cable' in four years, and for having got his whole crew home safely except for the cook – who was ill before he came on board. But Sakhalin's straits foxed even his Teutonic thoroughness. Approaching from the north, he ran out of water while still 200 miles away from Broughton's most northerly position, and agreed with his predecessors that Sakhalin must be joined to land.

Discovery of the straits finally fell three summers later to a 26-year-old Japanese explorer, Mamiya Rinzo. On behalf of the Shogunate, he and a colleague thoroughly surveyed, by land and by sea, Sakhalin's entire coastline, establishing beyond doubt that it was an island, and that the passage between it and the mainland was in fact navigable. For eighteen years, Mamiya's maps lay closeted in the Shogun's archives, until the arrival in Edo of an inquisitive Bavarian, Philip Franz von Siebold. Surgeon to the Dutch trading-post at Nagasaki, Siebold travelled to Edo in the train of the Dutch ambassador, posing as a 'mountain Dutchman' so as to circumvent Japan's ban on non-Dutch foreigners. In the capital he struck up friendships with several Japanese scholars, including Mamiya and the court astronomer Takahashi Sakuzaemon, one or other of whom allowed him to look over the Shogun's library and copy his maps. Two years later, for obscure political reasons, Mamiya denounced Takahashi as an informer and Siebold as a spy. Takahashi was imprisoned and Siebold deported, though he managed to smuggle out most of his papers. In 1834 he visited Petersburg, where he showed Krusenstern Mamiya's chart of Sakhalin. Spotting the straits, the old admiral is said to have slapped his forehead and cried, 'Les Japonais m'ont vaincu!' The Russian government kept the secret for another two decades, until poor Elliot discovered *Aurora* vanished from under his lee one foggy morning during the Crimean War.

The cartographical shenanigans over Sakhalin reflected its equally hazy political geography. Sakhalin, it has been said, is 'the Orient's Alsace-Lorraine'. In medieval times its indigenous people paid fur-tribute to the Chinese, at a fort at the mouth of the Amur. A hundred and thirty miles upstream, the ruins of a Buddhist temple could still be seen in the 1850s, inscribed in Chinese and Mongolian characters with the words 'The Temple of Eternal Repose' and 'May the Force of the Hand be Extended Everywhere'.[6] Barring a few shipwrecked Cossacks and a Dutchman in search of the Golden Isles, nobody else showed any interest in the island until the 1790s, when Japanese traders started building fishing-stations on its southern coast, opposite Hokkaido. One of the objects of Krusenstern's circumnavigation was to transport an embassy to Japan, which would establish trade relations and, if possible, claim Sakhalin for Russia.

Led by Nikolay Rezanov, founder of Russia's Alaskan colonies, the embassy was an unmitigated failure. Dropping anchor at Nagasaki, the Russians were stripped of all their weapons, down to the officers' personal fowling-pieces, and not allowed on shore except to take exercise along a fenced-off strip of beach. They could communicate with the port's Dutch traders only via loud-hailers, and were banned even from rowing round the harbour. Though Rezanov humbly removed his shoes and sword during an audience with a senior Japanese official, he was not given permission to travel to Edo, and his gifts and letters to the Shogun were returned unopened.

After seven months of rebuffs, Krusenstern came by a Dutch translation of an order banning all Russian ships from Japan, and immediately set sail for Sakhalin. His frustration comes through in his journal, in which he recommends annexing Sakhalin by force. Sakhalin was worth conquering, he wrote, for its fisheries, which were so rich that during the herring-run the natives caught their dinner in pails. Japan, moreover, did not have the resources to defend it – 'Two cutters of sixteen tons and sixty men would be quite sufficient, with a moderate air of wind, to sink the whole Japanese fleet' – so that the annexation 'would not cost a single drop of blood'.[7] Rezanov covertly ordered Russian-American Company employees to raid Japanese settlements on Sakhalin, Hokkaido and the Kurile Islands, in retaliation for which the Japanese government captured a Russian naval surveyor on one of the Kuriles and held him prisoner for two years.

Russo-Japanese relations deteriorated again in the 1840s, with the appointment of the expansionist Muravyov as East Siberia's governor-general. In 1849 he ordered a new survey of Sakhalin, confirming Mamiya's findings, and began to bombard Nicholas I with memoranda warning of Russia's need to consolidate her Pacific seaboard, given China's weakness and Britain's strength following the First Opium War. In 1853 cautious Nicholas capitulated, and allowed Muravyov to establish a garrison at Aniwa Bay on Sakhalin's southern coast. Two years later the Treaty of Shimoda divided the Kuriles between Russia and Japan, and gave them 'joint possession' of Sakhalin. In 1875 Russia exchanged her Kuriles for full sovereignty over Sakhalin, but allowed Sakhalin's Japanese settlers to retain their nationality and fishing privileges.

The next pass of the parcel came with the 1904–5 Russo-Japanese War, during which the Japanese army overran Sakhalin in three weeks, opposed by an unwilling draft of Russian convicts. The Treaty of Portsmouth of 1905, negotiated by Theodore Roosevelt, divided the island in two along the 50th Parallel, with the southern half, known as Karafuto, going to Japan and the northern to Russia. Fifteen years later, during the chaos of the Russian Civil War, Japan reoccupied the north, shooting or dumping into the sea its more obstreperous Bolsheviks. An American journalist who visited Sakhalin's former Russian capital, Aleksandrovsk, soon afterwards found it a queer mix of Europe and Asia: log-houses were divided with paper screens, stove-top beds furnished with hard lacquered pillows. Though closely chaperoned, she managed to chat with some Russian peasants, who grumbled about shortages of seed and jobs, but doubted that the Bolsheviks would have done any more for them. A Russian school-teacher similarly resented the Japanese, but admitted that they had improved the roads and drains. Most of the Russians on Sakhalin, she thought, 'if they could get some of the necessities of life and had a chance to make a decent living from their farms, wouldn't care a fig whether the island belonged to the Japanese or to Russia. The better class of people in Alexandrovsk are nearly all Poles, and consequently quite lukewarm as far as Russia is concerned.'[8]

In 1925 the old division of Sakhalin along the 50th Parallel was restored, though Japan kept its northern oil and coal concessions. With the rise of militarism in both countries in the 1930s, it turned into a closed border, whose guards exchanged messages using semaphore, or by wrapping notes around thrown stones. A Communist Japanese theatre director who defected across it in 1938 was promptly shot as a spy, and his lover, a celebrated actress, given four years in the Gulag.

Despite skirmishes on the Amur and the Mongolian frontier, Russia did not actually declare war on Japan until 8 August 1945, two days after America dropped the atom bomb on Hiroshima, one day before the destruction of Nagasaki. At Yalta, Roosevelt and Churchill had secretly pledged that in exchange for attacking Japan, the Soviet Union would receive southern Sakhalin and all the Kuriles. Now Stalin took them up on their promise, invading both. On 14 August Emperor Hirohito announced Japan's capitulation, but the news either failed to get through to Sakhalin, or was ignored. Reaching Esutoro (now Uglegorsk) on Sakhalin's western coast on 17 August, the Soviet army executed the town's mayor and police chief, and stood by as 170 civilians committed hara-kiri. On 20 August there was horrible fighting in Maoka (now Kholmsk), during which atrocities were committed by both sides, and more Japanese civilians, including the post office's six female telephonists, committed suicide. Two days later an anonymous submarine torpedoed Japanese refugee ships off Hokkaido, killing another 1,700 Japanese civilians, and Soviet planes continued to bomb refugee-packed Toyohara railway station until 23 August.

When the fighting finally ended, the Soviet authorities sent Sakhalin's entire Japanese middle class – civil servants, businessmen, lawyers, bankers, journalists and army officers – to labour camps on the Siberian mainland and in Central Asia. From 1946 to 1949 the island's remaining 312,452 Japanese were deported to Hokkaido, taking with them only as many belongings as they could carry. Repatriation from the Gulag took longer: in 1951 320,000 Japanese prisoners of war were still unaccounted for, and the issue dogged

Soviet–Japanese relations well into the 1960s. Today, Japan makes no direct territorial claim on Sakhalin, but insists that in principle at least, its status has yet to be determined.

On a sunny Sunday afternoon in September, Toyohara – now Yuzhno-Sakhalinsk – smells of hot asphalt and bad drains. In what used to be Ginza dori or 'Seat of Silver Street', and is now Kommunisticheskiy Prospekt, teenage boys squat on their heels round a watermelon, and a toddler runs through a flock of pigeons, sending the birds whirring into tired trees. Tall, melancholy army officers with sports bags and flying-saucer hats set the post office's doors gently flumping, and tinny rock drifts from the Adelaida Koktail-Holl, where Serb construction-workers fiddle with cigarettes and their girlfriends' breasts. The woman selling dried fish and cockroach chalk from a packing case on wheels wants to know who I am. 'A foreigner? Do *babushki* live like this with you, so badly?' She flicks stubby fingers at the town hall, its new façade of pink mirror glass flanked by frayed mosaics of border guards and fishermen. 'Over there, they get 2,000 roubles a month. But here, they just throw fifty roubles in our teeth. Why do you want to write about the Gilyaks? All they do is live in the woods. When I was little I went to school with them, up in the north. We got fleas from them, fleas that ate us. And now we don't even get pensions, not at all, not at all ...' The gesture takes in the pigeons, the post office, a Cable & Wireless billboard and a bearded beggar holding out a polystyrene tray. 'There's Russia for you! Write it down!'

Relics of the town's Japanese past are few. The best is the museum, a pre-war building whose upturned, pantiled eaves are guarded by stone lions with bulging eyes and curled moustaches. Inside, Japanese tourists are videoing one of the granite boundary-stones, carved with a double-headed eagle on one side and chrysanthemums on the other, that used to divide Sakhalin along the 50th Parallel. At the V. I. Lenin Art Gallery, formerly the Hokkaido Colonial Bank, a power cut has left a British Council-funded exhibition of Pre-Raphaelite portrait photography wilting, goitred, in the dark. In Gagarin Park, originally planted by a Japanese paper-pulp magnate, old men in string vests play dominoes under carmine maples. Deadest of all, in the hills above the town, is the resort that once hosted Japan's national ski-jump championships. Wild rhubarb blankets the remains of the cable-car, and a bare-chested man with tattoos yawns on the porch of a burned-out hotel. 'People used to come from Leningrad to jump here,' he says, 'to train for the Olympics. There were shops, a heating plant, a little *zoopark* even, with a fox and a bear. Now it's all fallen to bits. Russia's fallen to bits.'

In truth, of course, Sakhalin belongs neither to Japan nor Russia, but to its indigenous peoples. The most intriguing of them, early explorers agreed, were the Ainu. Heavily built, round-eyed and weirdly tattooed, they looked more Caucasian than Asian, and spoke an uncategorisable language. Their dogs served for food, clothing, transport and as hunting companions: according to one account, they were trained to swim out to sea and catch fish in their mouths. For their feasts they raised bears, as Whittingham saw, in log cages, and were said to suckle bear-cubs alongside their own babies. Most strikingly of all, Ainu men sported long, coarse and very un-Asian facial hair: as 'black and shiny', as one heavily humorous Victorian put it, 'as a highly polished boot',[9] and so thick that 'a double-teamed horse-rake could not have been got through it'.[10] Krusenstern found their appearance 'sufficiently ugly', but was much impressed by their hardihood and generosity. 'The characteristic quality of the Ainu,' he wrote, 'is goodness of heart, which is expressed in the strongest manner in his countenance.' Their manners were 'simple but noble', and it was hard to persuade them to accept payment for their gifts of dried fish. A family with whom he shared a meal appeared to live in 'the happiest state of harmony':

> We continued there some hours, and were scarcely able to distinguish the head of the family, so little assuming were even the oldest, towards its youngest members ... Here was no loud talking, no immoderate laughter, and still less any disputing. The satisfaction that appeared in all their countenances as they spread the mats round the hearth for us; their readiness when we were going away, to launch their canoes and carry us across the shallows to our boats ... but still more than all this, their modesty never to demand anything, and even to

accept with hesitation what was offered to them . . . all these uncommon qualities . . . make me consider the Ainos [*sic*] as the best of all the peoples that I have hitherto been acquainted with.[11]

By the end of the century, the 'Hairy Ainu' had become something of an anthropological *cause célèbre*. Scholars located their origins as far afield as Borneo and Australia, a Japanese professor had them making an Arctic odyssey from Europe via Iceland and Greenland, and there was the inevitable constituency in favour of the Lost Tribe of Israel. When St Louis decided to celebrate the centenary of Napoleon's sale of Louisiana with an exposition illustrating 'the upward course of human development, beginning with the Dark Ages of tooth and claw'[12] the Ainu were a star attraction, alongside Patagonian Giants and African pygmies (who had to be persuaded to wear more clothes during opening hours). Imported from Hokkaido with the help of a British missionary, three Ainu families drew crowds at all the railway stations from Seattle, and at St Louis's Episcopalian church. Scientists measured their heads and poked them with batons during educational lectures, and members of the public plied them, as a local paper observed, with questions 'pertinent and impertinent', which they answered 'without asking return information respecting the white people who were studying them'.[13]

Not all foreign interest in the Ainu was academic. When Krusenstern sailed by, they were already being employed by the Japanese to clean and dry herring, and trading sealskins for tobacco, lacquerware and pornographic prints. They seemed happier and richer, Krusenstern thought, the further north, and hence the further away from Japanese influence, they lived. Through the nineteenth century and later, both Russian and Japanese governments justified their various incursions on Sakhalin by claiming that the Ainu were being mistreated by the other side. In reality, Ainu seem to have felt more comfortable with the Japanese, for by the end of the 1800s many had migrated south to Hokkaido. The remainder scratched an increasingly meagre living from depleted hunting- and fishing-grounds, or worked as itinerant labourers. When the Japanese were expelled from Sakhalin in 1949, all but a few hundred Ainu chose to leave with them, joining compatriots on Hokkaido.

Fifty years later a Russian historian in Yuzhno-Sakhalinsk told me that there was one Ainu left on Sakhalin, Duludina Kuniko. I drove into her village behind a string of cows, which swung unherded into muddy gateways between shuttered wooden houses. Duludina's door was answered by her middle-aged, not noticeably hirsute daughter Irina. I could come in, she said, if I liked, but her mother had had a stroke six years ago and recognised nobody. Nor was it correct to call her the 'last Ainu', since she was really half-Japanese. Even Irina's 'clean Ainu' grandfather had tried to look as Japanese as possible, shaving close and plucking the hairs from the backs of his hands. No one in the family had thought of themselves as Ainu at all until 1989, when they were discovered by a Japanese professor. 'All the TV stations came here, the papers. We got our own television out of it, and a telephone.' Since Duludina's stroke, Last of the Ainu business had fallen off. Irina herself spoke nothing but Russian, had a Russian father and husband, and had chosen 'Russian' as the nationality entry in her passport.

Why?

'It was simpler, that's all.'

What about her children?

'No – I'm not interested; they're not interested. I'm sorry. I'd tell you more if I could.'

The native Siberians who do survive, 2,400 strong, on Sakhalin are the Nivkh, or as Russians still often call them, Gilyaks. Like the Ainu they fished, used dogs, held bear-feasts and spoke a unique language, remarkable for its twenty-six different methods of counting. Equally labyrinthine was their kinship system, which forbad sex between a man and his most distant cousin on his father's side, but allowed it with all his cousins on his mother's side, his older brothers' wives, and his wife's sisters and nieces. Though discreet, consensual extra-marital sex was permitted between all within-limits relatives, the taboo on relatives of prohibited degree was so strong that illicit lovers were expected to hang themselves. Many Nivkh never married at all, simply because no permitted individuals were available. Kinship limited even conversation. A man could give orders to his daughters or to his younger brothers, but not chat or joke with them. Growing up together in one-room huts, siblings of opposite sex were not allowed to look at each other, or to talk except via third parties.

The first Nivkh Krusenstern encountered were clearly afraid of white men. Led by a headman wearing an incongruously fine Chinese gown, they came to the shore making 'pantomimical expressions of friendship' but had filled a canoe with spears. When the Russians started walking towards the huts, they tried to block their way. The Russians persisted, and the Nivkh 'all ran on, giving evident tokens of their fear and terror'. Though Krusenstern removed his sword and held the chief's hand in token of friendship, at every other step the chief 'stopped short, and by the most pitiful looks gave me to understand his wish that we should return; and it was only by a fresh present of a piece of cloth that I could keep him at all in good humour ...' The Nivkh were already addicted, Krusenstern noted, to tobacco. One of his sailors was annoyed to see a silk handkerchief that he had traded for a native hat 'of no other value than as a curiosity ... immediately afterwards exchanged for a leaf or two'.[14]

Over the next half century many of the Nivkh settlements Krusenstern saw disappeared, wiped out by smallpox. But the Nivkh's real nemesis was Sakhalin's designation as a penal colony. Mainland Siberia, the scheme's proponents argued, would not prosper until freed of its transported criminals, who escaped from prison each spring and roamed the countryside in gangs, terrorising towns and villages. Sakhalin would be relatively escape-proof, and transportees could usefully be put to work cultivating its reputedly fertile soil and digging its newly discovered coal. A first batch of convicts was sent to Sakhalin to build gaols in 1873, and from 1884 all criminals with sentences of exile of more than two years and eight months were despatched there automatically. By 1900 the island's four to five thousand indigenous people were outnumbered by 13,500 convicts and another 7,000 officials, gaolers and 'settlers' – in practice, convicts who had served their terms but lacked the means to return home.

We have a superb account of Sakhalin at the period from Chekhov, who lived there from July to October 1890, researching penal conditions. Disconcerted by the success of his first play and saddened by the death of an alcoholic older brother, he took on the project as a penance and a distraction, collecting masses of data and filling in hundreds of specially printed questionnaires. The book in which he summarised his findings, *The Island*, was no match for his fiction. 'I have the feeling that my trousers don't hang right on me,' he complained to his editor, 'that I'm not writing as I should.'[15] The gruelling journey to Sakhalin probably also aggravated his incipient tuberculosis. But though fans of Chekhov's short stories found the statistics-packed *Island* disappointing, it shamed the government into despatching an investigatory commission, and with its combination of passion and detail must rank as one of the great social studies of its day, certainly of Russia.

Aleksandrovsk he describes as a tidy wooden town, remarkable only for the convicts who filled all the service jobs and for the absence of music or drunks on the streets in the evenings. Its officials were a vulgar bunch, 'boring and bored', who made him drink bad vodka, used the over-familiar *ty* instead of the formal *vy*, and talked from morning to night about nothing but escapes and floggings. The governor-general and military commander were better-bred but liars, claiming that corporal punishment was rare, forced labour not onerous, and convict life in general 'easier than anywhere in Russia'.

This, Chekhov quickly discovered, was nonsense, the state of the convicts who had completed their sentences and settled on Sakhalin being as pitiable as that of the serving prisoners, who were at least provided with prison rations. Hopes that Sakhalin would turn into another New South Wales were a chimera, for its soil was too poor for farming, and its schools and churches existed only on paper. Living in bark-roofed huts, bare save for a few food remnants in a saucer on the windowsill, 'a single pot and a bottle stuffed with paper', the settlers killed time card-playing and drinking, and adopted despairing aliases: 'Countryless', 'Forgotten', 'Twenty Years', 'Buried', 'Godless', 'Fetter'.[16] Among serving convicts, brutality was all-pervasive. Guards could give them thirty lashes for failing to sew the required three pairs of shoes a day or for doffing their hats too slowly. Chekhov forced himself to watch the flogging of an escaped murderer, but had to leave the room after forty-three lashes out of the prescribed ninety. Female convicts – outnumbered two to one by men – were forced into sexual slavery. Officials took first pick of the new arrivals, followed by clerks and guards, then by convicts with money or pull. Even free women who had voluntarily joined their convict husbands on Sakhalin turned to prostitution, there being no other work available. Neither age, ugliness, 'nor even tertiary syphilis' were impediments, and 'at the age of fourteen or fifteen the daughters, too, are sent out on the merry-go-round. The mothers haggle over them, and arrange for them to live ... with rich settlers or guards.'[17] Their ragged, diseased children played at beatings and chain-gangs. Chekhov relates a conversation with a barefoot ten-year-old:

> 'What's your father's name?' I asked him.
>   'I don't know,' he answered.
>   'How so?'
>   'He's not my real father.'
>   'What do you mean, he's not your real father?'
>   'He's my mother's cohabitant.'
>   'Is your mother married or a widow?'
>   'A widow. She came because of her husband.'
>   'What do you mean, she came because of her husband?'
>   'She killed him.'[18]

The Island's comments on the Nivkh are brief but revealing. Vague official estimates of their numbers had dropped from 3,270 in 1856 to 320 in 1889, partly due to smallpox and partly to their migration away from the west of the island, where Russians had usurped the best fishing-spots, to the east, where there were as yet no convict settlements and wild 'dark Gilyaks' were rumoured to kidnap stray travellers and fatten them for eating. The remaining 'tame Gilyaks' were employed as bounty-hunters and obliged to carry mail on their dog-sleds, which they did with scrupulous honesty. Otherwise, official contact with them was limited, especially since few Nivkh spoke Russian and the local authorities possessed only one, bad, interpreter. The Nivkh themselves appeared not to understand why the convicts were there, or the relative importance of different Russian officials. Out riding with Sakhalin's military commander, Chekhov was surprised when a passing hunter imperiously shouted 'Stop!', and asked if they had seen his white dog. He came across only two cases of Russians who had taken native wives, and only one half-caste child. Most Russians Sakhalin's indigenous people encountered, therefore, were traders or escaped prisoners. Five years previously, Chekhov was told, convicts had attacked an Ainu settlement, torturing its men, raping its women and hanging its children. In another notorious incident an escaped murderer, Blokha, had killed several Nivkh families.

Rather than recross Siberia, Chekhov returned home to European Russia by sea. His final comment on his government's treatment of the indigenous Siberians is from a letter to his editor describing a stopover in Hong Kong. He had been outraged to hear, he wrote, Russian fellow-travellers vilifying the English for exploiting the natives. 'Yes, the Englishman exploits the Chinese, the sepoys, the Hindus, I thought, but in return he gives them roads, water mains, museums, Christianity. You do your own exploiting, but what do you give in return?'[19]

The passage was deleted from the 1944–51 Moscow edition of Chekhov's letters, as were complimentary references to Hong Kong's streetcars, funicular, sailors' club and botanical gardens. Cut, too, was Chekhov's rapturous description, from Ceylon, of making moonlit love to a 'black-eyed Hindu girl' under swaying coconut-palms. In the 1963–4 edition of the letters Hong Kong's public amenities were reinstated, following adverse comment from abroad. The Sinhalese beauty stayed under wraps.

Today, most of Sakhalin's Nivkh live in Nogliki, a small town on the island's north-east coast. It was the usual muddle of decrepit concrete apartment blocks and careworn wooden houses, whose mongrel guard-dogs choked at the end of their chains at the approach of strangers. Faded murals shouted, 'Glory to the Soviet People!', '35 Years of the *Kolkhoz Vostok*!', 'CPSS – Party of Revolution! Party of Reconstruction!' The only vehicles on the streets were trucks and police jeeps, and in the biggest shop women in paper hats clacked at abacuses and tipped wrinkled beets into big mechanical weighing-machines. Behind their heads, vodkas sparkled: 'Citizeness Success', 'Diplomat', 'Bankir'. The wines had gentler names: 'The Gioconda's

Smile', 'Little Cossack', 'Foxtrot', 'Monastery Courtyard', 'Southern Night'.

An English PhD student living in Nogliki, Emma Wilson, took me to stay with her landlady, the Nivkh maths teacher Lidiya Kimova. Lidiya's flat had leatherette pouffes, a standard lamp with a violet frill, a reindeer-antler hat-rack and a glassed-in balcony in which she hung her underwear out to dry. The plasticised cloth on the kitchen table gnomically proclaimed 'Stockfarm' and 'My Lovely Hydrangea', and the doorbell – also from Korea – cheeped like a budgerigar. Everything smelt faintly of fried salmon.

Lidiya sat on the edge of a velour sofa, cracking pine-nuts into a bowl. She was born, she said, in 1935, on the *kolkhoz* 'First Five-Year Plan'. Her father was a traditionally minded fisherman; her mother hung the salmon fillets up to dry and read Party literature on the quiet. When Lidiya was aged six a woman from the next village came to call, driving a sled drawn by eleven dogs with bells on their harness. Presenting Lidiya's parents with rolls of silk and sides of smoked sturgeon, she said that she wanted her as a bride for her youngest son. Lidiya's father agreed, and to mark the betrothal, tied a cord around his daughter's wrist. That night Lidiya went to sleep wearing a hair-comb the neighbour gave her, but when she woke it had cracked in two. It meant that the betrothal was broken, and the woman drove away again, angry. Lidiya's mother was relieved. 'She hadn't wanted to give me to that family; she thought them lazy, ignorant. She was right. I saw the boy again a few years ago, and he was short – only up to here! And hunchbacked! And uneducated! And a drunk!'

Though Lidiya escaped a traditional marriage, through her child-hood the old kinship taboos still held firm. 'Everything about men was sacred; everything about women was dirty. If a man was sitting down it was wrong to step over his legs – it would bring bad weather when he was out hunting. If I or my sisters just touched a gun, we'd get such a scolding. I remember once, my father went out to check his traps, and didn't come back for a long time. We all sat there holding our heads, wondering what we'd done wrong.' All the treats went to Lidiya's older brother. 'But we got our own back by annoying him. He'd tell us to do something, and we'd do the opposite.' They also teased their Russian teachers, come to civilise the benighted north. 'There was this girl from Vologda, not much older than us. We'd sit in front of her tearing the skin off the salmon with our teeth, like this. She'd get so embarrassed; she used to go bright red. She taught us a song, a song about a "big, red poppy". And you know what "poppy" means in Nivkh? Female parts! Big red vaginas!' The Nivkh songs Lidiya's mother sang were sad ones, about boys lost at sea or girls sold to cruel husbands. 'They were always standing on the beach, weeping with the rain, sighing with the wind. It was proper opera.'

Nivkh shamanism, like Nivkh songs, had almost died out. 'Whenever my father caught a seal,' Lidiya remembered, 'he cleaned its skull, filled it with berries and threw it back in the sea, so that the next seal he caught would be a beautiful one, a spotted one. Nobody does that now.' The last time Nogliki had a bear-feast was sometime in the 1970s, down by the fishing-station. 'It was Russian-style. Women and children were allowed to watch, which is wrong, taboo. The bear was angry, a real fighter, and they couldn't kill him with arrows, like you're supposed to, so they took him into the woods and shot him there, with a gun.'

Other traditions, though, were coming back into fashion. 'There was this Nivkh recently, a mafioso. He'd bought a load of caviar and driven it to Khabarovsk. But when he got there half of it had gone rotten, so he couldn't pay the people here. He knew they would kill him, so he told his wife to burn him, the Nivkh way, once he was dead. If the smoke was in the shape of a bear, she should bury his ashes, and if it was in the shape of a deer she should throw them in the air. In fact, the smoke was in the shape of a skeleton. I'll show you the video.'

Cautiously, I read out some of Chekhov's less patronising comments on the Nivkh of 1890. What did Lidiya think?

She exploded: 'What did Chekhov know about us? Could he speak Nivkh? Of course he couldn't! It was all rubbish; stuff he'd picked up from the Russians!'

The other people Chekhov did not get to know on Sakhalin were its political prisoners. One of them was Lev Shternberg. Born in 1861 into a family of Ukrainian Hasidim, he was suffocatingly strictly brought up. 'I was deprived,' he wrote later, 'of all the joys of youth ... Conversations on morality and learning were among the only I had.'[20] Released into the intoxicating atmosphere of highly politicised St Petersburg University in 1881, he immediately joined People's Will, the anarchist group that had just assassinated Alexander II. The following year he was arrested during an anti-government demonstration and exiled to Odessa, where he continued his law course and secretly edited a revolutionary journal. In 1886 a newspaper-seller denounced him to the police, and he was gaoled for three years before being transported to Sakhalin.

The Sakhalin authorities initially put Shternberg to hard labour in Aleksandrovsk, but when they heard that Chekhov would be arriving they moved him to a small settlement sixty miles to the north, where he shared a cabin with three prisoners-turned-guards who spent their days looking out of the window for escaped convicts on whom they could claim a three-rouble bounty. With nothing else to do, Shternberg turned his attention to the local Nivkh. The first to catch his eye was 'a dishevelled shaman, with matted grey hair and a strange, cordial smile. Small boys surrounded him, shouting, "Look at the old shaman! He'll tell your fortune!" '[21] Relieved at Shternberg's change of interest, in February 1891 the administration put him in charge of a census of the inland Nivkh, allowing him to set off with two dog-sleds and an interpreter on what was effectively his first field trip.

One of the many books Shternberg had read in prison in Odessa was Friedrich Engels's *Origin of the Family, Private Property and the State*. Inspired by American research on the Iroquois, Engels had developed the theory that in its natural, primitive state mankind practised loose group marriage as well as communism. Monogamy had appeared only with capitalism, whose property accumulators wanted to be sure that their heirs were genetically their own. Rereading the book in his tent in the evenings, Shternberg realised that the Nivkh's complex family arrangements were examples of just the sort of group marriages Engels described. 'At first,' he wrote to a friend, 'I was afraid to believe it. But as I went from yurt to yurt, and from family to family making my census, I asked everyone how various kin members were addressed and who had rights to whom. Then I was convinced.'[22] He was amazed to discover that the wife of one of his native assistants, 'a pleasant woman, excellent housewife, and mother of children',[23] enjoyed fourteen lovers with the full approbation of her husband. The Nivkh were equally surprised that Shternberg found such arrangements unusual, asking him, ' "Is it possible that with you it is not so, that to sleep with a brother's wife is bad?" '[24]

In 1897 Shternberg was released, by which time his titillating findings – plus support from Engels, who was delighted to have living proof of his group-marriage theory – had won him a reputation in academic as well as revolutionary circles. In 1899 he joined Petersburg's Museum of Anthropology and Ethnography, and in 1905 was invited to New York by the great American anthropologist Franz Boas, who commissioned him to write the book, *The Social Organization of the Gilyak*, which contains much of what we know today about the pre-revolutionary Nivkh. Sidetracked into the Jewish-rights movement after 1905's democratic reforms, Shternberg turned back to ethnography with the 1917 revolution. Now, he and his generation of revolutionaries-turned-ethnographers believed, was their chance to put hard-won knowledge of the native Siberians to use, to do away with prejudice and exploitation and create a new Russia where all races, even the most backward, were equal, prosperous and free.

Their dreams were to be accomplished via two bodies: the Ethnography Department of the Institute of Geography, and the Committee for Assistance to the Peoples of the North, known for short as the Committee for the North. The aim of the former, headed by Shternberg, was to train a new generation of students-cum-activists, who would simultaneously study the northern native Siberians and gently introduce them to relevant aspects of Communism. Waldemar Bogoras, a Polish-Jewish former People's Will member who had served his term of exile in the far north-eastern tundra, joined as second-in-command in 1922. Though so similar in background, the two men could hardly have been more dissimilar in character. Whereas Shternberg was thin, sarcastic and scholarly, mumbling his lectures from file-cards, Bogoras was a fat, mischievous raconteur. Before the revolution, he had dodged the laws that made it hard for Jews to live in Petersburg by blithely declaring himself a convert to Lutheranism, and after it, he got hold of the Winter Palace servants' scarlet liveries so that his students could hand them out as gifts to native assistants.

Despite their differences and the surrounding political and economic chaos, the two men succeeded in creating a unique institution. In line with Shternberg's belief that the new science of ethnography encompassed the whole of human cultural evolution, the department's curriculum included Sinology, Egyptology, philosophy, theology and Freudianism, as well as history, folklore, archaeology and linguistics. Its students, many of them women, worked in freezing halls by the light of paraffin-lamps, but grew in number from 577 in 1918 to 1,530 in 1922. Graduates signed up to Shternberg's 'Ten Commandments of an Ethnographer', which enjoined them to abjure careerism, plagiarism, sloppy generalisations and hasty conclusions. 'Do not,' ran the last, 'impose your culture on the people you study. Approach them carefully and cautiously, with love and attention, whatever their state of development, and they themselves will aspire to the level of higher cultures'.[25]

From the department graduates went on to get their field experience working for the Committee for the North. Set up in 1924, its remit was to defend the interests of the 'Small-Numbered Peoples', meaning all the northern native Siberians excluding the Sakha, whose large numbers and sophisticated elites made them a special case. Its founder was another former exile, Anatoliy Skachko. The revolution, he told the Party's Central Committee in a barrage of memoranda in the early 1920s, had left the Small-Numbered Peoples even worse off than under tsarism. Most low-level Soviet officials in the north were rebranded fur-traders, and putting them in charge of native welfare was 'like entrusting a wolf with a flock of sheep'. Hence the need for a dedicated organisation in Moscow, whose specially trained operatives would be able to go over the heads of corrupt local bureaucrats, and have immunity from the bullying GPU.

In theory, the aims of the Committee for the North – the 'drawing-together' and eventual merger of native Siberians with modern Soviet society – were straightforwardly Communist and Russificatory. But in practice its values, like those of mellowed, middle-aged Shternberg and Bogoras, were voluntarist and gradualist, and the measures it proposed (alcohol bans, tax exemptions, limits on Russian settlement) little different from those promoted by liberal reformers under the tsars. Its most visible achievements were nineteen 'culture bases' or *kultbazy*. Consciously modelled on nineteenth-century mission-stations, each was equipped with a clinic, classroom, bath-house and 'House of the Native', where interested parties were shown Eisenstein films and given lessons on brushing their teeth. Like the old mission-stations, they concentrated their efforts on women, who were assumed to have most influence on native children, and more to gain from the abandonment of sexist traditions. Their smaller, mobile outposts were known as Red Tents. One young Red Tenter attracted custom by playing his balalaika; another devised competitions for cleanliness, awarding copper pots and cutlery as prizes.

In its wider aim of protecting northern natives' welfare, the Committee failed completely. Underfunded and possessing little Party clout, it did not have the resources to implement policy or to fight its corner against rival government departments. Out in the field, its young staff were pushed around by Party bosses and State Trading Committee employees, who were paid three times as much and regarded them as pious snoops. Their enthusiasm often wore off. 'Try spending,' wrote one, 'a whole year as a nomad – for that is how the doctors and veterinarians of the travelling detachments live. A whole year in a *chum* or a *yaranga*, in fifty below zero weather; endless blizzards that prevent you from venturing outside for days on end; inescapable smoke from the fire; inescapable dirt; no chance to wash yourself, and long weeks without taking off your lice-filled coat . . . All this has very little of heroism and a great deal of discomfort.'[26] Of the first cohort of Ethnography Department graduates, four actually died: one of typhoid on the lower Ob, one of tuberculosis in Kolyma, one by drowning in Chukotka and one of exposure and starvation on the Yamal peninsula.

Nor were the native Siberians themselves always grateful for the Committee's efforts. 'What is the October Revolution?', Evenk reindeer-herders plaintively enquired. 'Who are the bourgeois elements? What is technology? What is industry?'[27] A Chukchi clan declared that they didn't need any Red Tents, since their grandfathers had never had any, and lived better than they did. Especially unpopular was the Committee's system of 'tribal soviets', based on Speransky's reforms of a century earlier. 'Upon my arrival in the encampment,' reported a Chukotka-based activist in 1927, 'I invited the whole population to Rishchip's *yaranga* and declared that they ought to elect representatives to an encampment committee. They replied that they did not need a committee because they had always lived without one, and that if they elected one, the number of walrus would not increase.'[28] Koryak insisted that they already had their own leaders, and that if they were forced to hold elections they would just choose the same men again. Nenets scolded for taking orders from their traditional chief riposted, 'You Russians need the clan soviet, and we need our prince.'[29]

As the Leninist 1920s hardened into the Stalinist 1930s, Shternberg, Bogoras and their moderate, paternalist ilk found themselves increasingly out of step with the times. Early on, Bogoras had put himself out of favour with Stalin's Commissariat for Nationalities by arguing for American-style native reservations. 'Drawing together', of the Small-Numbered People and Russians, he had argued, amounted to 'a virtual end to the natives – they are crushed into smithereens like an earthenware pot tossed in with iron kettles'.[30] Such objections were now attacked as anti-Marxist and anti-Party, as 'old-fashioned populism' or 'fruitless theorising'. Starved of funds, in 1930 the Committee closed its *kultbazy* and sacked most of its staff. Five years later its responsibilities were transferred to the Main Administration of the Northern Sea Route, the organisation that was opening a shipping lane along the Arctic coast. Ethnically based 'national districts', created to give the Small-Numbered Peoples administrative autonomy and control over Russian settlement, were first handed to the Far Eastern Construction Trust, the innocuous-sounding organisation that ran the north-eastern Gulag, then dissolved.

The Ethnography Department survived, but turned from an academic institution into a training centre for indigenous Communist cadres. Of its 1922 student intake of 1,530, only twelve had been Bolsheviks. In the mid-1920s a class-based quota system was introduced, and the curriculum politicised. Bogoras, no longer so plump and jolly, spent his time inventing native-language neologisms for terms such as 'The Five-Year Plan in Four Years' and 'The First of May' – for which the Chukchi, embarrassingly, insisted on using the

English word 'Christmas', picked up from American whalers. 'Middle peasant', in Nivkh, persisted in coming out as 'someone living in the middle of the village', or 'man of middling height'. Newly codified native languages were taken out of the Latin alphabet and into Cyrillic, and reading-primers exhorted children to join the Pioneers and the Communist Youth League. One Nivkh-language primer even singled out for disapproval the same shaman, a man called Koinyt, who forty years earlier had sung songs for Shternberg in exchange for food and shelter. In 1938 a government review of schoolbooks published over the previous ten years still found room for improvement. A Mansi-language book overlooked the vanguard role of the proletariat before 1917. One for the Nenets mentioned Lenin only once in eighty-eight pages; and a Koryak one said nothing about 'Stakhanovites, Shock Workers, or the warriors of socialist labour discipline',[31] being filled instead with fairy tales about foxes. All these distortions were the fault of poor oversight by the People's Committee on Enlightenment, and of sabotage by bourgeois nationalists and Trotskyite-Bukharinist gangs.

In 1936 a journalist on the London *Times*, Harry Smolka, visited the revamped department, by then renamed the Northern Institute, at its summer school in the country. The indigenous students were divided into three faculties. 'From No. 1 faculty,' he wrote, 'come the future organisers of nomad Soviets, political agitators and instructors; from No. 2 faculty the chiefs of trading stations, organisers of collectivisation; from No. 3 the teachers for the native colleges and schools.'[32] He watched them learning how to play billiards and dance the foxtrot, and listened to them sing 'folksongs' relating how they had been led from darkness into light by

> Wisest under moon and sun,
> As great as the world,
> Man and leader as great as Lenin,
> Great friend of the peoples of the world – Stalin![33]

The students' biographies, which Smolka asked them to write down in brief, were in the same genre. A Nanai related how her family had tried to force her into a traditional marriage:

> In my grief I went to a Komsomol girl who led a Pioneer group in

our village. She helped me to run away and come here to this Institute. I have learned to read and write, can speak Russian fluently, and have read much literature: Tolstoy and Pushkin, and, of course, Gorky. I have also been to Moscow and seen the new underground railway. Soon I shall go back to my people and teach them how to become free from their old superstitions and the whip of the shaman.[34]

A Khant boy pulled up his shirt to show Smolka a tattoo of Stalin. He had had it done, he explained apologetically, while still at home, but had since learned that it was an 'uncultured' demonstration of loyalty, and that he should be wearing Stalin's portrait in his heart rather than on his skin.

The foxtrotting students' relatives back home were meanwhile suffering collectivisation. 'Everyone,' as a Nivkh fisherman put it half a century later, 'had to give their things in; one person a net, another a boat ... After that it was all *kolkhoz, kolkhoz, kolkhoz*. It was all about potatoes and *kolkhozy*. About how to give your things in.'[35]

The Committee of the North fought a valiant rearguard action. Over-hasty 'total collectivisation', Skachko warned, would destroy the Small-Numbered Peoples' traditional economies, forcing them into dependency on state hand-outs. Nomadism might be backward, but destroying it on principle was ridiculous. Theoreticians who thought that deer could be replaced with cattle, or fur-trapping with market gardening, did not know what they were talking about. Moreover, the Small-Numbered Peoples possessed no exploiters and exploited in the Marxist sense of the words. Owning a hundred deer did not make a man a kulak; prospective sons-in-law working out their bride-prices were not hired labourers; a shaman was not the same thing as a priest.

His protests fell on deaf ears, and all over the north Party activists, realising that unless they found class enemies among the native Siberians they risked becoming class enemies themselves, set to work rooting out counter-revolution. A Nenets who provided food for hungry neighbours was denounced as a kulak, as was a Nivkh boat-owner who took a larger share of the catch than his crew. Tables were produced giving approved deer/deer-owner ratios for different regions, according to which 73 per cent of the Kolyma tundra's herders turned out to be 'feudal lords'. One Komsomol leader used the 'bear principle', which damned as a kulak anyone found fattening an animal for the bear-feast. Where threats, fines and confiscations failed, collectivisers resorted to violence. Among the Nganasan, they threatened that 'soldiers from Krasnoyarsk will come and lock you in an iron box'.[36] On Kamchatka, they staged mock executions and interned critics in a specially organised camp. Elsewhere, unco-operative individuals were beaten up or simply disappeared.

To what extent the northern native Siberians resisted col-lectivisation is unclear. The protest killing of reindeer was certainly widespread, contributing to domesticated deers' fall in number from three million in 1926 to 1.8 million in 1934. The campaigning Russian ethnographer Aleksandr Pika found a local NKVD report of an incident which he thought to have been typical, judging by anecdotal evidence from elderly interviewees. In 1934 a Khant soviet chairman, Ivan Yernikhov, summoned a meeting by sending, in the traditional way, an arrow carved with his personal sign around nearby settlements. Twenty-nine Khant duly gathered, and wrote a petition asking for the return of abducted relatives, an end to the persecution of 'kulaks' and shamans, cancellation of state procurements of fish and furs, fresh elections to the local soviet and closure of the local *kultbaza*. At the meeting's end they ritually sacrificed fifteen deer. Soon afterwards Yernikhov and 150 angry followers set off with the petition to the nearest town, Kazym. On the way they were met by officials who calmed them down, promised negotiations and told them to return to their camps. When they continued to hold protest meetings the Kazym authorities retaliated by sending seven armed men to establish a fishery on a sacred lake. The men were strangled by persons unknown, at which point the NKVD intervened, arresting Yer-nikhov and eighty-seven of his supporters. Three Khant, including Yernikhov, died under interrogation, and fifty-one were sent to labour camps.

They were far from the only northern natives to be swept into the Gulag, for Stalin's terror decimated walrus-hunters and reindeer-herders just as it did every other category of Soviet citizen. Particularly badly hit were the Ainu and Nivkh of Sakhalin, whose mobility and proximity to the Japanese border were presumed to make them useful to Japan as spies. During the 'Islanders' Affair' of 1934, the NKVD arrested and shot 115 inhabitants of northern Sakhalin, forty of whom were Nivkh. From 1937 to 1938 they arrested another 200 Nivkh men from the island's north-western shore, a third of the area's adult male indigenous population. More must have been arrested elsewhere, since the NKVD report on the episode talks about 'maintaining pace' with quotas for the rest of the island.

The Nivkh likeliest to be targeted, ironically, were the very people Shternberg's and Bogoras's students had trained up as future cadres. 'All the good people,' a survivor remembered, 'all the people who spoke at meetings, those were the kind of people they put away.'[37] One victim, the chairman of a local soviet, had been praised in the press for his role in a 'relay-race against illiteracy', and for organising garbage-ditches and a bath-house. This did not prevent him from being charged with counter-revolution and shot – possibly, as his grand-daughter told an American anthropologist fifty years later, because he owned a Japanese watch. Wearing spectacles was dangerous, and Nivkh women buried their Chinese silk gowns, daring to dig them up again only under Khrushchev. Sometimes it was enough just to have found a Japanese sweet wrapper floating down the river: 'People would ask, "Where did you get that from?" Or they wouldn't ask at all, and the police would come all the same … They would come in one of those big trucks, a five-ton truck, the kind they used on the *kolkhoz* for moving nets. They just came up to the door and said, "Let's go! Get ready!" Where to, nobody asked.'[38]

Similarly engulfed by Stalin's terror were several hundred anthropologists, ethnographers and ethno-linguists: moderates, hardliners and Vicars of Bray alike.[39] In 1936, having done his best to turn himself into an orthodox Marxist, 71-year-old Bogoras was taken into custody by the NKVD and never seen again. Skachko disappeared around the same time. Nina Gagen-Torn, a 26-year-old Ethnography Department graduate and an expert on indigenous costume, was charged with having 'anti-Soviet conversations' about shortages of research funding and sentenced to nine years in camps and another four in exile. In 1937 another graduate student of Shternberg, Erukhim Kreynovich (who had written the first Nivkh-language schoolbooks and contracted tuberculosis because he was too polite to refuse Nivkh offers of tea), was accused of membership of a 'Trotskyite-Zinoviyevite spy ring'. For five days NKVD guards beat him in relays and allowed him no sleep, until he signed a paper confessing to terrorist bombings. He was sentenced to ten years in the Kolyma camps, at the end of which, when he was sentenced to another ten for the same 'crime', he attempted suicide and was transferred to a prison near Leningrad. Two years after Stalin's death, after a total eighteen years in gaol, he was released for 'lack of evidence'. As late as 1952 the Northern Institute's expert on the Evenk, Glafira Vasilevich, was accused of promoting 'reactionary linguistic theories' and 'coarse, vulgarised dictionaries',[40] stripped of honours won during the siege of Leningrad and sentenced to ten years' hard labour, only one of which she actually served before Stalin's death released her also.

Shternberg was luckier, dying of heart disease at home in his dacha in 1927. His headstone in Petersburg's Preobrazhenskoye Jewish Cemetery is engraved with the words 'All humankind is one'. The quote is from Bartolemé de Las Casas, the brave, eloquent Dominican monk who exposed the *conquistadores'* atrocities against the Aztecs and Incas, shaming Spain into temporarily halting its conquest of America.

With Stalin's death in 1953 the purges ended. His successor Khrushchev closed the bulk of the Gulag, freeing a camp population of about eight million. But for the northern native Siberians, Khrushchev's policies proved in the long term almost as destructive as Stalinism. From 1957 until the mid-1980s they were subject to *ukrupneniye* or 'centralisation', jargon for their forcible transfer from small, old, traditional settlements to large, new, Soviet ones, whose shops, Russian-language schools, fur-farms and fish-processing factories were supposed to turn them into new, Soviet men. The result was a slow social and cultural disaster. In the shoddily built, thoughtlessly sited new villages, Russians or the sort of Russified natives still contemptuously called *chinovniki* or 'placemen' took the few good jobs. The large majority of native Siberians turned from tough, self-sufficient herders, hunters and fishermen into bored, browbeaten manual labourers. Bereft of their cultural identity, self-respect and often of their children, many succumbed to the sort of passive, alcohol-soaked despair familiar from the Australian outback and sadder parts of Alaska. Unemployment, illegitimacy, suicide and murder rates rose. Life expectancy and literacy fell.

In Nogliki, Emma arranged for us to visit Nyivo, one of 700 Nivkh villages emptied by *ukrupneniye*. The Nivkh couple with whom we were to stay, Stas Nitkuk and Rita Buldakova picked us up in their dinghy, and we motored out of the river Tym into a low-lying estuary, sheltered from the Pacific by a sandspit that curved north as far as the eye could see. Nyivo consisted of a string of tar-paper shacks, crouched between dunes and water. Nowadays it was inhabited, Stas explained, only for a few weeks each summer, when Nivkh families came to fish the annual salmon-run.

Our first day there felt like a Hebridean holiday: beach wide, white and windy; blueberry bushes tweedy carmine; sky pale and feathery with cirrus. Stas scrubbed out barrels while his daughters, bandy-legged in outgrown dresses, played tag round driftwood logs and scratched their names in the quartzy sand. All next day rain swept across the bay, and the girls trounced Emma and me at card-games by the light of a paraffin-lamp. When the smoke from the stove became unbearable we stood outside under the dripping eaves, watching Stas work back and forth along his nets. Rita squatted on the doorstep, rocking cornelian beads of salmon-roe through a sieve. No, we couldn't help. The recipe was called *pyatiminutka* ('five minuter') because it only took five minutes to make, and because if you got it wrong, you had five minutes to run to the privy.

The following morning the weather cleared, and Stas took us in his boat to visit his oldest neighbour, Galina Zevina. Squatting in the marram-grass, her cabin looked even more like a tumbledown garden shed than Stas and Rita's. Outside, it was hung with drying rosehips and sides of salmon; inside, it was insulated with flattened cardboard boxes covered with stickers of girls peeling off their knickers. A man and a woman rolled out from under blankets and started pushing at each other with their elbows. Both were very drunk. Galina, a bent old lady with speckled hands and precise lips, was spreading bramble leaves to dry on sheets of newspaper. 'My children,' she said.

When Galina was growing up Nyivo had already been collectivised and renamed the *kolkhoz* 'New Life'. It was, she remembered, a 'nice settlement', with three fishing-brigades, a club, a shop, a *banya* and a kindergarten. Each family had its own team of sled-dogs, and discipline was 'strict but good' – not like now'. Hard workers were rewarded with Japanese rubber boots. In 1966, Galina went on, 'Party people came and called the brigade-leaders into a meeting. When they came out they told us that we were moving to Nogliki, and that we had a week to pack.'

Could people stay if they wanted to?

'Of course not! The Party decided everything! Nobody wanted to go, especially not the old people. But they just said that Nyivo was a bad place, that there would be typhoons, that the sand wasn't right for building on. It was rubbish of course. We'd lived here for thousands of years.'

Did they protest?

'No, we're obedient people. They said, "Go!" and we went, like dogs.'

Nogliki was not what had been promised either. 'We were going to take our spades and saws with us, but they said, "You won't need them, everything will be provided, you'll be living like Russians." And of course we regretted it, because for our stoves, all they brought us was one big log, which we had to chop up ourselves. Water, you had to get it from wells, and keep it in barrels. The men were away all the time – it was "Go fishing and fulfil the Plan!" – and the women were left on their own.' The local Russians were unfriendly. 'We'd be standing by the shop, chatting. And they'd say to us, "What language is that? If you can speak Russian, speak Russian!"' All this, though, was ancient history – 'a long time ago, a long time ago'. What Galina really wanted to talk about were the new fishing-quotas, which meant that she could legally catch only 100 kilograms of salmon each year. One of her neighbours, 'Nastya, in that house over there, next to the old *elektrostantsiya*', had been attacked by the interior ministry's riot troops, the OMON, for fishing out of bounds. 'They burned her nets, and shot up her boat with their guns. Now it's all holes. Why don't they just let us fish? It's our food, like theirs is bread and potatoes.'

Galina pushed her leaves into a pile; she had talked enough. With evening the wind had dropped, and the breakers on the other side of the dunes sounded louder and closer. Her son and daughter shambled after us, begging cigarettes. We gave them the end of a packet and they propped each other up, like comedy drunks, at the water's edge, waving goodbye.

The oddest place on Sakhalin was what locals called the 'oilmen's village' on the outskirts of Yuzhno-Sakhalinsk. I couldn't go in, the uniformed guard on the electronic gates told me, without a permit. Over his shoulder, surrounded by wire-topped walls, lolled a slice of suburban America: smooth lawns, shiny houses, fat-wheeled, candy-coloured land-cruisers. The scene seemed unnaturally bright and sharp, as though on a newly retuned television. The village, the guard said, had its own generator, its own sewage system and its own water-purification plant, and a shop where you could buy Hershey bars for dollars.

Foreigners have been chasing Sakhalin's oil since the 1880s, when a Russian trader got British backing to follow up Nivkh stories about an inky 'lake of death' in which seabirds drowned. In 1922 a crooked Oklahoma oilman, Harry Sinclair, won a thirty-year lease on Sakhalin's oilfields from the Bolsheviks' evanescent Far Eastern Republic, and was dismayed, two years later, to see his geologists turned away by the island's real-life rulers, the Japanese. When the Bolsheviks recovered Sakhalin's northern half in 1925 they reneged on their agreement with Sinclair, and handed his concessions to Japanese firms, which continued to exploit them until the late 1930s. Foreign investors returned with the collapse of Communism. Two multi-national consortia, involving most of the world's big oil companies, started drilling offshore in the summer of 1999.

In the evenings, the *Amerikantsy* ate ribs and tortillas at Yuzhno's Pacific Bar. My contact Kerry worked for a firm that imported drilling equipment. Thirty-something and drinking Baileys with ice, she did not like me much; perhaps because of my snooty accent, perhaps because I was not the one stuck in Siberia. The oilmen were plump and moved slowly. They said 'howdy', had round, mild faces and wore extremely clean pastel clothes. In their placid, masticating groups they resembled hippopotami, or one of the herbivorous species of dinosaur. Mike from Exxon gave me a stopwatch enamelled with his consortium's logo. Bill from Marathon produced a perspex cube containing a tear-drop of real Sakhalin oil. Indigenous people were something they knew all about. 'Up in Alaska,' said Bill, 'I was in this petrol station. These two young native guys bent through the window and said, "Look at his smile!" They couldn't believe my teeth!' Back home in Oregon, Kerry had an Indian reservation right next door.

Bill grimaced sympathetically: 'A casino, or a used-car lot?'

'A casino. And now my mother goes there every night. I'm sending her money, so I'm, like, put it down for an apartment or something, puh-leez!'

She had a scheme to start Nivkh women knitting ethnic jerseys, which her mother would sell at Seattle craft fairs. 'It could be big. And it would keep her away from the fucking slot machines.'

Up in Nogliki, the notion that locals – Nivkh or Russian – might be able to stop or substantially benefit from the oil-drilling seemed as sweetly innocent as the grand plans of the utopian-socialist ethnographers of the 1920s. Under Communism, the public had no say in such matters at all. Today, the oil companies negotiate directly with Moscow and Yuzhno-Sakhalinsk, bypassing the small towns near which drilling actually takes place. Though in theory they are obliged to hold public consultations on new developments, in practice they often fail to do so, and the meetings that are held are badly attended and have no legal force.

Nogliki's mayor was Russian, and a Communist. He had a square face, small eyes and hairy hands curled into two fat fists on his gimcrack desk. I put it to him that oil-drilling was hurting Sakhalin's fisheries. Dead seals were washing up on the beaches oftener than usual, and people complained that the salmon smelt of chemicals. Did he expect protests?

He did not. 'There will be no protests, because there have been no violations. Of course our people here are worried. But that doesn't mean that they should go off to meetings, be indignant. We, the district authorities, will ensure that all ecological norms are met.'

What about the salmon quotas? Shouldn't the Nivkh, who were here thousands of years before the Russians, be allowed to fish as they liked?

The mayor disagreed. Sakhalin's Russians were indigenous too, and special privileges only encouraged Nivkh to slack. 'In Alaska, the aborigines get compensation just for being aborigines. So they expect the state to do everything for them. Why should they be treated better than the people who developed the country, the ones who did all the work?'

Finally, I brought up the riot troops' intimidation of Galina's neighbour on Nyivo. Wasn't using OMON – associated, in Gorbachev's day, with the violent suppression of pro-democracy demonstrations – to scare old women an overreaction, especially since elsewhere professional poaching-gangs were laying nets quite openly?

Yes, the mayor admitted, the fish-inspectors had been bolstered by 'detachments of special designation, who don't stand on ceremony'. But mine was 'a foreigner's view. Every state has its own laws, its rules, its traditions. Maybe for you in England it's not clear why we do this. But here it's normal.'

Back at the flat, Lidiya thought I was taking a foreigner's view too. Of course nobody protested against the oil companies or the fishing quotas. With people like the mayor in charge, it would do no good. 'When there's a noise from above they obey. When it's from below it's useless, like the buzzing of a mosquito.' The mayor, I pointed out, would argue that special fishing quotas for Nivkh were a bad thing anyway, that everybody should be treated the same. Lidiya stood firm: 'I say, "All invaders get lost." He's an invader too. We're the locals here, and we didn't ask them in.'

The native Siberians most affected by oil-drilling on Sakhalin to date are the Uilta or 'reindeer-men'. Close relatives of the Evenk, they number, according to the 1989 census, only 190, half of whom live in and around the village of Val, fifty miles north of Nogliki.

The drive there took us through scrubby pine forest, intercut with heath and bog. The leavings of the Soviet-era oil industry were everywhere: nodding donkeys, gas-flares, charred trees, a pipeline sagging across a river. Thanks to the industry's migration offshore, the villages we passed were all dead or dying: messes of shattered glass, burned-out cars and telegraph-poles tumbled into overgrown allotments.

The last of the reindeer-men had retreated to the end of a track, where the ground dipped and the pines grew tall. Leaving our car, we walked over springy needles, following the chink of bells. Before we saw them the deer were there in front of us, camouflaged by the dappled shade. In charge of the herd was Viktor Innokentiyev, a quick, inquisitive old man in a comic knitted hat and rolled-down waders. The boy with him had the vague smile of the mentally handicapped and hung back under the trees.

Pleased to have company, Viktor rocked on his heels by a camp-fire, gesticulating with one hand, cupping his cigarette in the other. To scrape a subsistence income of fifty dollars per month, he explained, a family needed between eighty and one hundred deer, and each of those deer needed at least fifty hectares of grazing. Thirty years ago there had been enough free land on Sakhalin to support 2,000 deer and more than a hundred herders. Now there were 150 deer and seventeen herders. The decline was mostly due to the oilmen, whose spills, roads and forest fires had destroyed the grazing-grounds. But it was also the fault of the Uilta themselves, who had grown lazy and careless, letting their animals fall into holes, become riddled with ticks or be rustled by poachers. When I asked why, Viktor's gappy grin faltered and he snapped a finger against his throat. 'What do you think?' His collective – renamed a 'clan enterprise' – neither provided him with petrol nor helped sell his meat, so might as well not have existed at all. 'We cursed Soviet power, but at least they thought about production. It was, "Here's your gun, here are your rounds, here's the Plan!" Then in '91, "Hoorah! Democracy! For all the aborigines, it'll be better!" And it turned out – Pooh!' The oil companies were planning new pipelines that would cut across the remaining grazing-grounds. Would Viktor campaign to stop them?

'Campaign? If I had an economics education I'd go to Nogliki and check those papers. But I can't drop everything and leave. You need a *spetsialist*, someone with a good head. People come and say, "You'll get some money." But they're lying. Compensation will never arrive. Even if it's actually paid it'll never get past the administration.'

By the time Viktor stopped talking the woods had turned a ferny, aquarium green-gold, still as the sea-floor. Mosquitoes swam through slanting sunbeams, and the deer's mossy antlers branched above the undergrowth like weed-grown coral. Their names, a mixture of Uilta and Russian words, translated as 'Splotchy', 'Stupid', 'Obedient' and 'Twisty Tail'. The big white stag was called Ivanhoe, after Valter Skott. When he was a child, Viktor said, people used to sacrifice white deer to the gods, and even now Uilta herders were buried with their favourite riding-deer, gun and saddle. 'Oh yes, it carried on through Soviet times. When I go, they'll kill Ivanhoe for me.'

CHAPTER 7

THE CHUKCHI

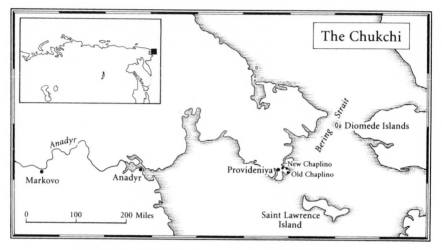

You are Russian people; God gave you the Russian faith and horses;
therefore you have Russian faith and horses, while God is in the
sky. We are the Chukchi people; God gave us the Chukchi faith
and reindeer; therefore we have the Chukchi faith and use reindeer,
while God is in the sky. And so you Russians worship the Russian
way and keep your horses, while we Chukchi will worship the
Chukchi way and keep our reindeer.
– Chukchi shaman to an Orthodox priest, 1880s

Even a small mouse has anger.
– Chukchi proverb, early 1900s

The Chukchi are in Anadyr to collect fourteen steel dinghies given
them – it is election time – by the regional government. Each morning
I find them drinking beer in the town's only café. The waitress glares
at their huddled backs, sniffing and clattering until they leave. The
rest of the day they hang about on the street corner by the fishing-
ministry building, hands tucked into the sleeves of their anoraks
against the cold. Even by local standards, they look conspicuously
poor, with home-sheared hair, ragged teeth, bow legs and off-centre

174

noses. Persuading them to talk is hard, and understanding when they do even harder, for they speak Russian badly, with a wild, blurry accent unsuited to the language's orotund phrasing and marching-tune emphases.

Down by the sea, where their boats edge the shingle next to the wreckage of an old fishing-station, they are more at ease. This summer, they say, they have killed sixty whales, 200 walrus and 600 seal, and would have caught more had they been given more fuel and bigger quotas. With a mixture of genuine pride and shrewd consciousness that it is what do-gooding Westerners probably want to hear, they assure me that their traditional skin boats are easier to handle than modern steel ones, and fur parkas better than high-tech wilderness gear. 'Last winter,' says one, 'we took these Japanese on an expedition, on sleds. There was a storm and they just sat there, shivering. But in our furs we were fine, we ran about!' The boiled whale-meat that someone produces from a carrier bag is delicious: dark, fibrous and tender, like the best beef.

Their plan for getting the dinghies back to their home villages, though, seems fantastical and slightly pathetic. Without charts or navigation equipment, they propose to motor along 500 miles of uninhabited coast, through fiercely tidal seas that are already, it being October, beginning to choke with ice. The boats themselves, emblazoned with the words 'Programme of the Governor' in patriotic red, white and blue, possess no cabins, buoyancy tanks, electronics, bilge-pumps or safety equipment of any sort. It seems quite likely that the world's last Chukchi whalemen will soon be drowned. The night comes down, the wind gets up, and the men scavenge planks for a camp-fire. Most drink tea, but the youngest, a sweet-faced boy in an absurdly large and womanish fur hat, fills and refills his jam jar with vodka, laughing and stumbling stupidly. The others sink into silence, gazing into the wind-thinned flames.

Chukotka is as far away from Moscow as it is possible to get while remaining on Russian soil. The plane there from the capital swoops a third of the way round the earth's circumference to the top right-hand corner of the map, where Russia and America almost join in a chilly air-kiss, fifty miles apart. The flight takes nine hours, and when you arrive you skip forward a day in your diary, never to regain the lost time unless you catch a plane on to Alaska, where east morphs into west again and the hands of the clock spin backwards 360 degrees. From a window-seat on a clear day, the view on the way freezes the blood. Inland, the Arctic tundra scrolls away like marbled paper, its rivers scattered into a confetti of silvery ox-bow lakes. Over the coast, the landscape fades to subtlest white-on-white, to abstract zig-zags, pleats and scallops, perfect as incised porcelain. When fluffy pink clouds intervene, the kitsch comes as a blessed relief.

Chukotka's indigenous people, the Chukchi, were once equally wild and fierce. A map of 1765 labelled their France-sized peninsula 'Chooktchi natio ferocissima et bellicosa, Russorum inimica, qui capti se invicem interficiunt' – 'a savage and warlike tribe, enemies of the Russians, who often kill themselves when captured.' An eighteenth-century Russian encyclopaedia listed them as 'the most savage, the most barbarous, the most untractable, the least civilised, the most rugged and cruel people of all Siberia . . . naturally as wicked and as dangerous as the Tungusians [Evenk] are mild and gentle'.[1] Something of this reputation lingers on in today's Chukchi jokes, still as standard among Russians as Irish jokes used to be among the English. Most turn on the Chukchi's supposed stupidity. (Question: What does the Chukchi riding the Moscow underground do when told that he is going the wrong way? Answer: Turn round and face backwards. Question: What does the Chukchi say when his taxi-driver knocks down a pedestrian? Answer: 'Chukchi hunter, he get both of them.') But others accord them a certain amused respect. In one, the Chukchi declare war on China. Puzzled, Beijing sends a delegation to find out who they are. The envoys come upon two men sitting in a skin tent eating a seal.

'Are you Chukchi?'

'We are.'

'And you want to fight us?'

'That's right.'

'You know that there are a billion Chinese?'

'Really! Wherever shall we bury you all?'

The Chukchi way of life, before the Russians' arrival, was stone-age man's. Inland tribes herded deer, and coastal ones hunted sea-mammals, using equipment fashioned from stone, bone, wood and hide. They lassooed wolves with cords of plaited sinew, and downed migrating geese with throwing-balls. On rocky promontories they built towers of antlers, which Chukchi women ascended, seal-oil lamps glowing under translucent fish-skin capes, to guide their husbands home through storms. Raw meat made up the bulk of their diet, supplemented with berries and deer-maggots in summer, and with blood-pudding mixed with roots and fish-heads in winter. They often made war on each other, tattooing their arms with a dot for every enemy killed. For fun they raced, wrestled, lifted heavy rocks and fought with spears, and to show affection, called each other 'little penis' or 'hairy anus'. The old or sick asked to be ritually stabbed or strangled, and believed that they would spend the afterlife playing ball with a walrus skull in the aurora borealis. When the head of a household died his relatives ate his flesh, and kept his bones as amulets.

No less tough and vital was the Chukchi's mental world, which was peopled with a bestiary of 'clever ones' or *kelet*. Lurking in clefts and hollows, *kelet* grabbed at unwary travellers with long tongues and hairy insect legs. One, an eight-pawed polar bear, lounged on passing ice-floes, wailing and beckoning. Another, a giant underwater worm, squeezed whales to death. Their wives were grotesquely fat, with breasts in their armpits and hair that glowed in the dark. All could change size at will; small as a mosquito one moment, so large the next that they used the cliffs as seats. The heroines of Chukchi folktales had red faces and bushy pubes, fed their mothers soup laced with bone splinters, pushed their fathers off precipices and refused marriage, trysting instead with a penis that lived in a lake. Chukchi heroes shrugged off arrows, pushed aside icebergs with fists the size of larch-boles and tore at their food like wolves. Villains were harpooned, flayed alive, dragged over stones or staked to the ground and sprayed with urine. In one such tale a father's only loyal son wins a team of obsidian-hoofed deer. Driving them to the top of a mountain he finds a girl asleep 'in a position convenient for copulation', whereupon he defecates between her legs, she giggles, and they lie down 'close as oysters', before feeding his perfidious brothers to a *kelet*.[2]

Folktales told, too, of the coming of the Cossacks. 'Our people,' a Chukchi told the exiled Bogoras,

> were very much afraid of them ... Their whiskers stuck out like those of the walrus. Their spear-heads were a cubit long, and so broad that they obscured the sun. Their eyes were of iron, round and black. All their clothing was of iron. They dug in the ground with the butt-ends of their spears, like angry reindeer-bucks, inviting our warriors to single combat.[3]

The first whiskery ironman to attack the far north-east was Vladimir Atlasov, a Cossack commander, as a near-contemporary put it, 'of very bad character and conduct, and exceedingly avaricious'.[4] Having come to royal notice when he accompanied the tribute to Moscow, he was given command of Anadyrsk fort on southern Chukotka's river Anadyr, from which he set off in late 1697, with a force of 120 Cossacks and loyal natives, to conquer Kamchatka. The peninsula's indigenous people – Yukagir, Koryak and Itelmen – descended on their attackers on dog-sleds, one man firing arrows while the second drove. Cornered, they retreated to hilltops, barricaded themselves behind boulders and pelted the Russians with stones. Over two years, Atlasov nonetheless subjugated most of them, and explored Kamchatka almost to its southern tip, returning with a spectacular haul of 3,640 sable pelts and a shipwrecked clerk from Osaka, who had cried with joy on being liberated from the natives, but was to spend the rest of his life trying to teach Peter the Great's boyars Japanese.

Delighted with Atlasov's discoveries, Peter rewarded and promoted him, and authorised a second, bigger, Kamchatka campaign. But on his way back east Atlasov could not resist plundering – in true Yermak style – a passing river-merchant, and when he tried to sell the stolen goods in Yakutsk the theft was discovered and he was put in gaol. The native Kamchatkans had meanwhile recouped their forces, and massacred two Russian garrisons as well as two relief forces. The leaderless surviving Cossacks ran wild, indulging in an orgy of rape and pillage. In 1707 Atlasov was released from prison and sent back to Kamchatka to restore order. Six months after his arrival at Upper Kamchatsk fort his own soldiers mutinied against him, citing, in the vindication they sent to Yakutsk, his release, in exchange for bribes, of native hostages, embezzlement of government stores and violent rages. Atlasov fled downriver to Lower Kamchatsk, where he held out for four years until the mutineers took control of that fort also, and murdered him in his bed.

The violence, during which Russians and natives fought among themselves as much as they fought each other, continued all through the 1720s. It was fuelled in part by Vitus Bering's first expedition in search of the North-East Passage, in the course of which hundreds of natives were impressed for transport labour and stripped of their winter stores of dried fish. We have a description of the ensuing 'Great Rebellion' from Stepan Krasheninnikov, a young botanist attached to Bering's second expedition, of 1733–41. The rising's leaders were the Itelmen chiefs Chugotche and Fetka Kharchin, the latter of whom had worked for the Russians as an interpreter and taken baptism. Unusually, they prepared their campaign well, doing the rounds of native villages to raise support, and arranging a coastal blockade so as to prevent communication with Anadyrsk. Having waited for part of the Russian garrison to sail for the mainland with the tribute, Kharchin descended the Kamchatka river to Lower Kamchatsk fort, set it on fire and killed 'almost every person, without sparing either sex or age'.[5] The next day he and his followers gave thanks for their victory, dressing themselves in looted Russian clothes and performing a pidgin Orthodox mass as well as shamanist rituals.

The celebrating stopped when Chugotche arrived with news that the tribute party had been delayed at the coast by headwinds, heard news of Lower Kamchatsk's capture, and was now returning to take revenge. Two days later a boatload of sixty Cossacks appeared. Their captain offered an amnesty, but the Itelmen 'would not give ear to him: nay, Harchin, their chief, told him that he had no business there, and that he was commissary of Kamtschatka, and would himself gather the taxes, so that they did not want any Cossacks among them'. Loosing their artillery, the Cossacks made a breach in the fort's outer walls, through which Kharchin fled, disguised in women's clothes. Of the remaining Itelmen thirty surrendered, but Chugotche and his followers carried on fighting until a powder-magazine exploded, reducing what remained of Lower Kamchatsk to ashes. By the day's end four Cossacks lay dead and many more wounded, but 'how many Kamchadales were killed was not known, their bodies being consumed in the fire. Not one escaped alive, for those who surrendered were killed by the Cossacks, in revenge for the loss of their wives and children.' Kharchin was pursued and taken captive, and his lieutenants split. One was killed by his own people. Another, Teghil, 'having defended himself a great while, at last murdered his wife and children, and killed himself'.[6]

Krasheninnikov landed on Kamchatka in 1737, when memories of the rising were fresh. An Enlightenment man to his bones, he found its indigenous people intriguing but repulsive. They ate their own lice, he complained, washed in their own urine, shared dishes with their dogs, smelled of fish and could not count beyond three without using their fingers, before moving on to their toes. Their wit was obscene and their religion 'extremely silly', consisting of 'many ridiculous anticks'.[7] He nonetheless paid full tribute to their bravery and technical ingenuity, and admitted that although young native women were beginning to adopt European clothes and powder their faces white with rotten wood, older ones thought themselves 'the happiest people in the world', and looked upon the Russians 'with contempt'.[8] Krasheninnikov's accounts of European civilisation they regarded 'as so many lies and fables; for, say they, "If you could enjoy these advantages at home, what made you take so much trouble to come to us? You seem to want several things which we have. We, on the contrary, are satisfied with what we possess, and never come to you for any thing." '[9]

Krasheninnikov was lucky not to sail off in search of America with Bering. In the Admiralty's eyes Bering's first, five-year expedition in search of the North-East Passage had been inconclusive. He had succeeded in getting tonnes of supplies and equipment all the way to Avacha Bay on Kamchatka's eastern coast, there building two ships and sailing them north until the land curved away, apparently for ever, to the west. But he had not actually seen the coast of Alaska, which on the vital days through what was later to be called the Bering Strait had unluckily been shrouded in fog. His vastly expanded second expedition was intended to remedy the omission. Again Bering traversed Siberia, with even more men and equipment. Again he crossed the Sea of Okhotsk, and hauled cable and anchors over Kamchatka's volcanoes. By the time he got to Avacha Bay, eight years after setting out, he was aged sixty, and mentally and physically exhausted. When his new ship, the *Saint Peter*, finally sailed into view of Alaska's Mount St Elias on 16 July 1741 he could hardly be bothered to come on deck to look, and the expedition's naturalist, Georg Steller, had publicly to threaten complaints to the Admiralty to get his permission to make even a brief landing.

Four weeks later, after a desultory survey, Bering turned the *Saint Peter* back towards Kamchatka. Autumn's westerly gales had come early, so that she made slow headway, and her sailors began one by one to fall sick with scurvy. When dark cliffs loomed out of the snow at the end of October, Bering decided to give up hope of reaching Avacha Bay before winter, and drop anchor. The cliffs were not, as he had hoped, Kamchatka's, but those of a small uninhabited island 400 miles to the east. His depleted crew staggered to shore, where they had to defend their baggage from packs of bold and curious Arctic foxes. As more men perished, the animals took to nipping the toes and noses off their unburied corpses. Bering himself died on 8 December, lucid to the end and regretting, with his last words, that the expedition had not been commanded by a younger man. Fresh seal-meat restored the strength of the rest, and they survived the winter playing cards and whittling pipes in shelters dug out of the foxes' burrows and roofed with sails. When spring arrived they built themselves a new, smaller boat from the wreckage of the *Saint Peter*, which had been driven on shore during a gale. Planting a wooden cross over Bering's grave, they set off west again on 13 August, and pulled into Avacha Bay, baling frantically, thirteen days later.

The news they brought with them – of a route to America, and of islands packed with animals so unused to man that they sat waiting to be slaughtered – sparked a second fur-rush. In two years on the Aleutians one merchant came home with the skins of 1,662 sea otters, 840 fur-seals and 720 foxes. In three years on the Commander Islands – where Bering had died – another killed 790 otters, 447 fur-seal cubs and an astounding 7,044 foxes.[10] At least two species – a flightless cormorant and a giant manatee – were driven to extinction, barely a decade after Steller had discovered them.

Almost as severe was the devastation wrought upon the north-east's indigenous peoples. Overcoming the gentle Aleut, a fur-trader reported, was easy. On one island their entire stock of weaponry consisted of twelve flint-tipped spears and a bone dart. Another particularly notorious trader amused himself, according to a nine-teenth-century account, by 'standing twelve Aleuts in a line, one behind another, and firing a gun at them to see in which Aleut the bullet would lodge. He learned through experience that the bullet would pass through nine and lodge in the tenth.'[11] On Kamchatka, warfare, impoverishment and disease killed nine-tenths of the Itelmen in seventy years. At the beginning of the 1700s Atlasov had found them living in settlements of several hundred huts each, and estimated their numbers at 25,000 on a single river. A tribute-census of 1773 recorded only 706 adult men, suggesting a total Itelmen population of 2,000–3,000.

In 1799 Catherine the Great's mad son Tsar Paul gave a monopoly on the Pacific fur trade, together with jurisdiction over much of the north-east, to the partially state-owned Russian–American Company. Establishing its headquarters, named Petropavlovsk, on the site of Bering's old Avacha Bay shipyard, it rapidly acquired a reputation for greed and brutality. Meticulous Krusenstern was disgusted by the whole operation. The Company's ships, he wrote, were carelessly built and equipped, and its captains took no precautions against scurvy. Ashore, its sailors lived like savages, covered with greasy furs and venereal sores. Though he did not visit its Aleutian or Alaskan colonies, he was told that just as its senior employees mistreated junior ones, even its lowliest agents were 'allowed to tyrannise with impunity' over the 'crouching Kodiakers and people of the Aleuti'.[12]

Twenty years later, the Scottish explorer Cochrane spent eleven months on Kamchatka and thought Petropavlovsk a 'contemptible place', hardly deserving to be called a village, let alone a town. Its fifty-seven buildings were 'emblems of misery and wretchedness', and its society so bad that an exiled Cockney forger was received in every house. As for the priest and schoolmaster, one was 'a great rogue, and the other a greater sot'.[13] On his journeys inland he found the natives ravaged by alcohol and smallpox, and by cheating tribute-collectors who underpriced their furs and impounded their possessions if they defaulted. As elsewhere, they were also obliged to provide free transport for supplies, mail and officials. 'Of the conduct of these travelling gentlemen,' Cochrane wrote,

> it will be sufficient to give a specimen:
>
> The officer, upon arriving at a village, is received by the Toion or Chief, and conducted to the warmest and cleanest part of the yourte. His upper garments are taken from him, cleared of the snow and put out in the open air for the night ... The landlady, or Toionsha, is also engaged in scraping the boots of the travellers, to prevent the heat of the room from melting the snow which adheres to them. The best provisions are then got ready as fast as possible ... The Toion then comes in with a reluctant smile and a pair of handsome sables, and bowing to the officer, places them upon the table for his acceptance. Dinner being at length served up, the officer may be considerate enough to give the Toion a glass of spirits, and permit the family to partake of the tea-leavings. Having finished his dinner, the officer asks the Toion if the chase has been good, and how many sables he has got ... which he accordingly takes for as many handkerchiefs, pieces of nankeen, pounds of tobacco, or a small quantity of tea and sugar. The dogs of the village are at last ordered out and the officer departs in perfect complacency with his conduct and condescending demeanour.[14]

Most pitiful of all the north-eastern peoples, nineteenth-century observers agreed, were the Yukagir. In legend so numerous that their camp-fires resembled the stars in the sky, by 1800 they had been driven virtually to extinction. Cochrane was told that there was only one full-blooded Yukagir, an old woman, left on the whole of Kamchatka. The exiled revolutionaries of the 1880s and 1890s found a few more families on the Kolyma river, so 'rotting alive with syphilis and scurvy' that other natives made long detours to avoid them.[15] To Bogoras, it seemed that they had lost the will to live, patiently submitting to regular famines and displaying 'a dull aversion to managing and having a family. "It is more convenient thus," was the answer of every one of them to all my questions: "the more children, the more care." '[16]

The exception to all this misery were the Chukchi, who managed to avoid direct Russian rule well into the twentieth century. Their reputation for fierceness was made in the 1600s, throughout which they regularly raided the tribute-paying Yukagir and Koryak to their south, and gathered in armies several thousand strong to fight off the Cossacks' retaliatory sallies. Their attacks on outlying Russian settlements are commemorated by place-names: 'Massacred' village; the rivers 'Lost', 'Tormented' and 'Murdered'.

Petersburg's efforts to subjugate the Chukchi culminated, in the 1730s and 40s, under the infantry-major Dmitri Pavlutsky. His first campaign, undertaken to avenge the murder of his commanding officer, was resoundingly successful. From March to October 1731, a force of 400 Cossacks and loyal natives, equipped with 700 sled-loads of weapons and provisions, made a 900-mile sweep from Atlasov's old fort of Anadyrsk to the Arctic Ocean and back. In the course of the expedition they destroyed several Chukchi camps and fought day-long battles with three large war-parties, killing nearly 1,000 Chukchi warriors and capturing several hundred women and 40,000 reindeer.

Ten years on the Chukchi were as troublesome as ever, raiding the tribute-paying Koryak and periodically besieging Anadyrsk. Pavlutsky, by now commander of Yakutsk, was recalled to active service and ordered to 'attack and uproot completely' all the insurgents. Peaceful Chukchi were to be deported south and distributed 'amongst different fortresses, or into places where loyal people live'.[17] But by now, the Chukchi had learned guerilla tactics, and never approached Pavlutsky's force in large numbers, leaving him to wander aimlessly about the tundra. Having eaten all their deer, eleven of his Cossacks and thirty-nine of his native auxiliaries died of starvation, and the rest scrabbled for roots and grass. His third campaign, of 1746, was equally disastrous, since during the entire expedition he found only six Chukchi tents.

Pavlutsky met his nemesis late the following winter. On 12 March 1747 a party of 500 Chukchi raided Anadyrsk, boldly driving away seven herds of deer. The same night, with ninety-six Cossacks and thirty-five loyal Koryak, Pavlutsky set off up the river Anadyr in pursuit, leaving the rest of his men to follow. At dawn on the morning of the 14th he caught up with the Chukchi where they had taken a stand on a hill near the present-day town of Markovo. Pavlutsky was unsure whether to wait for reinforcements or attack immediately, but a Lieutenant Gornitzyn goaded him on, saying, 'It seems that our Cossacks are warlike only at home.' Piqued, Pavlutsky ordered his men to advance. It was a fatal error, for they had fired only one volley when the Chukchi rushed down the hill with their spears, slaughtering most of them and capturing their muskets, field-piece and standard. A few Russians escaped on sleds – Gornitzyn, according to legend, being the first to flee. Five days later Pavlutsky's body was recovered and brought back to Anadyrsk, where it was encased in wax and kept in a cellar before burial in Yakutsk.

We have no portrait of Russia's General Custer, and few Russians today have even heard of him. But for the Chukchi he remained an awesome figure. In the folktales Bogoras collected he is as tall as a tree, wears armour that shines white like a seagull, tears women apart as though they were dried fish, and tortures men in such a way that they castrate themselves. One has him loading his victims' fur hats on to twenty sledges and taking them to the tsar, to whom he declares, 'There are no more Chukchi left; I exterminated them all.' The tsar replies, 'No, there are more little birds hidden in the grass' and sends him back to finish the Chukchi off. When the Chukchi finally beat Pavlutsky to the ground they are unable to find a chink in his armour, and have to stab him in the eye. In a second version he is roasted to death over a fire; in a third, stripped naked and made to run around in the snow, like an unbroken deer. The Chukchi word *quchaumel* ('Cossack-like') meant 'badly' or 'cruelly'.[18]

With the Pavlutsky disaster, Russian enthusiasm for heroism on the north-east frontier waned. By 1755, after more failed campaigns, the Yakutsk authorities were ready for negotiations, and when Chukchi chiefs arrived at Anadyrsk with an offer of one fox pelt per head in exchange for an end to all further incursions into their territory, officials accepted it. In 1771 Petersburg decided to abandon Anadyrsk entirely,[19] since over the previous fifty-four years it had cost 1.4 million roubles to maintain, and produced only 29,152-roubles' worth of tribute. To the sorrow of its Cossacks, who were loath to see their long-defended homes go up in smoke, its five cannon were buried, its eight church bells removed, and its buildings fired.

Seven years later Russo-Chukchi relations were codified in two treaties, making the Chukchi the only northern natives who succeeded in forcing Petersburg into a formal truce. In exchange for nominal tribute, the tsars were to allow no soldiers into Chukchi lands, nor any merchants except those attending closely regulated annual fairs. Russia's legal code of 1857 stated that the Chukchi paid 'tribute in quantity and quality according to their own free will', and were 'governed and judged according to their own customs and usages', being 'subject to Russian law only in case of murder or pillage committed on Russian territory'.[20] The article on tribute-payment was rescinded in 1876, but the legal exemption remained in force until 1917. Attempts to influence the Chukchi by co-opting their chiefs failed hopelessly. The 'Kings of the Chukchi' travellers encountered, comically dressed in antiquated dress-coats and cheap brass medals, were equally figures of fun to their own communities. As one observed to Bogoras, 'Now I am a chief, and have this dagger and a package of papers. But where in the world are my people?'[21]

Left to their own devices, the Chukchi flourished. Taking censuses in the 1890s, Bogoras noted that their numbers and their deer-herds were growing, and spreading south and west. In two centuries, he happily concluded, Russification of the Chukchi had made 'no progress at all'.[22]

It was not quite true. Almost all the Chukchi Bogoras met were familiar with alcohol, sold them by Russian and Sakha merchants who evaded restrictions by labelling their wares 'for personal use only', or by freezing vodka bottles into blocks of cream. Tobacco was so universal that mothers stuck pipes into the mouths of their screaming infants. Coastal Chukchi also came into regular contact with American whalers, who traded furs for rum and Winchester rifles, and employed them as deckhands, taking them as far afield as San Francisco. The American journalist George Kennan was surprised to find a portrait of an American major-general, cut from *Harper's Weekly*, hanging with the icons in a baptised Chukchi's tent, and his boatman sang 'Oh Susannah!', strumming along on a frying-pan.

Inland, however, it was still easy to find people who had never seen a white face. Money was unknown – the Chukchi word for it, literally translated as 'variegated paper', denoted any paper with writing on – and in places the old 'mute trade' carried on, whereby wares were exchanged on the points of spears. Stone knives, Bogoras noted, had dropped out of use only a generation previously, and remote clans still used fire-drills and bows and arrows. Though women's necklaces were strung with buttons, cartridge-bottoms and the handles of broken teacups, traditional dress was worn everywhere. Shamanism flourished, for although the clothing rather than the flesh of the dead was now shared out at funerals, dog sacrifices were still common, and the taboo on alien fires so strong that Bogoras could not persuade his Chukchi hostesses to boil his kettle. He was often asked, in the 'most naive and shameless way',[23] to join group marriages, and heard of at least twenty instances of traditional ritual euthanasia, the usual practice being for the sick man's wife to wrap his head in a shawl, while friends pulled at a cord wound round his neck. 'In one or two cases,' Bogoras wrote, 'I listened to a description of strangling from the lips of women who had held the head of their dying husband on their knees. They spoke of it with much composure, and related how the strangled man kicked with his hands and feet, and how they kept him quiet.' When he asked Chukchi why they chose to die thus, their reply was, 'We want to die fighting, as if we were fighting the Russians'.[24]

Chukotka's present-day capital, Anadyr, is situated on the tundra-bound estuary of the Anadyr river. At its foundation in July 1889 it was called Marinskiy Post, after Alexander III's Danish wife Maria. A photograph of the event shows a naval honour-guard, cap-ribbons snapping in the wind, standing to attention next to a wooden cabin buttressed with sods. Their two-masted gunboat, the *Razboynik* or 'Brigand', makes the bravest show it can in the bleak surroundings, fluttering pennants and puffing smoke. A little way off stand three skin tents, whose ragged inhabitants have been marshalled into solemn family groups, children in front, parents to the rear. An officer smiles down at them, cap tipped back and hands in greatcoat pockets. The bolder Chukchi must have been persuaded to come aboard the *Razboynik*, for another picture shows them squinting up from the deck through a cat's-cradle of shrouds.

Since then, Anadyr has grown and died again. Under Stalin, Chukotka was ruled by Dalstroy, the NKVD department that ran the north-eastern Gulag. Shipped in via the port of Magadan, a total of somewhere between two million and three million people died working in Dalstroy's mines and logging-camps, killed by starvation, exposure, disease, overwork, beatings and shootings. The north-east's indigenous people, besides ending up in the Gulag themselves if they resisted collectivisation, were impressed for transport and employed as bounty-hunters. According to Solzhenitsyn, when the Kolyma camps first opened the local Sakha were happy to shelter escaped prisoners, but began turning them in once they took to stealing their food and livestock. Captures were rewarded with flour, tea, cloth or dried herring, so that children shouted, 'There's a herring coming!' on sighting a stranger. If a runaway could not be taken alive, his head or right hand was cut off as proof of identity. Otherwise, Gulag slaves and native Siberians had little contact. Camp memoirists mention the native Siberians only rarely, and native Siberians claim that their reputation for bounty-hunting is exaggerated, and that they kept as far away from the camps as possible.

After the Gulag closed, Russians worked in the far north only if well paid to do so. Young couples moved to towns like Anadyr for a few years, saved their hardship pay and went home again – little caring, as environmentalists began to complain, what mess they left behind. The artificiality of their presence became glaringly apparent with the economic collapse of the 1990s, during which their subsidised jobs folded and they fled back to European Russia or to southern Siberia in hundreds of thousands. Chukotka's population halved, falling from 140,000 in 1990 to 73,000 in 2000.

Standing on the runway at Anadyr airport, I could see why they went. In every direction, the view was composed of three ingredients: stones, sea and snow. The wind chopped like an axe, so cold that even the ocean smelt of nothing at all. Across the bay, the town exhausted the synonyms for dereliction. About one in five of its apartment buildings stood empty, doors swinging and windows blank. The random spaces between them were filled with wrecked trucks and discarded building materials, criss-crossed by raised walkways bolted together out of concrete slabs. Signs of human habitation – pop music from a lighted window, a pram in a stairwell – felt as out of place as they would have done in a war zone. A peeling billboard outside the abandoned Party headquarters showed a dam, a satellite dish, pylons and rockets. Another spelt out the word 'ROSSIYA', the overblown capitals alternating with portraits of the classic Russian heroes: curly-headed Pushkin, coat-tails flying; Lomonosov, in a forest of retorts; Alexander Nevsky, waving a broadsword at slitty-eyed Tatars. In the half-light of a supermarket, handwritten flyers advertised emigrants' belongings: a Tula electric samovar, a nearly new sealskin hat, the collected works of Charlz Dikkens, Dzhek London, Mark Tven.

My interpreter Mikhail was a gawky middle-aged Russian, one of the many who could not afford to leave. The son of a Soviet general, he had come to Anadyr to work for a state-owned trading company, in the days when the north paid the 'long rouble'. His life had imploded with the Soviet Union: since its collapse his job had vanished, his wife had left him and he had lost his savings twice, first to hyperinflation and again to 1998's banking crash. Now he made a living out of Western journalists and wilderness tourists, arranging interviews and hunting trips. Over breakfast in his flat, with its view of motionless cranes, smokeless chimneys and the airport ferry scrunching its way through the sea-ice that had blown in overnight, he explained why he had not arranged, as promised, for me to go and stay with Chukchi reindeer-herders. The tundra, he said, was too wet, petrol too expensive, the herders too uncivilised. 'Very bad smell! Very dirty people! They just think about how to get a drink, not about your shaman stuff!' I muttered something about deracination, culture loss. 'Culture? Primitive! You mean dancing round a fire, banging on a drum, like this? There's a tent in the museum! You can go and sleep in that!' His pale eyes began to glitter; his Adam's apple to jerk up and down. I had lived in Kiev, had I? Well then, I should know that the Union's fall was a joke, a mistake. Even the Balts wished they were back with Russia now. After all, who did they buy their oil from? But Ukrainians voted for independence in a referendum, I protested. And the Balts wanted to join NATO and the European Union. Mikhail radiated bitterness like a fever. It was all lies what I had been told; lies put about by Ukrainian nationalists. Young, female, unable even to speak Russian properly, how could I think I knew better?

Escaping him took three days, while storms held up the flights to the smaller towns to the north. The families packing the airport killed time with expert resignation, filling in crosswords, boiling eggs in jam jars and watching Brazilian soaps. A drunk taking his wife and Persian cat home to Sverdlovsk kept saying 'I love you' in English and stroking my leg with a dried bear's-paw. The café sold Korean pot noodles and stale éclairs.

Tamara was going the same way as I, to the port of Provideniya, 125 miles short of the Arctic Circle. Plump and cheerful, she sat with her legs apart and her fists on her knees, telling stories. She was astonished that I was in Siberia at all – 'You can run round the whole world, and you come to our Chukotka!' – and even more so that I was interested in its indigenous people, who were 'like children, weak, not proper Siberians'. The Chukchi woman on her staircase was a nuisance, always making a mess, but the one at work was quiet, a normal person. 'You know why? Because she's got a Ukrainian husband, and he's beaten her into shape!' The other reason she was sober was that she had joined the Baptists, the ones who were everywhere now, grabbing people or paying them to go to church. I said that I wasn't too keen on Baptists either, that I disliked their denial of Darwinism. This did not bother Tamara. The pyramids proved that mankind had arrived on earth from outer space. Whites had come from one planet, *negry* from another.

Provideniya, when we got there, was even sadder than Anadyr. More buildings stood empty, more drunks shambled about the streets, more women dared you to stare at their swollen cheeks and black eyes. I stayed in an abandoned flat, in one of the few blocks still provided with electricity. Heating came from a two-ring hotplate plugged into the wall, and the rust-brown, ice-cold tap water had to be filtered through a bucket stuffed with towels, from which it emerged mustard yellow. Ten years ago, my landlady said, the town had everything: a meat-processing plant, a dairy, a tannery, a breeze-block factory and a film studio where a real director, from Leningrad, made nature programmes. The shops were full of fruit, the buildings were repainted every year and the beer from the brewery was the best in the world. Then it all vanished, just like that, poof! Everyone who could had moved back to the mainland, and Moscow didn't bother about those left behind. There was a saying for it: 'They closed the town, but the people remained.' Her friend, a nurse at the local hospital, chipped in. Her beds were full, she said, of tuberculosis and scurvy cases, and God knew what was happening out in the smaller settlements, because the helicopters that used to ferry in patients had packed up long ago. She had dealt with seven suicides so far this year, all Russian boys. The Chukchi were likelier to kill each other, with knives. When I asked about alcoholism rates both women burst out laughing. 'Alcoholism! Just look out on the street!'

What, meanwhile, of the native Chukotkans, whose proportion of the region's population has grown from 12 per cent in 1990 to 23 per cent in 2000? Until the late 1980s, official doctrine was that their lot, like that of all northern native Siberians, was every day and in every way getting better and better. Ethnographers, including indigenous ones trained up in Leningrad, toed the line, routinely asserting that the Small-Numbered Peoples were now model and modern Soviet citizens. The Chukchi writer Yuri Rytkheu was typical in extolling his home village's 'comfortable, modern'[25] dwellings, the replacement of seal-oil lamps with electricity from the Bilibino nuclear power station, and the 'remarkable flowering'[26] of Chukchi-language literature. Contact between Russian and American Eskimo (who until 1956 had been allowed to camp together on the sea-ice off the Diomede Islands) had been discontinued, he assured the Canadian native-rights campaigner Mowat, at Washington's insistence, because it did not want American Eskimo to see how well Russian ones lived. Similarly, ethnographers denied or ignored the continued existence of un-Soviet practices such as shamanism. A Sakha archaeologist told me how she used to refer to sources from the 1920s, rather than to her own fieldwork, when explaining traditional funeral practices, because if she had admitted that traditional funerals still took place she would not have been published, and might even have lost her job. 'When I look back at my dissertation,' she said, 'I laugh. Whenever you mentioned shamanism you had to say, "And this is how ignorant and unenlightened we were." And you had to quote Brezhnev of course, and the Party Congress. As for alcoholism, unemployment, all those things, the most you could talk about was "a need for further perfection".'

The pretence ended with Gorbachev's glasnost. Far from flourishing, a slew of new publications abruptly revealed, the Small-Numbered Peoples suffered the worst health and living standards of the whole Soviet Union. At forty-five years for men and fifty-five for women, their life expectancy was a shocking eighteen years lower than the national average. To blame were poverty-related diseases such as tuberculosis, and spiralling rates of accident, suicide and murder. Half to two-thirds of all indigenous children were born out of wedlock, and native languages were dead or dying. Rytkheu's 'workers' settlements with all modern conveniences'[27] were exposed as outback slums: 3 per cent of households had gas, 0.4 per cent running water and 0.1 per cent central heating. Questions began to be asked (and remain unanswered) about the health effects of atmospheric nuclear testing over the Arctic Ocean island of Novaya Zemlya in the 1950s and 1960s. Radioactive particles, scientists pointed out, were absorbed in high concentrations by reindeer-moss, and hence by venison-eating humans.

New Chaplino is a mixed Chukchi and Eskimo settlement ten miles from Provideniya, one of several into which local people were herded at the fall of the Iron Curtain, for fear of contagion from Alaska. Drawn up by the sea on a plain of stones, it looked like an abandoned barracks. Anthropologists in Moscow had advised me to look up the village's schoolmistress, Mariya Sigunylik. Her face was authoritative, used to keeping a class in order, and her hands crabbed and red, apt to haul coal and water. Flustered at the intrusion, she clucked me past a litter of worn-out slippers, broken gadgets and empty jars into her kitchen. Damp had knocked the plaster from the walls and cold rose through the floor like gas. The only food on show was a twist of whale-meat, wizened as biltong. When I gave her a couple of apples she hid them away in a cupboard, as if they were precious things.

She grew up, she said, twelve miles away, in Old Chaplino. Eskimo had lived there for hundreds, perhaps thousands, of years. You could still see the ramparts they built against the Chukchi, in the days when they fought. Then Party people came and ordered everyone to move – 'for strategic reasons, they said'. Nobody protested: 'We're trusting people. If somebody comes and says, "Life will be better here", we just go.' But New Chaplino turned out to be a 'dead settlement', far from good fishing-grounds and whale migration routes. Unable to hunt, Mariya's father and brothers got jobs butchering whale carcasses dumped on the beach by a big ship from Vladivostok, or feeding offal to caged foxes. The chairmen of the *kolkhoz* and village soviet were Russian, as were the doctor, policeman and school head.

Then came the collapse of the Soviet Union, and the Russians 'ran away. They killed the reindeer, took everything with them. Then they said, "You manage things!"' Now the younger Eskimo were leaving too, to find work. In June Mariya's son had put his wife and baby into a dinghy and motored fifty miles across the Bering Strait to America's St Lawrence Island, where he was scraping an illegal immigrant's living fixing outboards and carving walrus-ivory. 'After that Provideniya sent us a border guard, to stop anyone else escaping!' But Mariya didn't want me to think that her life had been all bad. Here was her Veteran of Labour medal, reward for thirty-three years as a teacher. When she was young she wrote books too – Eskimo-language reading-primers. The one she got out for me was nicely designed and produced, the only bright, fresh thing I had seen for days. On the cover, an Eskimo boy skipped to school with a spotted dog. Inside, he flourished a bouquet against a montage of Kremlin spires and combine-harvesters. Telling Mariya how pretty it was, I carefully kept my eyes from straying to the window, outside which every visible thing was a sordid, abject grey. Nor did I ask whether the village children actually spoke Eskimo, for I knew that they did not.

To show me round, Mariya handed me over to another teacher, Yuri Ettyn, and his father Mikhail. Yuri had fine, clever features, incongruous inside the hood of his tramp's anorak. Mikhail's were as open as a child's: apple cheeks squeezed his eyes to buttons, and his hair stuck out horizontally from under his knitted hat. Though he reeked of vodka Yuri was kind to him, calling him Papi and helping him into the warmth of my van. Together, we bumped from wreck to wreck, in thickening smoke from Mikhail's *papirosy*. The collapsed wooden scaffolding here used to be the fox-farm; the burned-out sheds there the club, café and bakery. The shop stocked sugar, macaroni and sunflower oil. Now that you couldn't buy petrol, Yuri explained, people were relearning how to drive dogs. Cobbled together from planks and rope the new sleds look small and ramshackle, debased versions of the long, elegant ones in the museums.

Our last stop was the village cemetery, on a hillside high above the bay. At the head of each grave stood a wooden obelisk topped with a five-pointed Communist star. Beneath the obelisks lay the dead's most important belongings: for a housewife, an enamel saucepan; for a driver, a car door; for a boatman, a starter-handle; for a herder, a thicket of antlers. Their names and dates had been punched out with hammer and nail on small zinc plaques. Many died young – drownings, Yuri said, and suicides. One such, a nineteen-year-old, had liked photography and wanted to travel, so here, tumbled among snow-dusted boulders, were his camera-case, trainers and Russian–German dictionary. I should notice, Yuri went on, that the offerings were all torn up or broken, so as to prevent the dead from finding their way back to earth and abducting the living. The magic had failed, for here was the grave of another young suicide, Yuri's half-brother Anatoliy. He hanged himself last December, aged twenty-four. Yuri called his father, 'Here's Tolik!' Not hearing or not wanting to look, Mikhail shambled away among the posts and stones.

What did Tolik do for a living?

'He couldn't find work.'

Why did he kill himself?

'He was tired.'

Glasnost's revelations about conditions in the far north spawned a native-rights movement. The most influential of a clutch of new organisations was the Association of Small Peoples of the North, led by the Nanai Supreme Soviet deputy Yevdokiya Gayer and the Nivkh writer Vladimir Sangi. Its founding congress, held in a Kremlin palace and attended by Gorbachev, demanded protection for traditional land and water use, the establishment of legally empowered 'councils of elders', better native education and healthcare, and ratification by the Soviet Union of the International Labour Organisation's convention on tribal peoples.

Briefly, it seemed that the movement might acquire the same clout as its equivalents in North America and Australia. In 1990 the Supreme Soviet passed legislation allowing for the creation, in areas where the majority of the population voted in favour, of district- and village-level ethnic councils, whose consent would be necessary before land was logged, mined or drilled for oil. In 1992 a presidential decree promised 'clan-based communities' preferential rights to logging and drilling licences, and a programme of federal aid. But like so many other Russian reforms, none of these measures, even when fully enacted into law, took practical effect, sinking instead into a morass of apathy, muddle and maladministration. The Association of Small Peoples splintered, and its second congress took place not in the Kremlin, but in a shabby hotel in the Moscow suburbs. Among the wider Russian public, newfound concern for indigenous peoples, as for the environment, waned with rising poverty.

Today's few Moscow-based native-rights groups are small, weak and Western-funded. Nor, arguably, do they have much connection with places like New Chaplino. Ensconced in bright, light city-centre offices, their organisers tended to blush and mumble when I asked when they had last actually been to Siberia. They could not visit their home villages, several complained, because they lacked the money – before going on to name-drop about the latest conference in Anchorage or Copenhagen. The Soviet-era institutions that might have led the movement are still dominated by old-style token natives. Taking a cigarette-break in the stairwell of Petersburg's Institute of Anthropology and Ethnography, a Russian interviewee pointed upward. 'Look at our boss – a Nivkh. How do you think he got there? By being an orthodox Communist, of course. Ten years ago he was saying that the survival of the Nivkh was all thanks to Soviet power.

And now people like him talk about how everything Russian is bad and everything indigenous is good. They haven't got any ideas, haven't done any serious research of their own, so they just say what they think people want to hear.'

Even if the native-rights movement were better run and funded, to make a difference it would have to change minds not only in relatively liberal Moscow, but also in places like Anadyr. Chukotka's 'minister' for nationalities, Nikolay Novikov, looked every inch the middle-ranking, late-middle-aged provincial apparatchik. His office contained a spider plant, a stack of rough, tea-coloured typing paper and a large rotary telephone. On top of the coat cupboard stood a portrait of Lenin; not a leftover from the old days, but a new, coloured, smiling one, in a twiddly gilt frame. Racial tension, he assured me, did not exist in Chukotka, this satisfactory state of affairs being 'an echo of former times, when we all lived peacefully, in one family'. The Small-Numbered Peoples did have lower-than-average life expectancy, but it was their fault for having too many children, unlike 'us white people, who plan our families'. He had statistics on suicide and alcoholism, but thought it 'unnecessary to talk about them. We don't know you; you can paint the picture however you want.'

Novikov's then boss, since replaced as governor by a shady oil and metals billionaire, was notorious for stealing fishing quotas and federally subsidised fuel, and for an internal visa regime that kept out critical outsiders, Russian as well as foreign. Landing in Provideniya I was met by three young policemen, who escorted me into their office, told me that my papers were not in order, and that I should get back on the plane and return immediately to Anadyr. If the citizeness refused they would use force, and ban her from the Russian Federation for five years. I made a fuss, they lost their nerve and the plane left: I could stay until the next one, in three days' time. I still had to report daily at the police station and to the deputy mayor, an infinitely weary, infinitely charming man who could remember his parents bolting the shutters to listen to the news that the Israelis had kicked Britain out of Palestine, and who had come to Chukotka as an ardent young teacher, seduced by a book titled *Pink Wings of the Seagull*. Each morning, when I told him where I was going, he would sigh that it was very far, very difficult, and that I would do better to visit the museum. Each evening he would ring again, and ask just who I had interviewed and what they had said. If I had known Russia in the 1970s, it would all have been delightfully nostalgic.

On my last day – whether I liked it or not – in Provideniya, a Chukchi acquaintance, Ivan Tanko, drove me to Avan, a deserted whaling settlement out beyond the airport between a salt-water lagoon and the sea. Like Old Chaplino, Avan was closed in the 1950s. Before that, according to archaeologists, it had continuously existed for between 1,000 and 2,000 years. Now all that remained of it were the whalebones from which the hunters built their crofts: driftwood-grey skulls, jaws and ribs, some in heaps, others pointing at the clouds. The cliff below the site was full of whalebones too; layer after layer of them, twenty feet down to the shingle. The earth smelt strange and nasty. Centuries' worth of discarded blubber, Ivan explained, had collected here, thawing only when erosion exposed it to air. Someone had anchored a wire noose to a whale's vertebra to snare the foxes that came to eat it. What looked like a root turned out to be a piece of plaited baleen, a man-made rope perhaps two millennia old. Turning round, Avan suddenly made sense, for there in the shallows, mobbed by gulls and almost close enough to touch, was a whale. Rolling and blowing, it flourished one barnacled flipper then another, like a fat bather contemplating his toes. Suddenly I felt absurdly happy, for here at last was a creature thoroughly enjoying itself and at home, neither dying of drink nor dreaming of life anywhere but Siberia.

Back in the van, Ivan unwrapped spam fritters from newspaper and asked about my book. Chaplino, he said, used to have a strong shaman. He was dead now, but had been skilled at recovering guns dropped through ice-holes, and once appeared from nowhere on the Provideniya post-sled during a storm, guiding it to safety. There had been another shaman in Ivan's own reindeer-brigade, in the days when he was a *brigadir*. Though the man was a good story-teller, Ivan and his colleagues had not realised that he was a shaman until they went to meet him one autumn at the herding-ground, and found nothing but the prints of his snowshoes. Next spring there he was again, cheerful as ever. Since he couldn't have survived the winter in the mountains, their conclusion was that he had turned himself into a crane and flown away down south. Ivan, graduate of Magadan's Higher Party School and of the Leningrad Agricultural Institute, could vouch that the story was true. He had seen it all with his own eyes. As he turned the van around, I took a last look at our whale. He was heading out to sea, the double arabesque of his flukes unfurling above the waves in a slow, superb goodbye.

AFTERWORD

With Moscow 5,000 miles behind me and Alaska sixty miles ahead, what had I found out about the native Siberians? Some caveats. First, they were so various that few generalisations held true of all of them. The pathetic last few Chukchi could not be bracketed with the confident, numerous Sakha, nor the smouldering Tuvans with the comfortably Russified Buryat. Second, my impressions of them were subjective and partial, drawn from a haphazard series of encounters with nine out of thirty-odd Siberian nationalities, rather than from broad, statistically sound pollsters' or government data. Academic anthropologists, used to spending every summer in the field, would rightly think me presumptuous in reaching continent-sweeping conclusions based on a few months' travel.

What I was sure of, though, was that my journey had not been a wild goose chase, that the native Siberians did still exist. I had not found merely Russians with Asian faces, but distinct nationalities whose identities had strengthened with Communism's collapse. In the cities, the traits, besides physical appearance, distinguishing them from their Slav neighbours were subtle: a more reserved manner, exotic holiday food, a stronger sense of obligation towards the extended family. In the country, where they were likelier to be in the majority and to speak their own language, the differences were obvious. In Buryatiya, each village's allegiance had been clear at a glance. Buryat houses were plainly built and widely spaced, with paddocks for livestock; Russian ones had fretwork shutters and huddled behind apple trees and cabbage-patches. As cities filled with rural native Siberians looking for work, and emptied, in some cases, of Russians, ethnic divides were widening there too. In Yakutsk, my interpreter Sonya had said, she used rarely to hear Sakha spoken in public. Now, she heard it almost as often as Russian.

So how did native Siberians and Russians get on? This was the question on which official data were scarcest, and the one on which my interviewees had been most prone to clam up or change the subject. The Soviet regime's refusal to acknowledge the existence of a race issue had deprived them of the vocabulary impersonally to debate it, and many thought, with justification, that they had better things to worry about, such as when they were going to get paying jobs and running water again. But there had been no mistaking, on the Vasyugan river, Aunt Motya's resentment at the racial insults thrown at her over the years, or Ludmilla's satisfaction, in Ytyk-Kel, in describing how her Slav neighbours had 'flown away'. Reciprocally, Russians called Buryat 'crows', made endless dumb jokes about the Chukchi and routinely damned – despite not being in the best position to throw stones – native Siberians for drunkenness and disorganisation. That I was interested in dirty, hopeless Ostyaks and Gilyaks rather than romantic Decembrists, rich oilfields or rare tigers they found puzzling, even faintly insulting.

How Siberia's ethnic relations develop in the future depends on its politics and economy. Currently, like most of provincial Russia, it is utterly moribund. When asking about this book, British friends commonly expressed surprise at my intrepidity in exploring Russia's Wild East. I was flattered, but had to tell them that most towns I visited offered less excitement than Bayswater on a wet Monday evening. Typically, literally their only sign of economic or social activity was the odd bunker-like kiosk, fronted, if the proprietor was especially enterprising, by plastic tables at which men in cheap leather jackets sat chewing toothpicks and contemplating the near-empty street. While faraway Moscow gossiped, bustled, shopped and hustled, Siberia seemed eerily quiet, like an aeroplane drifting through clouds following an engine failure. Whether it would crash, roar back to life again, or splutter on indefinitely at low altitude, scraping each oncoming tree and pylon, remained to be seen.

Assuming that Siberia stays airborne – that it maintains a semblance of democracy, that its economy does not shrink much more and that it escapes large-scale civil unrest – what will native Siberians' place in it be? Judging by the rest of the colonised world, they will sooner or later begin to assert themselves, demanding political and land rights, and increased respect and support for their cultures and languages. Though economic collapse has so far produced surprisingly little ethnic scapegoating (all nationalities are likelier to blame America), in times of crisis they may again take to the streets, sparking new race riots. In response, Russians will have to examine their consciences on race – on which, as on homosexuality, physical disability and women's rights, they are thirty years behind the West – and take a long hard look at their history, including the seventeenth- and eighteenth-century campaigns of conquest as well as the horrors of Stalinism.

Fitting native Siberians into post-Soviet Russia will be trickiest if Russians, having discarded Communism, replace it with Russian nationalism. Under President Putin, the country has already become more centralised and authoritarian. When Putin sees his popularity wane, he may be tempted to tap the deep vein of grievance and wounded pride that briefly made a career for the nationalist demagogue Vladimir Zhirinovsky. Judging by his cynical reignition of the Chechen war and contempt (in deed, if not in word) for civil liberties, it is not a card that he would be too fastidious or desirous of international respectability to play. Already, native Siberians find it hard to think of themselves as Russian citizens rather than Soviet ones. Conflating Russia with Russian-ness would squeeze them out completely.

And shamanism? How good an indicator for the survival of native Siberian nationalities had it turned out to be? Like broader native identity, it had been stripped down to its essentials by Russian rule and especially by Communism, reduced from a detailed, consistent way of apprehending the world to a rag-bag of vague, disconnected beliefs and rituals. It was also now in the process of reconstruction, with spare parts drawn from the West. Some of the rebuilding I witnessed had been a little self-conscious: the Buryat family who flicked drops of vodka to the four points of the compass before tucking in to their May Day dinner; the Sakha one who showed me round their spanking new *balagan*, copied from a Polish anthropologist's text; the Tuvan shaman who offered hypnotherapy alongside ceremonies for the recovery of lost cattle and success in university exams. But there had been nothing artificial about the sentiments behind these demonstrations, nor about the Chukchi whalemen's pride in their catch, Baibek's absorption in his throat-singing, or Dembik's tears in the ruins of Chadan monastery.

It has been fashionable for a while to think of all national identities as invented, to stress the artificiality of treasured national symbols and inaccuracy of not-so-ancient national myths. But the native Siberians are an example of the opposite phenomenon; of how hard it is to disinvent nationalities, of how they persist in the face of governments' best efforts at their destruction. To stretch a metaphor, the shaman bowing in front of the Russian flying-doctor is not donning his coat again, because although he hid it under a suit and tie for a while, he never really took it off.

NOTES

INTRODUCTION

1 George Kennan, *Siberia and the Exile System*, 2 vols., New York, 1891, vol. 1, p. 561.

2 Waldemar Bogoras, *The Chuckchee*, New York, 1904–9, Jesup North Pacific Expedition materials, vol. 7, p. 281.

3 Wenceslas Sieroszewski, quoted in Mircea Eliade, *Shamanism: Archaic Techniques of Ecstasy*, trans. Willard Trask, London, 1989, pp. 231–2.

4 Mariya Volkonskaya, quoted in Christine Sutherland, *The Princess of Siberia*, London, 1984, pp. 219–22.

CHAPTER 1: SIBERIANS AND *SIBIRYAKI*

1 Remezov Chronicle, in Terence Armstrong (ed.), *Yermak's Campaign in Siberia: a Selection of Documents*, trans. Tatiana Minorsky and David Wileman, London, 1975, pp. 206–8.

2 Valentin Rasputin, *Siberia, Siberia*, trans. Margaret Winchell and Gerald Mikkelson, Evanston, Illinois, 1997, p. 71.

3 Remezov Chronicle, in Armstrong, *Yermak's Campaign*, p. 208.

4 Ibid., pp. 98–9.

5 *L'Ouvrage de Seyfi Celebi, historien ottoman du XVIème siècle*, Paris, 1968, p. 88.

6 Remezov Chronicle, in Armstrong, *Yermak's Campaign*, p. 117.

7 Ibid., p. 101.

8 Stroganov Chronicle, in Armstrong, *Yermak's Campaign*, p. 46.

9 Remezov Chronicle, in Armstrong, *Yermak's Campaign*, p. 128.

10 Ibid., p. 161.

11 Armstrong, *Yermak's Campaign*, pp. 293–4.

12 Remezov Chronicle, in Armstrong, *Yermak's Campaign*, p. 191.

13 Stroganov Chronicle, in Armstrong, *Yermak's Campaign*, pp. 59–60.

14 George Lantzeff and Richard Pierce, *Eastward to Empire; Exploration and Conquest on the Russian Open Frontier, to 1750*, Montreal, 1973, pp. 117–19.

15 Adolph Erman, *Travels in Siberia: including Excursions Northwards down the Obi, to the Polar Circle, and Southwards to the Chinese Frontier,* vols. 2 and 3 of *The World Surveyed in the XIXth Century,* 3 vols., trans. William Cooley, 1848, vol. 1, p. 391.

16 J. G. Georgi, *Russia, or a Compleat Historical Account of All the Nations which Compose that Empire,* trans. William Tooke, 2 vols., London, 1780–83, vol. 2, p. 15.

17 Nikolay Polevoy's *Yermak Timofeyevich,* quoted in Mark Bassin, *Imperial Visions: Nationalist Imagination and Geographical Expansion in the Russian Far East, 1840–1865,* Cambridge, 1999, p. 53.

18 M. L'Abbé Jean Chappe d'Auteroche, *A Journey into Siberia, translated from the French,* London, 1770, p. 290.

19 Robert Massie, *Nicholas and Alexandra,* London, 1996, p. 445.

20 Giles Fletcher, quoted in *Purchas His Pilgrimes: in Five Books,* London, 1625, p. 460.

21 Johann Gmelin, *Voyage en Sibérie,* trans. M. de Keralio, 2 vols., Paris, 1767, vol. 1, pp. 89–91.

22 D'Auteroche, *Journey,* p. 104.

23 Jared Sparks, *The Life of John Ledyard, the American Traveller,* Cambridge, Mass., 1828, p. 201.

24 Richard Chancellor, quoted in *Purchas His Pilgrimes,* p. 215.

25 Basil Dmytryshyn, E. A. P. Crownhart-Vaughan and Thomas Vaughan (eds.) *To Siberia and Russian America: Three Centuries of Russian Eastward Expansion, 1558–1867,* 3 vols., Portland, Oregon, 1985–8. Vol. 1, *Russia's Conquest of Siberia of 1558–1700: a Documentary Record,* Portland, Oregon, 1985, p. 198.

26 Ibid., p. 202.

27 Ibid., p. 209.

28 Dezhnev's two reports of 1655, to the commander of Yakutsk fort and to Tsar Aleksey, are given in full in Dmytryshyn, *Russia's Conquest,* pp. 317–33.

29 Yuriy Krizhanich; his report is given in full in Dmytryshyn, *Russia's Conquest,* p. 430.

30 Mikhail Speransky, quoted in Marc Raeff, *Siberia and the Reforms of 1822,* Seattle, 1956, p. 42.

31 Quoted in James Gibson, '*Paradoxical Perceptions of Siberia: Patrician and Plebeian Images up to the Mid-1800s*', Galya Diment and Yuri Slezkine (eds.) *Between Heaven & Hell: the Myth of Siberia in Russian Culture,* New York, 1993, p. 68.

32 Rasputin, *Siberia, Siberia,* p. 133.

33 Quoted in Glyn Barratt, *Voices in Exile: the Decembrist Memoirs,* Montreal, 1974, p. 238.

34 Alexander Herzen, *My Exile to Siberia*, 2 vols., London, 1855, vol. 1, pp. 218–21.

35 Quoted in Mark Bassin, *Imperial Visions: Nationalist Imagination and Geographical Expansion in the Russian Far East, 1840–65*, Cambridge, 1999, p. 166.

36 An anonymous article in Herzen's *Kolokol*, quoted in Bassin, *Imperial Visions*, p. 168.

37 P. D. Gorchakov, quoted in Bassin, *Imperial Visions*, p. 122.

38 Bronisław Piłsudski, *Materials for the Study of the Ainu Language and Folklore*, Cracow, 1912, p. vi.

39 Vladimir Arseniev, *Dersu the Trapper*, trans. Malcolm Burr, London, 1939, p. 8.

40 Fridtjof Nansen, *Through Siberia, the Land of the Future*, trans. Arthur Chater, London, 1914, p. 348.

41 Arseniev, *Dersu*, p. 339.

CHAPTER 2: THE KHANT

1 Yesipov Chronicle, in Terence Armstrong (ed.) *Yermak's Campaign in Siberia: a Selection of Documents Translated from the Russian*, trans. Tatiana Minorsky and David Wildman, London, 1975, p. 80.

2 Remezov Chronicle, in Armstrong, *Yermak's Campaign*, pp. 162–4.

3 Johann Gmelin, *Voyage en Sibérie*, trans. M. de Keralio, 2 vols., Paris, 1767, vol. 1, p. 188.

4 Ibid., vol. 1, p. 244.

5 Ibid., vol. 2, pp. 186–8.

6 M. l'Abbé Jean Chappe d'Auteroche, *A Journey into Siberia,* translated from the French, London, 1770, p. 332.

7 Ibid., p. 276.

8 Ibid., pp. 283–4.

9 Ibid., p. 332.

10 *The Antidote, or an Enquiry into the Merits of a Book, Entitled 'A Journey into Siberia' translated into English by a Lady*, London, 1772, p. 4.

11 Ibid., pp. 8–9.

12 Ibid., pp. 78–9.

13 Ibid., p. 22.

14 Alexander Herzen, *My Past and Thoughts, the Memoirs of Alexander Herzen*, trans. Constance Garnett, Berkeley, 1982, p. 186.

15 Ibid., p. 199.

16 Ibid., pp. 185–6.

17 Peter Kropotkin, *Memoirs of a Revolutionist*, New York, 1917, p. 172.

18 Ibid., p. 213.

19 Three petitions from Sakha to Tsar Aleksey, of 1659–64. Given in full in Basil Dmytryshyn, E. A. P. Crownhart-Vaughan and Thomas Vaughan (eds.), *To Siberia and Russian America: Three Centuries of Russian Eastward Expansion, 1558–1867*, 3 vols., Portland, Oregon, 1985–8. Vol. 1 *Russia's Conquest of Siberia of 1558–1700: a Documentary Record*, Portland, Oregon, 1985, p. 348.

20 Capt. John Dundas Cochrane, *A Pedestrian Journey through Russia and Siberian Tartary, from the Frontiers of China to the Frozen Sea of Kamchatka, performed during the years 1820, 1821, 1822 and 1823*, London, 1824, p. 514.

21 Yuri Slezkine, *Arctic Mirrors: Russia and the Small Peoples of the North*, Ithaca, 1994, p. 49.

22 Ibid.

23 Novitsky's account is given in full in Russian and Hungarian in Grigorij Novickij, *Kratkoe Opisanie O Narode Ostjackom*, Studio Uralo-Altaica III, Szeged, 1973.

24 See Jean-Luc Moreau, 'La colonisation russe dans la poésie populaire des Ougriens de l'Ob' in Boris Chiclo (ed.) *Sibérie II: questions Sibériennes*, Institut d'Études Slaves, Paris, 1999, p. 405.

25 D'Auteroche, *A Journey*, pp. 283–4.

26 Gmelin, *Voyage en Sibérie*, vol. 1, pp. 170–71.

27 Quoted in Slezkine, *Arctic Mirrors*, p. 51.

28 Alexander Herzen, *My Exile to Siberia*, 2 vols., London, 1855, vol. 1, pp. 239–41.

29 Gmelin, *Voyage en Sibérie*, vol. 1, pp. 256–7.

30 Waldemar Bogoras, *The Chuckchee*, New York, 1904–9, materials of the Jesup North Pacific Expedition, vol. 7, p. 295.

31 Ibid., pp. 718–19.

32 Adolph Erman, *Travels in Siberia: Including Excursions Northwards down the Obi, to the Polar Circle, and Southwards to the Chinese Frontier*, Vols. 2 and 3 of *The World Surveyed in the XIXth Century*, trans. William Cooley, 3 vols., London, 1848, vol. 2, p. 98.

33. Ewa Felinska, *Revelations of Siberia by a Banished Lady*, 2 vols., London, 1852, vol 2, p. 318.

34 Annette Meakin, *Ribbon of Iron*, London, 1901, p. 59.

CHAPTER 3: THE BURYAT

1 Luigi Barzini, *Peking to Paris*, trans. L. P. de Castelvecchio, London, 1972, p. 134.

2 George Kennan, *Siberia and the Exile System*, New York, 1891, p. 108.

3 Basil Dmytryshyn, E. A. P. Crownhart-Vaughan and Thomas Vaughan (eds.), *To Siberia and Russian America: Three Centuries of Russian Eastward*

Expansion, 1558–1867, 3 vols., Portland, Oregon, 1985–8. Vol. 1 *Russia's Conquest of Siberia of 1558–1700: a Documentary Record*, Portland, Oregon, 1985, p. 206.

4 Nikolay Poppe, quoted in Robert Rupen, *Mongols of the Twentieth Century*, 2 vols., Bloomington, Indiana, 1964, vol. 1, p. 41.

5 Quoted in Rupen, *Mongols of the Twentieth Century*, vol. 1, pp. 201–3.

6 Roland Strasser, *The Mongolian Horde*, London, 1930, p. 265.

7 Ibid., p. 288.

8 Marguerite Harrison, *Red Bear or Yellow Dragon*, London, 1924, p. 192.

9 Quoted in Rupen, *Mongols of the Twentieth Century*, vol. 1, p. 85.

10 Ibid., p. 281.

11 C. R. Bawden, *Shamans, Lamas and Evangelicals*, London, 1985, p. 209.

12 Ibid., p. 235.

13 Ibid., p. 234.

14 Ibid., pp. 226–7.

15 Ibid., p. 251.

16 Kennan, *Exile System*, Vol.2, p. 82.

17 Ibid., p. 86.

18 Ibid., p. 88.

19 Ibid., pp. 94–6.

20 See Rupen, *Mongols of the Twentieth Century*, vol. 1, p. 158 for a table of them.

21 William Graves, *America's Adventure in Siberia*, New York, 1941.

22 Nicholay Poppe, *Reminiscences*, Bellingham, 1983, p. 95.

23 John Snelling, *Buddhism in Russia: the story of Agvan Dorzhiyev, Lhasa's emissary to the Tsar*, London, 1993, p. 234.

24 Poppe, *Reminiscences*, p. 99.

25 Nikolay Poppe, 'The Destruction of Buddhism in the USSR' in *Bulletin of the Institute for the Study of the USSR*, 8–7, Munich, July 1956, pp. 19–20.

26 Poppe, *Reminiscences*, p. 106.

27 Snelling, *Buddhism in Russia*, p. 249.

28 G. D. R. Philips, *Dawn in Siberia: the Mongols of Lake Baikal*, London, 1942, pp. 190–91.

29 Ibid., p. 5.

30 Poppe, 'The Destruction of Buddhism in the USSR', p. 20.

31 Quoted in Caroline Humphrey, *Karl Marx Collective*, Cambridge, 1983, p. 428.

CHAPTER 4: THE TUVANS

1 John Baddeley, *Russia, Mongolia, China*, 2 vols., London, 1919, vol. 2, p. 55.

2 Ibid., p. 56.

3 Ibid., p. 88.

4 Ibid., p. 93.

5 Ibid., p. 106.

6 Alexander Douglas Carruthers, *Unknown Mongolia: a Record of Travel and Exploration in North-West Mongolia and Dzungaria*, 2 vols., London, 1913, vol. 1, p. 44.

7 Ibid., pp. 95–6.

8 Ibid., p. 222.

9 Ibid., p. 142.

10 Ibid., p. 240.

11 Ibid., p. 166.

12 Ibid., p. 97.

13 Smirnov, quoted in Ronald McMullen, 'Tuva: Russia's Tibet or the Next Lithuania?, in *European Security*, vol. 2, no. 3 (August 1993), p. 455.

14 Otto Mänchen-Helfen, *Journey to Tuva: an eye-witness account of Tannu-Tuva in 1929*, trans. Alan Leighton, Los Angeles, 1992, p. 42.

15 Ibid., pp. 45–6.

16 Ibid., p. 5.

17 Ibid., pp. 41–3.

18 Ibid., p. 137.

19 Ibid., pp. 225–6.

20 Karl Schmückle, 'Ossendowski Redivivus: or a Mushroom Collector in Tuva', in *Moskauer Rundschau*, vol. 3, no. 38, 16 August 1931. Reproduced in full in Mänchen-Helfen, *Journey to Tuva*, Appendix A, pp. 237–42.

21 Mänchen-Helfen, *Journey to Tuva*, p. 135.

22 Ibid., p. 119.

23 Quote in Robert Rupen, 'The Absorption of Tuva', in Thomas Hammond (ed.), *Anatomy of Communist Takeovers*, New Haven, 1975, pp. 145–6.

24 McMullen, 'Tuva: Russia's Tibet or the next Lithuania?'

CHAPTER 5: THE SAKHA

1 Farley Mowat, *Sibir: My Discovery of Siberia*, Toronto, 1970, pp. 144–53.

2 William Pursglove, quoted in *Purchas His Pilgrimes: in Five Books*, London, 1625, pp. 551–2.

3 Isaac Massa, quoted in John Baddeley, *Russia, Mongolia, China*, London, 1919, p. 9.

4 Beketov's report to Tsar Mikhail, dated 6 September 1633 and sent from Yeniseysk fort. Reproduced in full in Basil Dmytryshyn, E. A. P. Crownhart-Vaughan and Thomas Vaughan (eds.), *To Siberia and Russian America: Three Centuries of Russian Eastward Expansion, 1558–1867*, 3 vols., Portland, Oregon, 1985–8. Vol. 1, *Russia's Conquest of Siberia of 1558–1700: a Documentary Record*, Portland, Oregon, pp. 136–48.

5 Petition of 1645, quoted in George Lantzeff, *Siberia in the Seventeenth Century: a Study of the Colonial Administration*, Berkeley, 1943, p. 80.

6 Isaak Shklovsky, *In Far North-East Siberia*, trans. L. Edwards and Z. Shklovsky, London, 1916. Reprinted as vol. 7 of David Collins (ed.), *Siberian Discovery*, 12 vols., Richmond, Surrey, 2000, p. 209.

7 Johann Gmelin, *Voyage en Sibérie*, trans. M. de Keralio, 2 vols., Paris, 1767, vol. 1, p. 377.

8 John Dundas Cochrane, *Narrative of a Pedestrian Journey through Russia and Siberian Tartary from the Frontiers of China to the Frozen Sea of Kamchatka, performed during the years 1820, 1821, 1822 and 1823*, London, 1824, p. 194.

9 Ibid., pp. 197–8.

10 Heinrich von Füch, quoted in Dmytryshyn, vol. 2, *Russian Penetration of the North Pacific Ocean, 1700–1797: a Documentary Record*, Portland, Oregon, 1988, p. 170.

11 Cochrane, *Pedestrian Journey*, p. 442.

12 Kate Marsden, *My Mission in Siberia: a Vindication*, London, 1921, p. 14.

13 Kate Marsden, *On Sledge and Horseback to Outcast Siberian Lepers*, London, 1893, p. viii.

14 Ibid., p. 119.

15 Jared Sparks, *The Life of John Ledyard, the American Traveller*, Cambridge, Mass., 1828, p. 210.

16 Ibid., pp. 240–41.

17 Cochrane, *Pedestrian Journey*, pp. 443–4.

18 Vladimir Zenzinov, *The Road to Oblivion*, trans. Don Levene, London, 1932, pp. 50–51. Reprinted as vol. 11 of Collins, *Siberian Discovery*.

19 Ibid., p. 51.

20 Ivan Goncharov, *The Frigate Pallada*, trans. Klaus Goetze, New York, 1987, p. 581.

21 Shklovsky, *In Far North-East Siberia*, reprinted as vol. 7 of Collins, *Siberian Discovery*, p. 225.

22 Wacław Sieroszewski, quoted in Antoni Kuczynski, 'La contribution

des Polonais au processus de civilisation de la Sibérie au début de la colonisation russe', in Boris Chichlo (ed.), *Sibérie II: Questions Sibériennes*, Institut d'Études Slaves, Paris, 1999, p. 245.

23 Zenzinov, *Oblivion*, p. 261.
24 Ibid., p. 187.
25 Aleksey Kulakovsky, *Snovideniye Shamana*, trans. Aita Shaposhnikova and Ruslan Skrybykin, Yakutsk, 1999, pp. 115–42.
26 Mowat, *Sibir*, p. 145.
27 Ibid., p. 151.
28 Vyacheslav Chornovil's petition of 30 August 1976 from the village of Chapanda: *Zayavleniye Ministru Vnutrennikhdel YaASSR o Mezhnatsionalnikh Konfliktakh v Yakutii*. Also Chornovil's article in *Svoboda*, 22 February, 1980.

CHAPTER 6: THE AINU, NIVKH AND UILTA

1 Capt. Bernard Whittingham, *Notes on the Late Expedition against the Russian Settlements in Eastern Siberia, and of a Visit to Japan and to the Shores of Tartary, and of the Sea of Okhotsk*, London, 1856, p. 78.
2 Ibid. p. 79.
3 Ibid., pp. 94–5.
4 Ibid., p. 109.
5 Ibid., p. 151.
6 Perry Macdonough Collins, *Siberian Journey: Down the Amur to the Pacific 1856–1857*, Madison, 1962, pp. 287–91.
7 Adam Johann von Krusenstern, *Voyage Round the World in the Years 1803, 1804, 1805 and 1806 by order of His Imperial Majesty Alexander the First, on board the ships Nadesha and Neva, under the Command of Captain A. J. von Krusenstern of the Imperial Navy*, trans. Richard Belgrave Hoppner, 2 vols., London, 1813, vol. 2, pp. 67–9.
8 Marguerite Harrison, *Red Bear or Yellow Dragon*, London, 1924, pp. 74–5.
9 Benjamin Douglas Howard, *Life with Trans-siberian Savages*, London, 1893, p. 8.
10 Ibid., p. 59.
11 Krusenstern, *Voyage Round the World*, vol. 2, pp. 70–76.
12 James Vanstone, 'The Ainu Group at the Louisiana Purchase Exposition, 1904', in *Arctic Anthropology*, vol. 30, no. 2, 1993, p. 90.
13 Ibid., p. 86.
14 Krusenstern, *Voyage Round the World*, vol. 2, pp. 163–8.
15 Quoted in Henri Troyat, *Chekhov*, trans. Michael Heim, London, 1987, p. 142.

16 Anton Chekhov, *The Island: a Journey to Sakhalin*, trans. Luba and Michael Terpak, London, 1987, pp. 32 and 132.

17 Ibid., p. 243.

18 Ibid., p. 258.

19 Letter to Alexey Suvorin, Moscow, 9 December, 1890, in Simon Karlinsky (ed.), *Letters of Anton Chekhov*, London, 1973, pp. 173–4.

20 Bruce Grant's foreword to Lev Shternberg, *The Social Organization of the Gilyak*, New York, 1999, p. xxix.

21 Ibid., p. xxiii.

22 Ibid., pp. xxiv–v.

23 Shternberg, *The Social Organisation*, p. 57.

24 Ibid., p. 62.

25 Yuri Slezkine, *Arctic Mirrors: Russia and the Small Peoples of the North*, Ithaca, 1994, p. 163.

26 Ibid., p. 169.

27 Ibid., p. 200.

28 Ibid., p. 174.

29 Ibid., p. 202.

30 Quoted in Bruce Grant, *In the Soviet House of Culture; a Century of Perestroikas*, Princeton, 1995, p. 70.

31 Ibid., p. 99.

32 H. P. Smolka, *Forty Thousand Against the Arctic: Russia's Polar Empire*, London, 1937, p. 119.

33 Ibid., p. 126.

34 Ibid., pp. 122–3.

35 Grant, *In the Soviet House of Culture*, pp. 90–91.

36 Slezkine, *Arctic Mirrors*, p. 175.

37 Grant, *In the Soviet House of Culture*, p. 101.

38 Ibid., pp. 101–2.

39 See A. M. Reshetov, 'Repressirovannaya Etnografiya: Lyudi I Sudby', in *Kunstkamera: Etnograficheskiye Tetradi*, Vypusk 4 St Petersburg, 1994, pp. 184–221, and Vypusk 5–6, pp. 342–68.

40 Reshetov in *Kunstkamera: Etnograficheskiye Tetradi*, Vypusk 5–6, p. 357.

CHAPTER 7: THE CHUCKCHI

1 J. G. Georgi, *Russia, or a compleat historical account of all the nations which compose that Empire*, trans. William Tooke, 4 vols., London, 1780–83, pp. 175–84.

2 See Waldemar Bogoras, *Chuckchee Mythology*, Jesup North Pacific Expedition materials, vol. 8, New York, 1910–13, p. 107.

3 Bogoras, *The Chuckchee*, Jesup North Pacific Expedition materials, vol. 7, New York, 1904–9, p. 651.

4 Stepan Krasheninnikov, *The History of Kamtschatka and the Kurile Islands, with the Countries Adjacent*, trans. James Grieve, Gloucester, 1764; reprinted Richmond, Surrey, 1973, p. 247.

5 Ibid., p. 259.

6 Ibid., pp. 260–62.

7 Ibid., p. 206.

8 Ibid., p. 180.

9 Ibid., p. 224.

10 See G. F. Muller and Peter Simon Pallas, *Conquest of Siberia, and the history of the transactions, wars, commerce, etc. etc. carried on between Russia and China from the earliest period*, London, 1842, pp. 146–51.

11 Pavel Golovin, *Civil and Savage Encounters: the Worldly Letters of an Imperial Russian Navy Officer, 1860–1861*, trans. Basil Dmytryshyn and E. A. P. Crownhart-Vaughan, Portland, Oregon, 1983, p. 107.

12 Adam Johann von Krusenstern, *Voyage Round the World ...*, trans. Richard Belgrave Hoppner, London, 1813, 2 vols., vol. 2, pp. 105 and 110.

13 John Dundas Cochrane, *Narrative of a Pedestrian Journey through Russia and Siberian Tartary*, London, 1824, pp. 416–20.

14 Ibid., pp. 410–11.

15 Isaak Shklovsky, 'In Far North-East Siberia', in David Collins (ed.), *Siberian Discovery*, Richmond, Surrey, 2000, 12 vols., vol. 7, p. 5.

16 Bogoras, *The Chuckchee*, p. 36 and pp. 570–71.

17 I. S. Vdovin, *Ocherki Istorii Etnografii Chukchey*, Moscow, 1965, p. 120.

18 Bogoras, *The Chuckchee*, pp. 651–3.

19 Sources conflict on the date of Anadyrsk's closure: I. S. Vdovin gives it as 1771; Bogoras as 1764.

20 Quoted in Bogoras, *The Chuckchee*, p. 701.

21 Bogoras, *The Chuckchee*, p. 706. See also George Kennan, *Tent Life in Siberia*, New York, 1910, pp. 188–90.

22 Bogoras, *The Chuckchee*, p. 732.

23 Ibid., p. 607.

24 Ibid., pp. 562–4.

25 Yuri Rytkheu, *From Nomad Tent to University*, Moscow, 1981, p. 24.

26 Ibid., p. 20.

27 Ibid., p. 28.

SELECTED BIBLIOGRAPHY

General histories

The benchmark for any English-language history of the native Siberians is James Forsyth's magisterial *History of the Peoples of Siberia: Russia's North Asian Colony 1581–1990* (Cambridge 1992). Benson Bobrick's *East of the Sun: The Epic Conquest and Tragic History and Siberia* (New York 1992) is a lively and scholarly general history of the region.

Ed. Galya Diment and Yuri Slezkine *Between Heaven and Hell: the Myth of Siberia in Russian Culture* (New York 1993) analyses Siberia's place in the European Russian imagination. Ed. Alan Wood and R. A. French *The Development of Siberia: People and Resources* (London 1989) and ed. Alan Wood *The History of Siberia: from Russian Conquest to Revolution* (London 1991) contain a variety of papers by many of the leading specialists in the field.

Early tsarist Siberia

The three volumes of orders, reports, petitions and memoranda comprising ed. Basil Dmytryshyn, E. A. P. Crownhart-Vaughan and Thomas Vaughan *To Siberia and Russian America: Three Centuries of Russian Eastward Expansion, 1558–1867* (Portland 1985–88) are an invaluable source on the conquest and early governance of Siberia. The Russian chronicles narrating Yermak's career are given, complete with facsimile illustrations, in ed. Terence Armstrong *Yermak's Campaign in Siberia* (London 1975). W. Radloffs' 'Die Sprachen der Türkischen Stämme Süd-Sibiriens und der Dsungarischen Steppe', vol. 4 of *Proben der Volkslitteratur* (St Petersburg 1872), includes Tatar folktales on the same subject. George Lantzeff and Richard Pierce's *Eastward to Empire: Exploration and Conquest of the Russian Open Frontier, to 1750* (Montreal 1973), and Lantzeff's *Siberia in the Seventeenth Century: a Study in Colonial Administration* (Berkeley 1943) are standard works, and *Archpriest Avvakum: the Life, Written by Himself* (Ann Arbor 1979) a rumbustious memoir of a Cossack expedition into Buryatiya.

Grigoriy Novitsky's account of an expedition to convert the Khant has been published in Russian and Hungarian as Grigorij Novickij *Kratkoe Opisanie o Narode Ostjackom* (Szeged 1973). The Khant's oral history of events appears in Jean-Luc Moreau's 'La colonisation Russe dans la Poésie Populaire des Ougriens de l'Ob', in *Sibérie II: Questions Sibériennes*. The Siberian fur-rush is exhaustively covered in Raymond Fisher's *The Russian Fur Trade, 1550–1700* (Berkeley 1943); Oleg Bychkov's 'Russian Hunters in Eastern Siberia in the Seventeenth Century: Lifestyle and Economy', *Arctic Anthropology* vol. 31, no. 1, 1994 and Janet Martin's paper's in ed. Boris Chichlo *Sibérie II: Questions Sibériennes* (Paris 1999).

Igor Krupnik's *Arctic Adaptations: Native Whalers and Reindeer Herders of Northern Eurasia* (Dartmouth 1993) demonstrates that native societies were in flux well before the Russians' arrival, and A. P. Okladnikov's *Yakutia before its Incorporation into the Russian State* (Montreal 1970) makes the case for the Sakha's origin in Central Asia.

Late tsarist Siberia

The standard works on Speransky's reforms are Marc Raeff's *Michael Speransky: Statesman of Imperial Russia, 1772–1839* (The Hague 1957) and his *Siberia and the Reforms of 1822* (Seattle 1956). Mark Bassin's *Imperial Visions: Nationalist Imagination and Geographical Expansion in the Russian Far East 1840–1865* (Cambridge 1999) traces the rise and fall of the 'Siberia as America' idea, and ed. Daniel Brower and Edward Lazzerini *Russia's Orient: Imperial Borderlands and Peoples, 1700–1917* (Bloomington 1997) contains insightful articles by Dov Yaroshevski on central government's relationship with the Buryat elite, and by Slezkine on the eighteenth-century's view of the native Siberians.

Nikolay Yadrinstsev's *Sibir kak Koloniya* (St Petersburg 1892) is the central text of the pre-revolutionary Siberian regionalist movement, more information on which can be found in Alan Wood's paper in ed. R. Bartlett *Russian Thought and Society 1800–1917: Essays in Honour of Eugene Lampert* (Keele 1984). The regionalists' present-day heir Valentin Rasputin is good on Tobolsk, Irkutsk, Kyakhta and the time-warp settlement of Russkoye Ustye in *Siberia, Siberia* (Evanston 1997).

John Stephan's *Sakhalin: a History* (Oxford 1971) and *The Russian Far East: a History* (Stanford 1994) survey the Pacific seaboard. His 'The Crimean War in the Far East', *Modern Asia Studies* 3, 1969 tells the story of the Pacific Fleet's escape through the unmapped Sakhalin straits.

Soviet Siberia

The outstanding book on early Soviet policy towards the native Siberians is Yuri Slezkine's *Arctic Mirrors: Russia and the Small Peoples of the North* (Ithaca 1994).

Robert Rupen's *Mongols of the Twentieth Century* (Bloomington 1964) contains valuable, though disorganised, material on the Buryat national movement. His 'The Absorption of Tuva', in ed. Thomas Hammond *Anatomy of Communist Takeovers* (New Haven 1975), shows how Stalin's 1944 takeover of Tuva acted as curtain-raiser for his post-war annexation of Eastern Europe. Nicholas Poppe's somewhat unreliable *Reminiscences* (Bellingham 1983) recall Stalin's repression of Buryat Buddhism and Leningrad academe. Better on names and dates is Poppe's 'Destruction of Buddhism in the USSR' *Bulletin of the Institute for the Study of the USSR*, 8–7, July 1956, pp. 14–20. The anthropologists shot or imprisoned under Stalin are listed, together with short biographies, in A. M. Reshetov's 'Repressirovannaya Etnografiya: Lyudi I Sudby' *Kunstkamera: Etnograficheskiye Tetradi*, nos. 4 and 5–6, 1994. William Grave's *America's Siberian Adventure, 1918–1920* (New York 1941) bears witness to the viciousness of Buryatiya's Civil War.

Recent books on the Sakha national movement include Ye. Ye. Alekseyev's *Istoriya Natsionalnogo Voprosa v Respublike Sakha (Yakutiya), Fevral 1917–1941* (Yakutsk 1998); T. S. Ivanova's *Iz Istorii Politicheskikh Repressiy v Yakutii* (Novosibirsk 1998); and Vladimir Pesterev's *Amga v Vikhre Grazhdanskoy* (Yakutsk 1997). Feliks Roziner's novel *A Certain Finkelmeyer* (New York 1991) satirises Soviet-era native-language publishing.

Post-Soviet Siberia

Perestroika allowed the publication of a flood of articles on the collapse of native societies in the far north. Amongst them were Alexander Pika and B. Prokhorov's 'Soviet Union: the Big Problems of Small Ethnic Groups', *IWGIA Newsletter* no. 57, May 1989; Pika's 'Spatial–Temporal Dynamic of Violent Death among the Native Peoples of Northern Russia', *Arctic Anthropology* vol. 30, no. 2, 1993, and his 'The Small Peoples of the North: from Primitive Communism to "Real Socialism"', in *Anxious North: Indigenous Peoples in Soviet and Post-Soviet Russia* (Copenhagen 1996). Nikolai Vakhtin's *Native Peoples of the Russian Far North*, published by the Minority Rights Group International (London 1992), gives a useful historical overview, and Yeremei Aipin's 'Not by Oil Alone' *IWGIA Newsletter* no. 57, May 1989 pleads for a halt to the oil-industry's destruction of the environment and of native society in the Ob basin.

Dmitri Gorenburg's 'Nationalism for the Masses: Popular Support for Nationalism in Russia's Ethnic Republics' *Europe-Asia Studies* vol. 53, no. 1, 2001 uses survey data to examine popular attitudes to native-language education and political devolution. Tanya Argounova-Low's Phd thesis *Scapegoats of Natsionalizm: Ethnic Tensions in Sakha (Yakutia), Northeastern Russia* (Scott Polar Research Institute, Cambridge 2001), looks at the post-Soviet Sakha national revival, as do Marjorie Mandelstam Balzer and Uliana Vinokurova 'Nationalism, Interethnic Relations and Federalism: the Case of the Sakha Republic (Yakutia)', *Europe-Asia Studies*, vol. 48, no. 1, 1996; Balzer's 'Homelands, Leadership and Self Rule: Observations on Interethnic Relations in the Sakha Republic' *Polar Geography*, vol. 19, no. 4, 1995; and her 'A State within a State: The Sakha Republic (Yakutia)' in ed. Stephen Kotkin and David Wolff *Rediscovering Russia in Asia: Siberia and the Russian Far East* (Armonk 1995).

Travel-books and exiles' accounts

Of the dozens of travel-books on Siberia, I found the most entertaining and illuminating to be the following: Stepan Krasheninnikov's *The History of Kamtschatka and the Kurile Islands, with the Countries Adjacent* (Gloucester 1764); Johann Gmelin's *Voyage en Sibérie* (Paris 1767); M. L'Abbé Chappe d'Auteroche's *A Journey into Siberia* (London 1770); John Dundas Cochrane's *Narrative of a Pedestrian Journey through Russia and Siberian Tartary . . .* (London,1824); Adolf Erman's *Travels in Siberia: Including Excursions Northwards towards the Obi . . .* (London 1848); George Kennan's *Tent Life in Siberia* (New York 1910), and his *Siberia and the Exile System* 2 vols., (New York 1891).

Adam Johann von Krusenstern's *Voyage Round the World in the Years 1803 . . .* (London 1813) is good on the Ainu and the colonial administration of Kamchatka. Ewa Felinska brings the Ob town of Berezov to life in *Revelations of Siberia, by a Banished Lady* (London 1852); Pavel Golovin does the same for an Alaskan fur-trading settlement in *Civil and Savage Encounters: the Worldly Letters of an Imperial Russian Navy Officer, 1860–1861* (Portland 1983). Alexander Douglas Carruthers's *Unknown Mongolia: a Record of Travel and Exploration in North-West Mongolia and Dzungaria* (London 1913) describes pre-revolutionary Tuva, and Otto Mänchen-Helfen covers its Sovietisation at the hands of Buryat Bolsheviks in *Journey to Tuva: an Eye-Witness Account of Tannu-*

Tuva in 1929 (Los Angeles 1992). The classic work on pre-revolutionary Sakhalin is of course Anton Chekhov's *The Island* (London 1987). A twelve-volume series of reprints, ed. David Collins *Siberian Discovery* (Richmond 2000), includes two colourful accounts of exile life in northern Sakha: Isaak Shklovsky's *In Far North-East Siberia* (vol. 7) and Viktor Zenzinov's *The Road to Oblivion* (vol. 11).

Anthropological works

Dmitri Shimkin's 'Siberian Ethnography: Historical Sketch and Evaluation' *Arctic Anthropology* vol. 27, no. 1, 1990 is a useful historiography of Siberian anthropology from the 1700s on. Waldemar Bogoras's great works on the Chukchi, *The Chukchee* and *Chukchee Mythology*, comprise vols. 7 and 8 of the *Publications of the Jesup North Pacific Expedition* (New York 1910–13). Lev Shternberg's *The Social Organisation of the Gilyak* (New York 1999) is the seminal text on the pre-revolutionary Nivkh; the edition includes an interview with Shternberg's last surviving former student. Wacław Sieroszewski's classic work on the Sakha is published in Russian as V. L. Seroshevsky *Yakuty* (Moscow 1993). Extracts can be found in English in 'The Yakuts: Abridged from the Russian of Sieroszewski' *Journal of the Royal Anthropological Institute*, XXXI, 1901.

Mary Czaplicka's *My Siberian Year* (London 1916) describes life among the pre-revolutionary Nenets; Caroline Humphrey's *Karl Marx Collective* (Cambridge 1983) the persistence of shamanism amongst Brezhnev-era Buryat. Sevyan Vainshtein's volume on the Tuvans, *Nomads of South Siberia* (Cambridge 1980), is typical of Soviet anthropology in giving much detailed information on clan structures and herding techniques, but nothing on religion or the effects of collectivisation and Slav in-migration. Bruce Grant's *In the Soviet House of Culture: a Century of Perestroikas* (Princeton 1995) contains moving interviews with Nivkh survivors of Stalin's terror.

On shamanism, the classic text is Mircea Eliade *Shamanism: Archaic Techniques of Ecstasy* (London 1989). More up-to-date surveys of the subject are Piers Vitebsky's beautifully illustrated *The Shaman: Voyages of the Soul; Trance, Ecstasy and Healing from Siberia to the Amazon* (London 1995), and Ronald Hutton's refreshingly analytical *Shamans: Siberian Spirituality and the Western Imagination* (Hambledon 2002).

INDEX